We Need Snowflakes

Also by Hannah Jewell

100 Nasty Women of History

We Need Snowflakes

In defence of the sensitive, the angry and the offended

Hannah Jewell

CORONET

First published in Great Britain in 2022 by Coronet
An Imprint of Hodder & Stoughton
An Hachette UK company

1

A CIP catalogue record for this title is available from the British Library

Hardback ISBN 9781473672130
Trade Paperback ISBN 9781473672147
eBook ISBN 9781473672161

Typeset in Sabon MT by Hewer Text UK Ltd, Edinburgh
Printed and bound in Great Britain by Clays Ltd, Elocraf S.p.A.

Hodder & Stoughton policy is to use papers that are natural, renewable and recyclable products and made from wood grown in sustainable forests. The logging and manufacturing processes are expected to conform to the environmental regulations of the country of origin.

Hodder & Stoughton Ltd
Carmelite House
50 Victoria Embankment
London EC4Y 0DZ

www.hodder.co.uk

For my silly parents

Contents

Preface

In the time between writing the first and second drafts of this book, there was a pandemic.

I mean, I say 'was'. There still *is* a pandemic. But in the many months between merrily sending off a first draft and finally forcing myself to sit down and make it better, COVID-19 killed millions of people worldwide.

Like many others, I watched with horror, but without surprise, as a public health crisis became the latest stage for a battle between those who believe in making minor sacrifices to their freedom to protect the vulnerable, and those who seem to fear that doing so is an expression of weakness.

Arguments about hand-washing, mask-wearing, social-distancing, vaccines, and even the existence of the disease itself became yet another way to divide 'us' from 'them'. Leaders who should have worried only about preventing mass death, sickness and economic fallout instead used their considerable power to spread xenophobia and attempt to prove their own machismo.

I watched on 12 March 2020 as Boris Johnson declared that the UK pandemic plan was simply to tough it out in the name of gaining herd immunity – a plan which was abandoned within ten days when it became apparent what a devastating toll this strategy would take.

In the United States, as the death count ticked past 180,000 on a hot August night in Washington, I stood outside the entrance to the White House south lawn, where guests of President Trump, dressed in their finest, smiling and maskless, crowded through security and into the grounds to hear Trump deliver an address for the last night of the Republican National Convention.

Crossing their paths were protestors headed to Black Lives Matter Plaza – a few city blocks renamed by Washington's mayor, just on the other side of the White House. They were mostly wearing masks, and were on their way to continue the summer's protests against ongoing police violence against black Americans. The gulf between the groups, their ideas about politics and public health and gender and race and each other, felt colossal.

In his convention speech – and in most other speeches delivered over four nights of the RNC – Trump referred to the pandemic in the past tense. While people died alone in hospital rooms, he reframed sensible precautions against the coronavirus into something else: a sign of oversensitivity. Of hysteria. Of political correctness.

I didn't know then whether Trump would win re-election, and I certainly couldn't have predicted quite how delirious and terrifying the weeks following that election would be. But I did know that the circumstances which had led to the failure of both the US and the UK to contain the coronavirus – and the forces which elected both nations' leaders – were going nowhere. Joe Biden is president now, and yet I am more sure of that than ever.

This is a book about a so-called 'culture war' that is often portrayed as funny and ridiculous, but which also unfortunately touches every aspect of our lives. I have watched it contribute to hundreds of thousands of deaths in Britain and America, both of my countries, where leaders and citizens did not take the threat of COVID-19 seriously because they did not want to be seen as fragile or vulnerable. They didn't want to be seen as special snowflakes.

The term snowflake is a profoundly cringeworthy one, used to accuse people of being overly sensitive, angry, or easily offended. But as I watched the horrible events of 2020 unfurl, I understood more than ever that these 'special snowflakes', 'sensitive snowflakes', and, of course, 'fucking snowflakes' are the ones who will make life better for all of us, if we let them.

Introduction

What older commentators and columnists today seem to long for, either explicitly or in complaining about young snowflakes or the ways things are 'nowadays', when everything has gone to shit, is the strength, moral purpose and all-round grit of previous generations. So let me tell you about my grandma, who would have hated this book.

Growing up in California, I didn't really get to know my father's mother, my indomitable, chain-smoking, whiskey-drinking grandma, until my twenties and her nineties, when I moved back to Britain for graduate school in the last few years of her life.

The official reason my parents moved to California when I was a baby was for my dad's job. He was a computer programmer, and his British software company was moving to the Bay Area, as software companies are wont to do. The unofficial reason was that my parents wanted to escape Britain with its cold, its damp, its misery, and, as my dad has put it to me, its 'society steeped in outdated attitudes under a crippling social-class-based system'. Without airing too much of the family baggage, they had plenty of pain to leave behind. So my parents picked up and moved to California to romp among the redwoods and brag to their friends back home about all the sunshine.

Every other year or so, though, we would make the trip back to England, where I, as a child, was disgusted by the fact that I sometimes had to wear a coat. Visits to my grandparents meant dipping my young toes into deep pools of family drama of which I understood very little. Visits to my grandma meant breathing in a *lot* of second-hand cigarette smoke, and listening to her tales, which often featured harsh judgements upon the world, her neighbours and her family. My grandma's bluntness was often funny. She believed forcefully in the way things should be done, from Christmas pudding to withholding verbal expressions of love. She was proud and stubborn and hated the things she loved to hate: sport of any kind, religion generally and oppressive men. She grew up in a Labour family but *loved* Margaret Thatcher in the 1980s. She hated Europe, politically and generally, and would have loved to see Brexit had she not died the year before the vote. She once complained to me that the news showed too many 'crying mothers' and not enough 'people just getting on with it'.

By the age at which she was almost completely blind, Grandma's body clock had replaced her need to look at a real clock: she could feel the arrival of noon each day, because that was the time for her whiskey and lemonade. Her suspicions of anything or anyone not British extended to her garden, where she derisively referred to a plant brought by her son who had settled in Galway as 'the Irish plant'. (She knew the full name of every other plant in her garden.) She was an old woman who loved nothing more than to smoke cigarettes (the doctors who said it was harmful were merely 'blinding you with science') and talk for hours about the world, whether a cringeworthy revelation of her xenophobia or the funny and unbelievable stories of giving birth at home to each of her children. ('The midwife couldn't make it, so I said to my cousin, "Boil the scissors."')

At other times, Grandma's overall coldness was painful. She had not been an expressively loving mother to my father. When my grandfather neared the end of his life, and began to grow a little senile, he told my grandma, his wife of over sixty years, that he loved her. I was sitting on the stairs at her house, listening, in my early twenties. 'We don't say that in this family,' she told him off. I wrote in my diary: 'I cannot believe her blood runs in my veins.' I could not understand what would make a person that way. I didn't think about its source. Grandma was just Grandma, and while she found other ways to show us she approved of us, or was even very proud of us, saying 'I love you' wasn't one of them.

Later in my twenties, when I returned to England for grad school and then for work, I had the opportunity for the first time in my life to get to know Grandma on my own terms, without the memories and the tension of the generation between us. Visiting her on my own was the chance to build a new relationship. She also met my husband, Sam, on our second date. He made her a strong cup of coffee and showed great interest in her life story. She approved.

On these visits I learned more about Grandma's life, her childhood and especially her experiences during World War II. When I was growing up, there were plenty of jokes between my parents about my mother's posh north-west London upbringing and my dad's working-class childhood on council estates across south London. But it wasn't until my long evenings with Grandma that I learned quite how acute the poverty of her upbringing, and my father's, had been.

Grandma heralded her impending death for many years. She would clear up after meals and mutter, 'One less meal.' Sensing the beginning of the end, she decided to write her memoirs. Barely able to see, she wrote down everything she could remember about her childhood in ninety pages of mostly all-caps lettering in a thick black pen.

I love these memoirs, written with my grandma's deader-than-deadpan matter-of-factness. They cover two notebooks and contain basically everything I know about my family tree on my father's side. This includes details such as: 'CAROLINE (MY GRAN) LIVED TO HER NINETIES. HER HUSBAND FELL OFF A CRANE WHEN

DRUNK (HE WAS A CRANE OPERATOR) WHEN THE CHILDREN WERE QUITE YOUNG.' It's important to learn and cherish your family history.

There are many tales of Grandma's mother, Grace, born in 1894. Grace worked from the age of fourteen in a laundry, as her mother worked as a maid in rich households. When both her parents died, a teenage Grace supported the entire family in their home in Greenwich, keeping the rent and bills paid somehow. When she married, her first child, Ella, known as 'Bubsie', died of diphtheria at eighteen months old. 'They were devastated, and my father often said that I saved my mother's life and sanity by starting when I did,' my grandmother writes.

The young family moved to a new home infested with bedbugs. During the Depression, Grandma's father lost his job as a foreman in a paint factory 'on the other side of the water', that is, north London. The family was financially ruined, and relied on a single charity meal each day, collected in her mother's 'largest pudding basin', filled to the top and shared out at home. They faced illness and insecure work, cold, hunger, and beyond this – as my grandmother does not record in her memoirs but would mention in passing to me during our visits – physical abuse from her father.

Grandma's dad had survived being gassed in the trenches of World War I. While many of her memories of him are of being 'walloped' at his hand, she also recalled the times he was her defender: When he convinced the local library to let her join even though she was not yet seven years old. When he called her a 'good girl' for looking after her younger siblings when he had to leave them alone at home to take up an offer of a street-sweeping job. When she earned a junior county scholarship to grant her admission and funding to go to grammar school, and her father supported her. Her mother, meanwhile, said, 'she'll only get married and that would make it all a big waste', when she could get a job instead. (The headmistress bought Grandma a school blazer with her own money.) She also remembers moving to a council house in

Bellingham in 1938. 'My dad couldn't believe his luck,' she says. 'The most wonderful bit was that we not only had electric lights for the very first time but a bathroom as well. It was like being a rich person.'

With the outbreak of World War II, Grandma remembers getting a gas mask. She was evacuated to the countryside, which she spoke about fondly for the rest of her life. For the first time, she could study and enjoy the fresh air of not-London, away from her difficult home life. But on her sixteenth birthday, Grandma received a card summoning her home to work and support the family. 'For after all, why should my younger sister be working so hard in order to help keep me in idle luxury?' she was admonished. She told me this tale countless times.

Back in London, Grandma worked in the Royal Arsenal at Woolwich and earned a pound a week, an amount that made her feel extremely well off. Throughout the war, she lived large. Grandma's war stories were often hysterical. She went on many dates with servicemen on leave, and once left her glasses in the pocket of an American soldier while they kissed goodnight and had to go back to his barracks to retrieve them the next day – to much merriment from the other soldiers. She once got a lift home from a dance with a milkman making his early rounds, who was horrified to see that the sequins she had glued to her dress had attached themselves to his vehicle's seats instead. The arrival of American G.I.s brought jazz to London, and Grandma took full advantage of wartime entertainments.

Still, though, she continued to live under the thumb of her father. 'I began to think about clothes and hair styles and make-up,' she writes in her memoirs, 'which in those days was only used by loose women! One lunch time I spent sixpence on a lipstick. I put some on and forgot to wash it off before riding home.' Her father was so furious that he grabbed her and scrubbed it off with a dishcloth. He told her she had brought disgrace to his house.

Other memories sound straight out of a film. One night during the Blitz, when bombs dropped and fires raged all around them, Grandma rode the train home with her youth-club friends, singing camp songs to keep up the carriage's spirits. At the end of the perilous journey, an older man on the train shook their hands and thanked them for distracting him from his sheer terror.

When telling these memories, Grandma would often drop in casual mentions of what, if you thought about it, were unbelievable horrors. She liked to tell of the time she and her friends were kicked out of their youth club at Charlton House in Greenwich early one night, because one of the 'more unruly boys' had sworn at the Charlton House warden. As they left and wandered down the path, stopping to look at constellations and meteors, a bomb hit the exit of the building which they had just passed through, at the time of night they normally would have been leaving the building. She told this as a story about mild coincidence, like running into an old friend at the shops, and not as the near-death experience it was.

In another story she apparently did not consider remarkable enough to include in her memoirs, Grandma decided to leave the Woolwich Arsenal for a lunch of fish and chips instead of using the workplace canteen as usual. While she was out, a bombing raid hit the arsenal, and many people died. She mentioned it to me once, as if it were a small story. I do not remember if she said her friends were among the dead.

It is easy to assume, as I have for most of my life, that back then – in the *olden days* missed by so many – people were much tougher. Narrowly escaping multiple bombings and suffering the war deaths of friends and family must not have hurt so bad, since it happened all the time. After all, people lived till thirty and lost half their children in *the olden days*, right? And so I assumed it was with Grandma. She was tough then, and she was tough for the rest of her life. She never grew emotional, even on her deathbed where she told me matter-of-factly that she was 'ready to go'. This alarmed me at first, until I realised what a rare privilege it was to be 'ready to go'. She expressed pride in her grandchildren and her great-grandchildren. She kept meticulous photo albums of her family and loved that the girls, in particular, had all achieved academic and career success, opportunities she had wanted for herself but had largely been denied. In hospital shortly before she died, I snuck her a whiskey and lemonade in a Sprite bottle. When she realised what it was, she grabbed my arm and told me that I should tell people that I take after my grandma. There was a time when this would have horrified me, but I'm pleased by it now.

I grew up believing Grandma's coldness and toughness were simply her character. That she had an innate grit which got her through a childhood of abuse and poverty and a young adulthood marked by war and the constant terror of bombing – like all Londoners then. Grandma was, and remains, the ideal image of what you could call resilience – the kind today's young generations allegedly lack in the eyes of their critics. I believed that she was the tough one and I would be the aberration if I was not tough also.

But was this really resilience? Was that toughness her true, original character? Would it have been so if not for her childhood and for war? Does resilience simply mean the ability to survive, and to stay alive, when your emotional life has been muted by adversity?

When people critique the lack of a certain hardiness in young people today, there is on the one hand a convincing case that this simply isn't true. Young people face new and different challenges to their grandparents. They have been young in a pandemic, denied over a year of the pleasures and rituals of youth. They have faced an unequal and unstable economic path. Many young people around the world face the same agony of war, or worse, experienced by young Londoners in the 1940s.

But there's another argument to be made: that the 'strength' of previous generations is *not* something to aspire to. It's not something we should necessarily emulate. It's something we should mourn. My grandparents, and yours, dealt with the traumas of their youth long before psychological trauma had entered into medical understanding, let alone common knowledge. What may look from the outside like resilience may sometimes have been a different kind of dealing with pain: suppressing and avoiding it, rather than acknowledging it and then healing from it.

What if my grandma had been allowed to be a bit of a delicate snowflake? How might her life have been different?

At the end of her handwritten memoirs, Grandma includes a section titled 'Summary', underlined in her thick black pen.

'On the whole I think I was lucky to have lived my childhood in those days,' she writes. 'We led a very sheltered life compared to the children of today. We knew nothing of the evils of the world as we now [know] them. I assume that sexual predators existed then, as now, that violent criminals and drugs barons, that the thieves and swindlers were around then. But we knew that the area's policeman would deal with all that, so it was nothing to do with us.'

It surprised me to discover, years after her death, when I finally sat down to read her memories, that in some regards Grandma thought she had it easier as a child than young people today. It's the opposite of the classic 'I walked fifteen miles to school in the snow and it was uphill both ways' elderly judgement. Grandma really did walk that proverbial fifteen miles in the snow, and yet she saw the difference between that kind of grind, and the different kind of murkier misery brought on by the modern world. When she said that she 'knew nothing of the evils of the world' as a child, you see how she was conditioned not to see physical abuse in her home, or even bombs dropping on her city, as first-hand knowledge of the evils of the world. That was simply how things were in those days.

Nevertheless, she died thinking it is *today's* kids who are forced to grow up too quickly. 'I think the children of today know too much about the evils of the world too soon,' she wrote. 'But I suppose it's my generation who made that happen by inventing devices like radio and cars and television and computers and mobile phones and cinema.

Have these things done more harm than good?' Forever the teacher, she concludes: 'Discuss!'

It's impossible to imagine my grandma without suffering, without poverty, without war, and without abuse. These are the things that she wove into her very being. They defined her view of the world and her assessment of all the people in it. But unlike so many who cannot survive and integrate their traumas into the stories of their lives, Grandma found purpose in her life story. She identified firmly as a tough old bird. She was not a perfect parent, certainly, and I remain grateful to have escaped the direct onslaught of her demons as a grandchild who grew up far away in sunny California.

But perhaps her past did not actually make her stronger. What if it simply made her better at hiding away whatever feelings she did have? She took the pain of her life and buried it somewhere it could not be accessed by any of us. For all her love of grumbling about the state of the world, it is remarkable that she still wished for better lives for her children and their children – and less suffering, not more.

What did she miss in life? What could she have experienced if she'd had the room to be a bit of a snowflake? If she had been safe, at home and on the streets of London? If her entire generation had learned how to feel? In terms of the scope of suffering experienced during World War II, Grandma got off easy. She was not a soldier or a concentration camp prisoner. Even so, there's no telling how her life might have gone otherwise if she hadn't experienced what she did. It seems safe to say, though, that she might at least have been able to express and receive love from her family. How different that might have made things for her children, and theirs.

The issues she faced are still faced today by millions of children, around the world, and in Britain, and on the very same south London estates where she lived, when they were shiny and new.

Is the trouble with kids today that they are not as tough as my grandma was?

We can think of my grandma, then, as the antithesis of what this book is about: the snowflake. The snowflake is the allegedly weak, pathetic, sensitive soul, who walks about the earth in a perpetually childlike form, without an ounce of Blitz spirit to her name. This imagined figure is a threat and an insult to The Way Things Used To Be, that is, a world inhabited entirely by romanticised versions of Grandma. Sturdy souls who didn't care for safety, or science, or friendliness, or feelings.

While I am happy to take after my grandma in so many ways, and while we must respect and understand and forgive all the Grandmas, we should not aspire to be exactly like them. Instead, we must reclaim not just the term 'snowflake' from its critics, but the idea of the 'snowflake' as it has existed over decades. It is, after all, only a recent iteration of an idea which has existed for each generation, stretching back to the first time old men looked at the young and were irritated by them.

Over two thousand years ago, Aristotle himself wrote of the way that young people tended to 'overdo everything', that they were know-it-alls, and that they were primarily guided by their 'strong passions' (that is, their horniness) and their 'exalted notions' about the world.[1] Sounding like a peeved columnist in the *Sunday Times*, Aristotle declared that young people were 'regulated more by moral feeling than by reasoning,' in contrast to the reason and wisdom of age. This wasn't all bad news, though, as Aristotle observed that 'whereas reasoning leads us to choose what is useful, moral goodness leads us to choose what is noble.' Today's commentators are not so gracious as to see nobility in the passions of youth.

Whether we call them snowflakes or long-haired hippies or garbage teens or overly passionate Athenian youths, though, the target is the same. Words like 'snowflake' serve a political purpose, to bully and denigrate the young (and their allies). These insults are a way to trample on the energy and solidarity of young people and snuff out their often radical ideas. To resist this trampling, we have to understand origins of the snowflake discourse – and reclaim the snowflake as a sympathetic, even noble figure.

To trace the origin of the word 'snowflake', to see what it can tell us about our troubled times, to try to reclaim it – all of this can feel like a futile task. Trawling through furious internet arguments and reading the books of pure, relentless idiots in search of great meaning can seem, at times, ridiculous. In trying to get to the heart of one of the key terms of the culture war and those who wield it, I may as well ask my cat for his thought process on projectile-vomiting his dinner onto my best wool blanket. Maybe we are all gripped by a human nature that cannot be changed, as Seymour is gripped by cat nature. Maybe nothing can stop us from tweeting terrible ideas or hurling up chunks of dried horse meat.

I know also how hard it is to change minds. Whether it's a friend's terrible boyfriend, a random internet troll, or a prominent commentator, it may be a lost cause to convince someone who uses the term 'snowflake' derisively to cut it out. Giving serious time and attention to the political and media figures who constantly use the phrase is often exactly what these awful people want. Maybe there isn't a way to dampen the pure delight some people take from cringeworthy name-calling. Maybe they don't want to consider a new perspective. Maybe they just want to post. Piers Morgan may know that the angrier he makes young people by calling them snowflakes, the more they will reply to his tweets calling him a bellend, and this is how he maintains his successful career. But notorious bellends aren't the only ones who use the term or carry the baggage that comes with it. As we will see, a piece of language such as 'snowflake' and all its attendant insults which begin on the far right can find their way into the mouths of widely read columnists, university presidents, prominent feminists and political leaders. And much of the time, the 'snowflake' insult also doesn't really seem to mean *anything*. It is an idea that evades critique. It transforms meaning and intent mid-air. It throws up a smoke screen of its own stupidity. And if you argue with someone claiming that you are *not* a snowflake, you will, in the eyes of your accuser, become an even bigger one. A big, wet, drippy piece of pathetic, laughable snow. Nobody wants to be this.

But by diving deeply into the meaning of what may appear to be a very shallow term, it turns out we can find out a lot about what has happened to our politics, our media and the way we treat each other. 'Snowflake' may be tossed around with thoughtless abandon, but it is never meaningless, even if it might appear so most of the time. So despite its stench, I am going to bend over that pile of sick, as it seeps ever deeper into my nicest wool blanket, which came all the way from my mother-in-law in New Zealand, and I am going to examine it. We must peer into the sick, to see what it has to teach us. and then take that blanket to the dry cleaner.

Here's the fundamental problem:

Every day, lots of commentators, most of them of a certain age, with a wide influence and a brand of *telling it like it is*, take to television and the radio and their well-compensated columns and very popular books, in America and in Britain and around the world, to say that young people today are simply *pathetic*. They can't argue like we used to. They are *struck down* with terror, fear and full-blown panic attacks at the mere suggestion of the *politically incorrect*.

They are horrible, like snowflakes, utterly weak and yet also, some-how, profoundly threatening to society. To these figures – who I will call the snowflake critics – the snowflake is a moany, spoiled, narcis-sistic youth who can't cope with the real world, was incorrigibly corrupted by a too-loving childhood and prevented from a toughening-up by health and safety regulations.

If this is what a snowflake is, you can see why nobody would want to be one. People don't want to be thought of as weak. We want to be thought of as brave and courageous. We want people to know we can carry *all* the bags of shopping from the car to the house in one go. Wanting to be a snowflake may sound like aspiring to be a failure. And because a snowflake is such a hateful, pitiable thing to be, it's a great term to wield against your own enemies. If Piers Morgan has called you a snowflake for being upset about, say, a new scheme by Boris Johnson to ban women from public office, then you might say that *he's* the real snowflake for getting so upset when people call him a prick on Twitter. It's a terrible and boring game of hot potato with no escape. In the end, everybody's covered in potato, and no one is happy.

You do not have to be a conservative to hate a snowflake, though the term rose to popularity from the social networks of the alt-right. Nowadays, though, plenty of liberals, centrists, and of course those media figures who consider themselves to be *perfectly unbiased, non-ideological bearers of universal wisdom* hate snowflakes just as much as your average internet Nazi does. Some are university professors who despise the snowflakes who question their all-knowing authority. Some are respected members of the anti-Trump liberal 'resistance'. They are not all older people who loathe the young, and they aren't only far-right lunatics, and they aren't only populists in the style of Donald Trump and his followers. Some seem to believe what they're saying. Some are charlatans who have discovered a quick way to gain attention and funding for their work. Some are simply writing what they're told to maximise clicks to the *Sun*. Wherever we find them, we can learn a lot about modern snowflakes by meeting their greatest haters. We can also learn a lot about the haters themselves, their vision of the world and their all-consuming anxieties.

The power of the 'snowflake' insult comes primarily from a fear of appearing weak. It's a fear of being whiny. But in truth, a snowflake is not the same as a whiner. Take for example Jessica, the girl in middle school whose name was not Jessica but had the same vibe as Jessica, who asked me in seventh grade to open her car door for her because she had hurt her finger in basketball practice (I was there, she had not). Or imagine the kind of man who blames his tools, rather than himself, for failing to complete a simple task, when it is clearly he himself who has failed. Imagine the guys who get really mad when they lose board games, or sulk because it's raining ever so slightly. Imagine the people who are consistently unwilling to try new things, without a good reason beyond thinking they won't be good at it. These characters may indeed be whiners. But a whiner is not necessarily also a snowflake, because a snowflake's complaint has a political purpose. That purpose is likely deeper than not wanting to open a car door.

Yet a snowflake critic will often dress up a critique of political expression as pure whining. This is the power of the word. It reduces political complaints to personal grievances. Snowflake critics look at a young person with a political idea, and say, *this is pure weakness*. This is *unbearable* grumbling. We shall see this over and over again! Dear reader, this is the very problem, the problem which has driven me to the brink, in classic snowflake form, at the ridiculousness of the entire world right now, and beyond into an ever-sillier future. The snowflake critic, in his critique of snowflake whiners, is himself being extremely whiny!

The thing is, the snowflakes I have known and loved were not weaklings, nor whiners, nor necessarily more sensitive than your average conservative man of a certain age, for example – though they may be sensitive about different things. And it turns out that there are in fact many ways to be strong and brave which don't entail being horrible to others. You can lift a large log. You can swim in cold water. You can face an uncomfortable dispute face on. You can be an incredibly strong person while maintaining compassion and sensitivity.

Over the course of my life and career I have again and again walked among many such bold and admirable snowflakes. I have lived among the naked vegans of UC Berkeley's co-operative housing. I have snapped my fingers in non-threatening agreement at the meetings of community activists. On the internet, I have written my snowflake takes. I have travelled across the United States to report for the *Washington Post* speaking to university students and intersectional activists and young socialists and ageing hippies – as well as Trump supporters and anti-maskers and all manner of conspiracy-addled souls. So I can tell you from my experience that those who get called snowflakes are not unwilling to face uncomfortable situations or ideas. They are often the *only* ones willing to face uncomfortable situations or ideas. They are not self-centred or over-privileged. They are relentlessly focused on others, and often come from unprivileged spaces to enter privileged ones. This is the tension of snowflakery. The person who gets called a snowflake is someone who has transgressed the status quo, in their actions, with their words, or simply by *being* in a space not built for them. Snowflakes, particularly those at universities, are usually characterised as privileged and spoiled. They're usually not. They're usually the ones whose identities are new to elite institutions. They're the ones who can't always afford the avocado toast.

They're also not particularly terrifying. If you fear snowflakes as some kind of terrible horde – the famous 'mob' we hear so much about – you probably *should* be more worried about causing offence. You probably should correct your speech from time to time. You probably *should*, on occasion, listen to the people you have pissed off. You should ask yourself: 'Am I at the mercy of a bad-faith "mob" – or am I the one with power that I'm wielding unfairly? Are my critics the ones who have shut their minds to new ideas, or have I?'

I don't mean to alarm you, but snowflakes are all around you. Sometimes they're loud. Sometimes they're yelling in the streets. Sometimes they are pulling down the statue of a seventeenth-century slave trader and hurling it into the Bristol harbour. But sometimes they're a lot quieter. Sometimes they are taking small steps toward justice in their communities or their workplaces or their families. Sometimes people are snowflakes just because of who they are.

If we were to generalise, though, we could say that a snowflake is someone who challenges hierarchies and the powerful inequalities which structure modern life. They threaten patterns of class power and of racial power and economic power, and this, fundamentally, is why they are demonised. They are also, on the whole, an easy target for those whom they threaten, because of their comfort talking about their feelings, their commitment to making change, and the way they look. Like the youths romping about Aristotle's Athens, they are guided by passion, and that can be a terrifying sight.

My job in this book will be to convince you that you should actually *want* to be a snowflake – or at the very least, you should admire snowflakes wherever you spot them. We will look at how snowflakes have been defined, and by whom, and how panics about university students in particular have shaped suspicion of young people. We will see how hypocritical arguments about free speech and 'cancel culture' work to protect financial, political and cultural power. We will see how the terror of feelings and the unaddressed trauma of previous generations has the effect of silencing and dismissing vulnerable people today. We will see how fear of snowflakes fuels hatred of trans people. And we will see how the snowflake's quest to build fairer and less awful workplaces enrages the beneficiaries of inequality.

In the end, if you are still not sure if you *are* a snowflake yourself, I hope you will understand why we need them.

Or at the very, very, *very* least, I hope you'll be less of a dickhead to young people.

The origins of the snowflake

What is a snowflake?

The short answer: when not referring to a merry little piece of actual snow, an impossibly beautiful crystal laying bare the majesty of all creation, it's an insult. Specifically, it's an insult meant to disparage young people (but sometimes also older folks) when they express concern about social justice issues such as racism, sexism and inequality, when they critique those in power who perpetuate those problems, or when they take action to protect their own comfort and happiness.

Snowflakes are most often defined by those who hate them. Those who earn their living by making sweeping generalisations about the Problems With Kids Today offer us endless commentary about the alleged generation of snowflakes that threatens us all. But I want to begin with some examples of how the term 'snowflake' is generally used, and how it feels to be called one. (Because snowflakes are nothing if not attuned to their feelings.)

I cast a net across the internet, sourcing stories of times that people had been called snowflakes, and why, and how it felt. As fellow internet users may be able to predict, I was swiftly owned for doing so. (For my mother: to be 'owned' is to be succinctly mocked for a foolish mistake online.) An early respondent to my questionnaire identified himself as 'Smedley Weetabix, 29, consultant'.

The form asked: When and why were you called a snowflake?

Smedley's answer: 'Every time I demand that I get free stuff that I am not willing to work for.'

Were you called a snowflake because of your race, ethnicity, sexuality or gender identity?

Mr Weetabix: 'I was called a snowflake for no other reason than because I demanded that I get free stuff and that others' free speech be curtailed if it is not the same as my opinion.'

How did you respond, and how did it make you feel?

'I held my breath, telling others to recognise that I deserve stuff that I am not willing to work for.' And so on.

Thank you, Mr Weetabix, for your contribution.

My non-Weetabix respondents, though, shared a range of tales from the front lines of the snowflake discourse. They showed how the term snowflake is used to make someone feel bad, of course, but is also meant to make the person who wields it feel more powerful. It is meant to disempower and humiliate, and to cast its user as tough and unflappable in contrast – despite the fact that a person calling someone a snowflake is more often than not *extremely* flapped.

For one woman, an administrator in New Zealand, Natalie Eskrick, the insult came after she made knowing eye contact with a young supermarket cashier, who was at that moment being berated by an American tourist because he had a problem with his credit card. The man rounded on Eskrick, and also called her a 'libtard'. (Here we have the conjunction of 'liberal' and the offensive term for people with intellectual disabilities.) Eskrick says she found the experience 'a bit odd'. After two delightful visits to family in New Zealand, I can confirm that this is not a usual Kiwi checkout experience. So what does Eskrick think her insultor meant to achieve by calling her a 'snowflake'? She told me:

I think people who use the term are articulating a resentment of being asked to moderate their own behaviour. Whether it's pronouns, or treating a retail assistant with respect, it seems like a way to denigrate someone who is asking to be treated in a different way than what they currently are.

Eskrick gets to the heart of the accuser's discomfort. It is easier to call someone a name, in any situation, than to change your own behaviour. Even in a supermarket, confronting a stranger who has made a face behind your back, the man did not call her rude, or mean – nor did he apologise for holding up the line in a rage. Inherent in the term 'snowflake' was an outrage that a woman appeared to be judging a man. He saw in her amused gentle mockery an entire politics, an entire world view, which was threatening to *him* and *his* politics and *his* world view. And it was an insult hurled with *rage* – a rage at a perceived loss of power in a situation, an overturning of gender roles, perhaps. It was a mad grasp at regaining respect and power in a situation that should have been as simple as purchasing some crisps with an alternative credit card. It was 'quite odd' indeed.

Another person who shared their story about being called a snowflake with me was a social media manager in her twenties, who didn't want to be named because her story touches on her job. We'll call her Sarah. She told me about the time she was out drinking with co-workers when a former colleague at her company joined the group and began complaining about another former colleague, who was a black woman, an activist, and friends with Sarah. Here's what Sarah says happened:

Knowing I'm gay, he switches to talking about how he believes in gays but not in trans people . . . I'm arguing a little because I feel that's the right thing to do, but being civil because I'm drunk, and I don't want to kill the vibe. At this point he starts questioning me about where I'm from and why my family came here and why I disagree with his views – he simply doesn't get it – so I make the mistake of (very civilly) saying that as a privileged white man it's hard for him to understand. And boy, he absolutely LOSES IT. He gets up, screams and screams at me about how I'm the whole reason this country is divided, he should've known better than to try to talk to someone who is friends with [the ex-co-worker he hates], and of course I'm a 'snowflake'. Though I'm arguing back, I start crying because I'm drunk and totally unprepared to be screamed at, and he says 'sorry for triggering you snowflake' multiple times before leaving.

As the only person of colour in an all-white social setting, Sarah became the target of a white man's anger and aggression. Her white colleagues did not do much to stick up for her, which was even more hurtful. In this situation, Sarah shared her thought that the term snowflake was wielded simply to be 'a derogatory term for someone you wish to intentionally provoke with outlandish statements but not engage in meaningful conversation with.' When Sarah attempted to push back, he erupted in a consuming rage. When Sarah cried, she became a snowflake – and was 'triggered'. It was Sarah who was pathologised with a mental health term, being 'triggered', rather than the man who had exploded at her. The result was a horrible experience on what should have been a simple night out with co-workers. She stuck up for a friend and was berated for it.

An events manager in her twenties who we'll call Olivia also shared her story with me about being called a snowflake, this time by a friend. It happened when Olivia said to her friend that the reason the Disney film *One of Our Dinosaurs is Missing* is never on TV is 'because it has white English actors with yellow painted faces, pretending to be Chinese'. You would think this explanation would be pretty self-evident. But pointing out someone *else's* racial sensitivity (in this case, television programmers) was enough to make her friend call *her* a snowflake. It made her 'angry and hurt' but Olivia recognised her dilemma: 'It's a catch-22, because if you respond by saying, "I don't like that you called me a snowflake," you are (to them) proving that you are sensitive.'

The people who may hurt us the most with the term 'snowflake' are those that are closest to us. I heard from a person whose own brother-in-law has called her a snowflake 'more times than [she] can remember.' This person, who we'll call Angela since we're talking about her actual family, says that when this happens, it 'usually has to do with [her] doing something he considered typical millennial behaviour.' Once, he called her a snowflake because she quit a new job 'where the boss seemed like a cruel drug addict.' Angela explained: 'I thought it seemed like a normal thing to do – quit a terrible job before it ruined my life – but apparently it was a snowflake move.' Standing up for herself at work was enough to be denounced as a snowflake – by a family member.

Others have told me they were called snowflakes for comments they left on news articles criticising powerful people and policies, or for tweeting their opinions. They identified being called a snowflake as a simple way to 'shut down discourse.'

A friend of mine, Amna Saleem, told me she thinks that calling someone a snowflake is a way to shut down conversation before it can threaten privilege. Amna is a Scottish-Pakistani writer who is frequently in the public eye and speaks often about racism and sexism. As a result, she gets called a snowflake or similar all the time. 'Usually what they actually mean,' Amna told me, 'is HOW DARE YOU MESS WITH THE STATUS QUO THAT BENEFITS ME?'

I have also heard from people who are white, male, straight, or all of the above – but they, too, have been called snowflakes for the times when they stood up for those with different backgrounds, or advocated for a political position meant to empower other groups. They were punished for breaking ranks with other white men and called snowflakes as a result.

Tom Ward is a PhD student living in Belfast. He's been called a snowflake twice. Once was at Manchester Pride in 2019, after shouting 'Fuck Boris'. The other happened when he was organising a rally at the University of York against what he called 'extortionate rents' for student housing. A member of the University of York Liberal Democrats, who were opposed to the cuts to student rent costs, called him a snowflake for organising the rally. How did Ward respond to each experience? At Manchester Pride, he simply shouted 'Fuck Boris' again. After the run-in with the Lib Dem, though, he says he just laughed. What does Ward make of the term snowflake, after being called one? Maybe, he said, it's 'an attempt to ground baseless prejudice in a baseless and meaningless phraseology.' In his encounters, that is, he felt that the insult meant basically nothing.

In many ways, the word snowflake *does* mean nothing. It can twist and morph its meaning as it goes, and slides between gaps in conversation like a noxious ooze. Its intent, though, matters a lot, whether it's wielded by an American tourist on a lovely visit to New Zealand, a Boris Johnson-loving Manchester Pride attendee, or even a Liberal Democrat. Calling someone a snowflake is a way, in each of these examples and the many more we will encounter, to draw a line between yourself and others.

Collins English Dictionary named 'snowflake generation' as one of its ten phrases of the year in 2016.[1] Looking back at the list, some of its other top words already seem dated. 'Mic drop' is now something said by supporters of white-bread boy-wonder Pete Buttigieg, former Democratic presidential candidate and newly minted US Transportation Secretary, when he has said something clever on Fox News. 'Dude food' was undoubtedly never more than a dead-inside marketing consultant's attempt to sell frozen meats. Other words from the 2016 list, though, have stuck around. The number-one word of the year was 'Brexit', which, I've heard, is still going strong. And then there's 'snowflake' which, with or without the 'generation' tacked onto it, has only grown more ubiquitous as an ever more frustrating term.

The Collins definition of 'snowflake generation' limits snowflakery to one subsection of millennials:

> the young adults of the 2010s, viewed as being less resilient and more prone to taking offence than previous generations.[2]

While snowflakes may be of any age and ilk, the snowflake *generation* was, at least in 2016, those who came of age in the 2010s in a maelstrom of weakness and offence-taking. It was me and my terrible, pathetic friends. This definition, though, doesn't name the source or the cause of this embarrassing class of young adults. You have in this definition a sense of the delicacy of the real-world snowflake, which melts at the slightest touch. It also takes a passive approach to the person who has 'viewed' in this way. Who views the young adults of the 2010s this way? *They* do.

This definition of the 'snowflake generation' doesn't, however, give us the other important metaphor of the snowflake for pitiful youths: our specialness. As the snowflake is crystallised into an infinity of unique designs, my lamentable and inadequate generation sees ourselves as impossibly *unique*. We believe that each of us is different, and what could be more grotesque than that?

Over in the *American Heritage Dictionary*, meanwhile, we find a definition that includes this awful sense of individuality. A snowflake is 'a person who is considered to be overly sensitive or too easily offended, especially as a result of believing himself or herself to be unique or special.'[3] This definition names cause and effect. The fragility is caused by the sense of specialness. The snowflake's sense of being a unique individual, different from anyone else who has ever lived, is the source of her undoing. She is unable to experience her lived reality without succumbing to offence. What offence? We aren't told. Offence about *things*.

The *Oxford English Dictionary* takes a similar look at the snowflake. The *OED*'s snowflake is 'originally: a person, esp. a child, regarded as having a unique personality and potential. Later: a person mockingly characterised as overly sensitive or easily offended, esp. one said to consider himself or herself entitled to special treatment or consideration.'[4] The *OED* definition reminds us that it didn't always have to be this way. Being called a snowflake was once like being called a gifted and talented child. Once upon a time, a snowflake was a bright young thing. It was little Priscilla who excelled at the pianoforte, before Priscilla grew up, shaved her head and started a new feminist society at SOAS.

Again, the *OED* definition leaves us without context. Snowflakes feel entitled to special treatment or consideration. What kind of special treatment? Does this special treatment or consideration mean 'a ramp into shops for wheelchair users'? Or does it mean 'not having to do the washing up because Priscilla is such a precious young child, and she mustn't spoil her delicate fingers'? We don't know, and it isn't, apparently, an important distinction to the definition of the snowflake. Snowflakes simply feel entitled to *stuff*.

An October 2019 explainer in the *Sun* illustrates the popular understanding of snowflakes quite well, describing one as an 'overly sensitive person who thinks the world revolves around them.'[5] An example helps expand the point: 'Snowflakes gasp in horror when they hear an opinion they don't like.' Snowflakes furthermore 'believe they have a right to be protected from anything unpalatable.' It is not said what the unpalatable thing might be. It could be a racial slur, it could be a rude glance, it could be a dead body. The content of the unpalatable thing does not matter to the *Sun*. What matters is the sensitivity, the self-centredness, the demand for protection and, of course, the gasp of horror.

The *Sun*'s definition of snowflakes, unlike the dictionaries', leans heavily on the imagined antics of the modern university student: 'Sensitive uni students are often labelled snowflakes because they receive "trigger warnings" on books and lectures that might contain upsetting subjects.' The loathed sense of specialness is tied closely to receiving a university education. It's true, some people who go to university are in many ways an elite, or on their way to join the elite. But that isn't what is at issue here. It isn't about a university student's lack of understanding of or contact with the majority of the country. It's that they're upset. The *Sun* explainer brings up some other key themes that swirl around the snowflake discourse: free speech and safe spaces. 'Today, many of these unis are hostile to free speech and determined to shield students from any ideas they don't like,' while 'students unions demand "safe spaces" – areas where people cannot disagree with or challenge your ideas.' (This, it must be said, is not what safe spaces are, but we'll get to that.)

The *Sun* adds that snowflakes are 'self-obsessed and fragile, easily offended, or unable to deal with opposing opinions.' Opinions about music? Films? Or whether girls can do science? No matter. And finally, a photo caption in the *Sun*'s piece helpfully adds: 'Many "snowflake" young people took the result of the Brexit referendum personally.' At last, a hard example: snowflakes are not just angry about Brexit, they are making it all about themselves. The snowflake believes that the biggest political event in Britain in a generation has something to do with them. Because they are too sensitive. And so they *gasp*. There isn't any inherent reason that different characteristics like 'supporting Britain's member-ship of the European Union' and 'being self-obsessed' should go together. The force of the word 'snowflake' serves as a shorthand to place many disparate attributes together. It adds 'easily offended' to 'overly sensitive' to 'wanting to be able to live and work in twenty-eight countries.'

This didn't happen by accident.

*   *   *

In these various 'official' definitions a conflicted picture of snowflakery begins to emerge. In some definitions, you could imagine loving a snowflake. Who doesn't sometimes enjoy an over-sensitive person, for example? Like the hot guy at my high school who cried every single time his basketball team lost a game. Tender, sensitive and tall. He was a testament to the beauty of the human soul, among other things. But for most of these definitions so far, the person is not sensitive because of external factors. They are sensitive because of how they feel about themselves. In considering themselves special and unique, it's implied, but not stated, they think they are *better* than everyone else. And that's not sexy, or tall.

The reason for someone being sensitive or offended or entitled should surely be at the centre of any definition of a snowflake, but it isn't. You'd feel quite differently about someone who is offended by a chipped teacup and someone who is offended by a politician demanding the return of the whipping post to town squares across Britain. (Then again, it can be difficult to predict the priorities of the British populace.) But the act of being offended *itself* is how we understand the modern snowflake. As it happens, someone can be called a snowflake for appearing sensitive about anything from 'people being slightly rude' to 'the election of Donald Trump'. Not all offences are ridiculed equally, but being offended at all is enough to be deemed a snowflake.

But by the time an informal insult has made it to the dictionary, or, indeed, the *Sun*, it's already had a long journey through the culture. In the case of snowflake, its pejorative use has gone back as far as our understanding of what an actual, physical snowflake is. It's drifted across the centuries like a cold front bearing down on us from a frozen-over hell. It was taken up by politicians during the Civil War and by the mean girls of Tumblr in the early 2000s. It has burst from the darkest corners of the internet into the mouths of the most powerful people in the world.

Where does the term snowflake come from in the first place? Who brought us this term, and why?

The earliest use of the term snowflake to refer to a human being was most likely in Missouri in the 1860s. During the US Civil War, Missourians fought both for the Confederacy and the Union. As the state grappled with the slavery question and whether or not to enter the Civil War, three political factions emerged in the state legislature.

There were the Charcoals, radicals who believed in 'prosecuting the war vigorously and wiping out slavery as soon as possible,' as described in a history of Missouri written in 1876, the thrilling *Saint Louis: The Future Great City of the World* by one L. U. Reavis.[6] The next faction was the 'moderate war men', known as the Claybanks due to the middling colour of the local clay. And finally, you had the 'snowflakes', who were opposed to the abolition of slavery and to the Civil War generally. 'The anti-war and pro-slavery men gloried in the name of "snowflakes",' writes our friend L. U. Reavis. According to Merriam-Webster lexicographer Emily Brewster, this is probably due to the fact that snow is white, as these men favoured whiteness above all.[7]

Brewster writes that the Missouri usage did not seem to spread beyond the state or the historical context. After its usage in that time and place, snowflake only meant, for a while, little bits of snow. While the Missouri usage was the first consistent usage of the term, snowflake was also sometimes used interchangeably as far back as the 1780s with the derogatory 'snowball', defined in *Bartlett's Dictionary of Americanisms* as 'a jeering appellation' for a black person. It was an ironic way to refer to a black person as something white, in the pinnacle of 1780s racist humour.

Fast forward to the 1970s, when 'snowflake' was used as slang for cocaine, as an insult for white people, or for a black man who 'acted white'.

Over the years, 'snowflake' has had a large number of meanings, but today's insult doesn't emerge from any of the above usages. The modern snowflake appears on the scene much more recently, slowly dressing itself in new connotations over the years.

There was a time when 'snowflake' was a nice thing to be called. It could be a positive and uplifting term. If someone called you a snowflake, they probably wanted you to feel wonderful and precious. A snowflake in this age of innocence was something a kindly elementary school teacher might call you. It might appear in a self-help book, or on a poster on the wall of a therapist's waiting room, set over a picture of some pleasant pine trees. In 1983, the term appeared in the evangelical writer and minister J. MacArthur's *Spiritual Gifts*. In this religious study, MacArthur writes: 'You are a snowflake. There are no two of you alike. God cannot trade you for anyone.'[8] God loves a special snowflake – that's why he made us this way. If you're into that kind of thing.

A snowflake was once a nice thing, but the time of nice things has passed. We have *Fight Club* by Chuck Palahniuk to thank for this, at least in part. In the book version of *Fight Club*, which came out in 1996, we find the line: 'You are not a beautiful and unique snowflake. You are the same decaying organic matter as everyone, and we are all part of the same compost pile.'[9] A saying you would probably *not* find on a poster over a picture of pleasant pine trees in a therapist's waiting room. Unless your therapist was also an angry 15-year-old boy.

In the 1999 film version of *Fight Club*, we get an even bleaker version of the same line: 'Listen up, maggots. You are not special. You are not the beautiful or unique snowflake. You are the same decaying organic matter as everything else. We are the all-singing, all-dancing crap of the world. We are all part of the same compost heap.' While you could argue that no two maggots are alike, either, and indeed all part of the same miracle of creation, this is hardly an uplifting message.

Whether he got the idea from someone else, or it sprung fully formed into his brilliantly twisted mind, Mr Palahniuk was happy to claim credit for the resurgence of the term 'special snowflake' to the *Evening Standard*'s Londoner's Diary in January 2017.[10] Presented with a listening ear, Palahniuk also took the opportunity to reprimand today's young people. He has some friends who are high school teachers, and *they* say that students these days 'are very easily offended.' And that's not all. 'There is a new kind of Victorianism,' he told the *Standard*. Palahniuk sees snowflakery as a problem of the left, who are 'always reacting to things'. This is a grave sin in the eyes of a man who wrote a book about men punching each other in the face for no reason whatsoever.

In the *Fight Club* universe, we see another source of people's discomfort with snowflakes. Perhaps being a snowflake is just a bit *girly*. Feeling things? Girl stuff. Weakness? Definitely feminine. Punching Jared Leto in his beautiful face? Real man shit. For a certain subset of commentator, hating snowflakes is just another way to defend one's masculinity. As Dana Schwartz wrote in GQ in February 2017, the purpose of the 'snowflake' insult 'is dismissing liberalism as something effeminate, and also infantile.'[11] Schwartz writes of snowflake hatred as a dismissal of the lessons you learn in primary school: 'sharing is caring' is communism, and 'feelings are good' is contrary to the cold and rational universe of facts and graphs to which the snowflake hater subscribes.

Schwartz finds another away to connect the multivariate meanings of the snowflake: 'Calling someone a snowflake combines every single thing a college freshman loves: trolling people on the internet, a self-satisfied sense of the superiority of one's own impeccable powers of reasoning, and *Fight Club*.' It's fine that a college freshman would love all of the above. Being young is a wonderful time to be awful and superior. That's what youth is for. But the snowflake insult has sadly escaped the realm of the awful young and found its way to the lips of those who should know better.

*   *   *

After getting beaten up in *Fight Club*, the meaning of the snowflake dusted itself off and continued to develop. Throughout the noughties and early 2010s, a derogatory 'snowflake' stayed alive with Palahniuk's general meaning. The *New Statesmans'* Amelia Tait writes that 'special snowflake' was tossed around the social network Tumblr in this time, when it was used 'to insult those with dyed hair and alternative gender pronouns.'[12] A snowflake on Tumblr was seen as someone who thought they were special, or someone sensitive – but that's not all. They were also someone bending gender norms on the internet. This is a key aspect of snowflake hatred today, as we'll see in a future chapter. Perhaps the fastest route to being called a snowflake in Britain today is to challenge a binary, biologically determined understanding of gender.

But the evolution of the snowflake insult didn't stop with the mean teens of Tumblr. In the years leading up to the social and political upheaval of 2016, the most significant source of the current understanding of a snowflake came from the so-called alt-right.

The alt-right is something of a catch-all term. If you trawl the depths of the internet and reel in that particular net, you'll find a wide variety of unpleasant creatures and bottom feeders. First, you have the Gamergaters. If you don't know what Gamergate is, you probably have clear skin, go for lots of runs, eat five servings of vegetables a day and are a loving son or daughter to your parents. Gamergate began in 2014, when a conspiracy in the world of video games (bear with me!) claimed that the gaming press was in cahoots with certain feminist game developers. As in all good conspiracies, there were allegations of trading sex for positive reviews, with the general idea that women and progressives were entering the world of gaming by sleeping their way to the top. And, once they got there, they had the nerve to make female video game characters *less busty*. Female characters in games no longer had their tits fully out, all the time, while fighting wars in space. This, to those who would become known as Gamergaters, was a travesty.

Two women game developers, Zoë Quinn and Brianna Wu, along with the journalist Anita Sarkeesian, became the targets of an online harassment campaign. This was Gamergate. A sort of war against there being too much feminism in video games, fought online, with real-world consequences. Gamergate was both deeply silly – people getting furious about feminist gamers! – and totally horrifying. Quinn, Wu and Sarkeesian faced thousands and thousands of death threats, the hacking of their accounts and leaking of their personal information, and a vast organised attempt to derail their careers and their personal lives. For her criticism of sexist depictions of women in video games, Sarkeesian had to cancel speaking events after threats of mass shootings. Brianna Wu had to leave her home after her address was published on the platform 8chan. The FBI got involved.

What Gamergaters really stood for was never totally clear. The official line – 'this is about ethics in gaming journalism' – has become a sort of joke about men grasping for 'ethical' reasons to hate feminism and women generally. Gamergate can be thought of above all as the first great gathering of reactionary politics on the internet, one of the first coordinated attempts among consumers of media which had nothing to do with politics – video games! – to push back against the revitalised cultural power of feminism and social justice. It is from Gamergate that we get the idea of the 'Social Justice Warrior' or SJW. This term gave a name to a figure who is paramount to future critics of snowflakes generally: the person who has made it their personal battle to fight for social justice. This may not sound like such a bad thing to be to the untrained ear, but it is to a large swathe of the alt-right, the internet and beyond – the same people who call their enemies 'snowflake' to this day.

Gamergaters, though, make up only one part of the alt-right. You also have the dwellers of social networks 4chan, 8chan and certain corners of Reddit. You have men whose identity is formed primarily around their ability or inability to have sex with women. You have on the one hand the pick-up artists, who believe themselves cunning manipulators of women, able to convert the low self-esteem of women into sexual opportunity. On the other hand, you have the 'incels', short for those who are 'involuntarily celibate'. For these men, the women who apparently owe them sex are instead having sex with beautiful, stupid 'Chads', which is crazy given what 'nice guys' incels often claim themselves to be. This is of course classically funny, to think of men being furious that they aren't getting laid and creating whole identities and communities around this fact. But these communities have birthed real-world violence, as in 2014 when a self-described incel killed six people in the college town of Isla Vista, California, in 'retribution' for his rejection by women. He would not be the last self-identified incel to kill.

The alt-right encompasses multiple identities that often overlap. It can also encompass old-fashioned white supremacists and neo-Nazi groups who have found a presence online. The term alt-right has been taken up enthusiastically by these groups in particular, who supposed that they might find more widespread credibility being called alt-right rather than being called white supremacists or neo-Nazis. They were right – and several prominent leaders of the alt-right have received lengthy profiles in mainstream press, complete with flattering photographs and comments about their 'dapper' clothing.[13] The strategy of far-right leaders using their image to make themselves palatable to the mainstream is nothing new. The former Ku Klux Klan leader David Duke did exactly this when he attempted to revitalise his political career in the late 1980s, and media profiles referred to him as a 'clean cut' and 'well-dressed' man.[14] This is apparently a convincing strategy to members of the press more offended by bad aesthetics than bad politics.

For the modern far right, or alt-right, the snowflake is more or less the same as the social justice warrior. It's the person who isn't as *hard* as they are online. It is the person who is fragile and believes they are special when they are *not*. The alt-right defines itself by what it hates. It hates the snowflake and in doing so holds itself up as the anti-snowflake – a movement of strength and hardiness and callousness and comfortable, outward racism.

But the use of the term snowflake does not only come from a place of hatred. It can also come from a place of irony. Indeed, as the *New Statesman*'s technology and culture writer Sarah Manavis told me, it may be that a 'significant minority (if not most) of the alt-right don't use the term snowflake in actual anger or sincerity, but with trolling as the main motivation.' While it's true that the alt-right (and the right more generally) have political differences with liberals, Manavis said, they also 'simply enjoy watching them lose it at being insulted.'

But this urge to get a rise out of liberals and leftists does not mean that the alt-right cannot also be invested in violence and dehumanisation. When a gunman killed 51 people at two mosques in New Zealand in 2019, he not only live-streamed his attack on Facebook, but shared a manifesto which seemed to mingle both sincerely held far-right beliefs, and jokes and memes meant to troll and mislead the press.[15] While taunts and trolls may have an ironic motivation, the line between performance and reality is not always easy to find, nor an effective barrier against real-world consequences.

Ironic or not, the alt-right created a powerful political force in the act of creating and opposing the figure of the snowflake, one that hasn't gone unnoticed or untapped by mainstream politicians in the US and the UK alike.

In the years leading up to 2016, the term snowflake erupted from the backrooms of the alt-right internet to take up its place in the popular consciousness and in mainstream media. It made that journey through the pages of the far-right press.

A large portion of the blame for the constant, pejorative use of 'snowflake' can be placed at the presumably disgusting feet of Steve

Bannon, who co-founded the conservative website *Breitbart News* in 2007. By 2016, the campaign chairman and soon-to-be senior counsellor to President Donald Trump declared *Breitbart* to be 'the platform for the alt-right.'[16] Under Bannon's leadership, the website had indeed transformed into a vehicle for delivering white nationalist talking points into the social media feeds and news programmes of more mainstream journalists and readers.

A constant theme of *Breitbart* content in the years before and after 2016 was that the snowflakes of the left were threatening to destroy the world through both their authoritarianism and their utter frailty. The rejection of 'political correctness' is among the site's key motivators. To hate the 'politically correct' is not to simply think it is a bit tiring to accommodate different types of people in your day-to-day life, or to use inoffensive language. It is to see the existence and empowerment of different types of identities beyond straight white maleness as a threat to your position in society. This is an explicit, stated concern of the alt-right.

The alt-right can be thought of as a movement by primarily young white men who reject traditional conservatism in favour of outright white supremacy. They see themselves as defenders of whiteness and maleness, groups they see as under threat from feminism and from a 'white genocide', the conspiratorial idea that immigration, globalisation and abortion rights are part of a plot to eradicate white people from the earth. They are anti-immigrant and consider themselves anti-establishment – even after the ascension of Trump to the US presidency, who wholly embraced the alt-right as part of his base. Steve Bannon would call his politics a 'nationalism' without explicitly adding a 'white', but the alt-right he helped to champion deals in explicitly racist memes.

Bannon left *Breitbart* to chair the Trump campaign in August 2016, then returned to the site after his ousting from the ever-churning White House one year later. Just a few months after that, in January

2018, Bannon was also ousted from *Breitbart* after the publication of journalist Michael Wolff's questionably sourced *Fire and Fury*, in which he was quoted as saying that Ivanka Trump, the president's daughter, was 'dumb as a brick'.[17] This apparently created some tension between the president, Bannon and the brick. But even after Steve Bannon was dismissed from his role in the White House in August of 2017, as McKay Coppins observed in *The Atlantic*, President Trump continued to use the kind of language popularised on *Breitbart* in his day-to-day business and understanding of the world.[18] He referred to his own aides as 'globalists' and his former Secretary of State as 'establishment'. These, writes Coppins, are 'distinctly *Breitbart*ian terms'. While these words might seem innocent enough, they are in fact among the 'strongest epithets' of the *Breitbart* world, summing up what the alt-right opposes – with strong anti-Semitic overtones of a shadowy, globalist Jewish elite.

In any case, during his stint in the White House and at the helm of *Breitbart*, Bannon presided over a shifting of the Overton window – a phrase for what society considers acceptable discourse – far to the right. With this shift, the alt-right's lexicon reached a much wider audience. Some members of the alt-right are explicitly attempting to shift the Overton window to include their beliefs and their language, and so far they're doing a pretty good job.

The modern pejorative use of snowflake – and the political intent behind its use – has launched from the darkest corners of the internet into the mainstream, and into the language of not only the alt-right's supporters, but also some of its critics on the left and the right.

The language of the alt-right is vast and replete with hidden meanings and inside jokes. It deals in symbols and phrases which criss-cross the divide between the ironic and the serious. As Joe Bernstein wrote at the end of 2015 for *BuzzFeed*, 'like any counterculture, this one has developed its own social norms, accepted truths, sense of humour, methods of communications, and even terminology.' 'Snowflake' is among them, but unlike other terms such as 'white genocide', it has seeped into the vernacular of those who would like to think themselves very far in attitude, comportment and political belief from the racist alt-right.

How did this language creep occur?

In 2015 and 2016, mainstream media outlets frequently invited prominent alt-right figures onto their programmes, like the once popular but now irrelevant British far-right provocateur Milo Yiannopoulos, and the American far-right extremist Richard Spencer. In Britain, Yiannopoulos appeared on Channel 4 and the BBC. On Sky News, Yiannopoulos participated in a debate about whether or not women make rubbish scientists.[19] Richard Spencer was interviewed on Channel 4 for a segment on whether the alt-right were 'testing the limits of free speech' at American universities.[20] In the US, Richard Spencer was interviewed on the staid evening public programme, *PBS NewsHour*, and the progressive magazine *Mother Jones* tweeted out a long profile of him with the teaser: 'Meet the dapper white nationalist riding the Trump wave'.[21] (That article was updated with an editor's note after Spencer gave a speech proclaiming 'Hail Trump, hail our people, hail victory!' just a few weeks later to a crowd of seig-heiling onlookers.) With the sheen of credibility granted them by these platforms – even when challenged by the channels' most eminent presenters – more and more people felt justified in picking up the opinions and the terminology of the alt-right. In a 'both sides' understanding of media, in which debates are framed as civilised discussions between competing, equally legitimate good-faith actors, it becomes easier for an average person to empathise at least a little with an ideology as extreme as the alt-right. Figures such as Yiannopoulos and Spencer couch their extremism as 'politically incorrect' – something many watchers will aspire to be. (Even those with 'politically correct' views don't normally want to frame themselves as 'politically correct'.) And so you have an audience of regular people who can watch figures such as Spencer and Yiannopoulos and think, 'these guys aren't politically correct – and neither am I.' What else might they have in common, then? (One of the things Donald Trump's supporters enjoy about him, and also enjoy about these alt-right figures, is indeed their explicit objection to 'political correctness'.)

Yiannopoulos wrote in a November 2015 article for *Breitbart* titled 'Why I'm Winning' that every time he entered a new platform or internet subculture, 'I immediately begin hearing the same grievances about you, the progressive media establishment.'[22] He wrote about how many times he had been profiled by the media, and promised to 'continue to lead the charge for free speech and freedom of thought,' as well as 'the internet's right to comment on a woman's weight or to post Hitler memes because *words don't hurt* and *I don't care about the feelings of special snowflakes* and it's precisely the most offensive and obnoxious speech that needs to be protected with the most ferocity.' It was a taunt to the press from a man enamoured of his own invulnerability. It framed his fans' inelegant desires, such as the right to call women fat, as a noble crusade in the name of free speech.

Since writing 'Why I'm Winning', though, Yiannopoulos has been banned from YouTube, Twitter and other platforms, and is no longer invited to speaking events at universities. The final straw was his apparent endorsement of paedophilia in an old video that came to light in 2017. In the video, he said that sexual relationships 'between younger boys and older men' could be a beneficial, 'coming-of-age' experience.[23] Yiannopoulos blamed 'deceptive editing' and 'British sarcasm' for the scandal, apologised for 'imprecise language', and clarified: 'I do not endorse paedophilia.'[24] As a result of his deplatforming, however, people don't really talk about him anymore. I mostly think about him nowadays when remembering one of the all-time greatest Twitter threads, sparked by journalist Jeb Lund, who called Yiannopoulos a 'Barney-wearing-a-teen's-poplin top,

Wonka-accident amazing-gobstopper-ass motherfucker', among other, well, politically incorrect things.[25] Yiannopoulos is now so defunct that in writing about him here, I fear I may inadvertently summon him back to life, like saying 'Candyman' in front of a mirror. But the fact is, despite the many media panics centred on the idea that 'no-platforming' figures such as Yiannopoulos will only make them stronger, his banishment from respectable institutions and media platforms hasn't made his him sexier and more dangerous. Instead, he's gone from being one of the leading voices of the far right in Britain and America to being millions of dollars in debt after his book deal was retracted and his public writing and speaking engagements dried up. 'Do you know how successful you have to be to owe that kind of money?' Yiannopoulos boasted on Facebook.[26] 'Two years of being no-platformed, banned, blacklisted and censored . . . has taken its toll.' As of 2018, he was spotted selling milk thistle extract nutritional supplements on the conspiracy-mongering web show *InfoWars*.[27]

There's plenty more to say about Yiannopoulos, unfortunately, so keep your children safely hidden. But for now, we can see the way that with his precipitous rise into public consciousness in the middle of the 2010s, Yiannopoulos was one of the many carriers of the term snowflake from the fringe of the racist internet to the centre of public discourse. Indeed, the term and its attendant ideology has outlasted him, and grown larger than he ever was. While Yiannopoulos now feels like an unsavoury footnote to the last decade, the forces that led to his rise remain largely unchanged – both the mainstream outlets whose attention he enjoyed, and the 'politically incorrect' ideas he espoused.

Whether or not Yiannopoulos finds a platform again, his time spent in the spotlight was bright enough and long enough that his arguments gained a foothold across the political spectrum. *Breitbart* writer Allum Bokhari saw this process take place, writing about critiques of university student snowflakery in particular. 'It is no longer uncommon to see condemnations of student censorship in liberal publications such as the *Guardian*, the *New York Times*, and the *Daily Beast*,' he wrote in March 2016.[28] As a result, he says, 'left-wing activists now face hostility from the left, the centre, and the right (who, after years of warnings about radicalism on campus, are no doubt feeling a great sense of vindication) as well as mainstream media.'

The racist clowns of the internet formed a flexible mould for the snowflake character, which now can be filled in by anyone in need of a straw man or an enemy. This straw man was put to good use in 2016.

The far right originated the snowflake insult and aired its hatred of snowflakes to an ever-wider audience through 2015. But it was in 2016, with Britain's vote to leave the European Union and the election of Donald Trump as US president, that the term emerged from hiding in the far-right corners of the internet to take its place at the forefront of political debate in both the US and the UK. Some of the main characters of that year have risen to greater power or fallen by the wayside, but the hatred of snowflakes churns ever onward, nowhere more relentlessly than in the British press.

It was in 2016 that author Claire Fox published her book '*I Find that Offensive!*', an explicit assault on the idea of the snowflake, and a popular article in the *Daily Mail* outlining its top lines before a wide audience. Fox's well-timed publicity tour meant that by the day of the Brexit vote, the British public was primed to see snowflakes everywhere, particularly among the ranks of young people most upset about the referendum result. As the leaders of the Leave campaign from Nigel Farage to Boris Johnson took their victory lap, they defined their defeated opponents as emotional, fragile and overly politically correct. Those who had voted to Remain in the EU were a rich seam of snowflakes to be mocked and hated.

In '*I Find that Offensive!*' (and its thrilling sequel, '*I Still Find that Offensive!*') Fox introduced a hatred of snowflakes to an ever-widening audience. So, what do snowflakes find so '*offensive!*'? Once again, their offendedness matters more than what offended them. In fact, Fox sees offence-taking as something snowflakes *enjoy*. She says that snowflakes are 'dangerously thin-skinned' but have an 'almost belligerent sense of entitlement'.[29] She tells stories of 'teenagers who believed that words really hurt and that contradictory opinions to their own beliefs were the cause of real harm.' Her proof of this comes from two poorly received school talks she gave: one about Islam to a ninety per cent Muslim school, and one questioning whether the ostracisation of footballer Ched Evans after his imprisonment for rape – and later, his acquittal – was 'social justice' or 'mob rule'. As a result of her talk about rape, Fox says, 'a group of emotional girls suggested that maybe as an older woman I needed to be more sensitive to the plight of younger women and that I obviously had no empathy with women worldwide who are raped daily.' She describes the teenagers at both talks as 'shrieking' and 'screeching' and 'shrill'. She finds that the snowflake generation 'too often behave more like sulky, demanding children than young adults,' and says older commentators are worried 'that the young are becoming too mollycoddled and infantilised for the rough and tumble of real life.' Kids these days don't know how to pull a plough.

Fox's book is a quest to discover what has made young people gain their 'insidious deference to offence,' unlike her own and older generations, who, we must understand, were never offended about anything at all (other than, perhaps, the young). Fox's snowflake emits high-pitched noises, is belligerent, indulges in a childlike sulkiness, suffered a mollycoddled upbringing, has a fear of words, and, of course, has a soft spot for mob rule. This may seem a ridiculous vision of a *kids these days*, but Fox has articulated an easily hateful caricature of a young person and lobbed it into the political sphere. There, it's found many takers.

Across the Atlantic, the political cartoonist Ben Garrison has further filled in the picture of what a snowflake looks like, this time from the perspective of the favourite cartoonist of the alt-right.[30] Garrison's work centres on many figures of the left, and often depicts classic racist and anti-Semitic tropes. Congresswoman Alexandria Ocasio-Cortez, known popularly as AOC, makes frequent appearances in his cartoons. In one, the former bartender is pictured behind a bar serving up signature cocktails including the 'Venezuelan Surprise', the 'Late Term Abortion' and the 'Stalin Stale Ale'.[31] In a tiny, barely visible thimble, we see the less prominent cocktail, the 'Reason and Logic Liqueur'. It seems not to be a favourite of the hideous bartender, who wears a crop top which says, 'SOCIALISM IS SEXY'. 'Drink up!' the cartoon AOC implores us. 'Someone else will pay for it.' The cartoon is awful, but the bar sounds great.

In another cartoon we see a terrifying scene: the 'Attack of the Crybullies'.[32] Three enormous babies stomp down a university path. The first one wields a rattle which says 'RACIST!!' and a wooden sword labelled 'SOCIAL JUSTICE'. The second baby is a girl. She has dyed hair and 'SPECIAL SNOWFLAKE' across her belly. Behind her, a tattooed boy baby with a sign which says '#HOLD YOUR BREATH FOR JUSTICE'. They are all wearing 'pampered' diapers and they're all crying furiously about 'MY FEEWINGS'. Beneath their horrible stomping feet are a few unfortunate 'liberals'. In the background, another angry baby sits in his 'safe space', and in the foreground, we see a pile of burning books including one titled 'REASON', one called 'LOGIC', and the United States Constitution. The giant angry babies stomp through their fancy university campus, holding their breath and trampling respectable liberals and the founding document of the United States in their path. Yes, they are babies. But they're also giant monsters. The snowflake is both pathetic and fearsome. The snowflake is physically hideous. The cartoon is very stupid, but it's also intoxicating to those in search of an enemy to blame for their ills.

This silly, muddled cartoon shows us a world view which dictates political reality. It consolidates a hatred of certain characteristics and behaviours. While covering the 2020 election, from the crowded Democratic primaries through to the vote and ensuing crisis, I realised how often people vote for vibes (or against vibes) rather than for or against policies. This cartoon captures one such vibe, the vibe of the snowflake. Those who vote against this vibe produce Brexit and Trump and whatever comes next. It is hard for a very politically engaged person to realise how unengaged most people are. They are distanced from journalists, and from pollsters, by barriers of class and education. But those who still vote have to make up their mind somehow. They may see a cartoon like Garrison's and know immediately that they hate what it depicts. A politician such as Nigel Farage or Donald Trump is very good at signalling to such people that they, too, stand against the amorphous cry-babies. For so many Brits and Americans who have abandoned their faith in media and experts – often with good reason – this may be all they need to know. And once in power, a figure such as Trump can look at vanquished opponents and say not just that they are losers (though he also says that) – but that their reaction to their loss is a profound display of moral weakness. Nigel Farage and other leading pro-Brexit campaigners can and do say that the upset they witnessed after the EU referendum from Remain voters was a humiliating display of snowflakery.

Another quite ironic example of this could be found in a tweet from the American conservative media publisher Brent Bozell, who tweeted on 20 January 2021, the day of Joe Biden's inauguration as president, that 'unlike the snowflake left four years ago, today conservatives were able to survive without having to hug teddy bears, scream into pillows, fill in colouring books, find crying rooms and have therapy sessions.'[33] Well, Brent, maybe if they'd gone to therapy or done some colouring in, they wouldn't have violently stormed the US Capitol.

It is hardly a new phenomenon to be sad that your party or your candidate or your side in a referendum has lost. The very heart of political contest depends on people caring about different things, often deeply. But for the snowflake critic, expressions of sadness, anger and grief at a political loss is not merely a natural emotional reaction. It is an attempt – a *stifling* and *censorious* attempt – to undermine democracy. In expressing the sadness of losing, there is an imagined power grab, a violent attempt to threaten the winning side. The snowflake is cast as aggressive, and if the snowflake is aggressive, its opponents must be the victims of that aggression – even as they gained political power after the Brexit vote and in general elections in both the UK and the US.

Talia Lavin wrote of this phenomenon for the *Village Voice* in April 2018 in an article titled 'The far-right's ironic snowflake problem'.[34] Her piece was inspired by an incident in which Milo Yiannopoulos encountered members of the left-wing political organisation the Democratic Socialists of America, the DSA, in a bar in Manhattan. The DSA members bought his beers for him, and then sang the famous trade union anthem, 'Solidarity Forever'. Yiannopoulos claims he was shoved in the incident – though this was disproved by video evidence. The incident led to the conservative *Washington Examiner* writing about 'The far-left's ironic Nazi problem', which led to Tucker Carlson railing against left-wing 'fascists' on his Fox News show – the natural life cycle of an American snowflake panic. The argument was this: the right and the far-right are victims of the snowflakes of the left, who wield authoritarian power through their victimhood. But not just any power. *Fascist power.* Lavin imagines that this argument stems from the discomfort of any oppositional ideology achieving institutional power: 'Having found themselves in political power, but nonetheless without complete cultural dominance, these conservatives must manufacture a sense of powerlessness.' The battle over who does and does not *actually* wield power over whom is at the heart of arguments about snowflakes. Lavin writes that American conservatives, 'finding themselves in possession of all three branches of government, and a plurality of state governments too, find themselves so bereft of struggle that they must invent it.' The snowflake may be defined as weak, coddled and mentally frail. But if the snowflake critic wishes to wage a war against elite cultural forces, the snowflake can never be depicted as an underdog.

President Trump, and his right-wing comrades in Britain such as Nigel Farage, built their appeal at least in part on a willingness to stick it to these apparently culturally dominant snowflakes. The snowflake they claim to stand in opposition to can be anyone from a university student to Meryl Streep calling for more empathy in a Golden Globes acceptance speech. The snowflakes of 2016 and beyond are the protestors of the women's march, and the lawyers going to airports to assist the victims of Trump's travel ban against Muslims, and the Jewish social justice groups visiting the US border with Mexico to demonstrate against the separation of migrant children from their parents. In any of these iterations, the snowflake in the eyes of its critic wields weakness as a source of undemocratic power. As American conservative author Ben Shapiro tweeted the day after the 2016 US presidential election – 'Precious snowflakes think Trump won't assume office if they fuss? The real world doesn't pay them to believe in the power of their dreams.' The snowflakes of Shapiro's imaginary fuss like babies, and in doing so hope to overturn an election. With just enough crying, according to Ben Shapiro, snowflakes think they can overthrow a president. Once again, this claim grew ever more ironic in the wake of President Biden's election, which over half of Republicans still didn't believe was legitimate as of early 2021.[35]

In the hands of the former president and his allies, the snowflake insult and its cousins can also still retain the kind of ironic, trolling motivation so often present when used by the online alt-right. I was reminded of this by Trump's former communications director (of eleven days) Anthony Scaramucci when I interviewed him for the *Washington Post* in 2019. 'He likes lighting you guys up,' he told me, meaning the mainstream press. 'That's part of his move'. Explaining why Trump was so uncommitted to truth-telling, Scaramucci went on:

He wants everybody in the liberal press to sound like Charlie Brown's teacher. You follow? Like, he wants them hair-on-fire every night counting up all the lies he's told. Because he knows his base doesn't like those people, so they like seeing those people 'triggered', you see what I'm saying?[36]

The pleasure of the troll, for Trump as for online alt-righters, lies in pissing people off. Specifically, pissing off their political and cultural enemies. But again, a semi-ironic motivation does not preclude the real-world harms that such trolling can foster. It is a deft political calculation to know exactly which people to rile up, and how, in order to drum up a base. All that base needs is a term like 'snowflake' to stand in for any version of the figure they hate.

What are snowflakes, then, according to their greatest haters and most committed trolls? They are both fragile and belligerent. They make up a mob, but a mob of wussies. Snowflakes will kill you, and then cry because they've upset themselves. Snowflakes require trigger warnings before receiving any unpleasantness, but do not shirk their responsibility to persecute those who disagree with them. Snowflakes are brutal and obsessive and relentlessly unfunny. They shriek and wail like banshees. They are manipulative little babies. Snowflakes are obsessed with themselves, but more importantly, they are obsessed with everyone else falling in line with their opinions. They gasp in horror at offensive statements, and retreat to their safe spaces, from where they plot their totalitarian takeover of politics and society.

Let the contradictions pile up in your mind.

Have you ever met a person who fits this description? I don't think I have. I've met people who were sulky, and people who cried a lot, and people who very actively call out offensive statements of private and public figures. I've also met plenty of regular-degular assholes, and entitled people, and spoiled people, and self-centred people. I've met people who have devoted their lives to activism, and people who have devoted their lives to posting memes about communism on Instagram. I've met people who are extremely unfunny at parties. But I don't think I've met someone who does all of the above. Some reality television characters come close, I suppose – but they're not the ones clamouring for social justice. Does the complete snowflake package actually exist beyond the minds of the snowflake's critics? I don't think it does.

So what's the appropriate response to being called a snowflake? Can it be reclaimed, in the same way that LGBTQ+ activists reclaimed 'queer'? Can it be harnessed as a term to describe those who want to make respect and empathy and outrage and sensitivity a coherent, political force? Yes, it can be – and it should be. But it hasn't happened yet.

Rather than try to reclaim it, or spin it into something positive, many of those who get called snowflakes tend to lob the insult back at their detractors in a game of hot potato. When a conservative figure gets outraged that someone has been rude about a statue, for example, it may be tempting to call him a snowflake for getting so upset.

Perhaps the real snowflakes are the powerful conservative forces who themselves get offended by people getting offended too much. In this iteration, the snowflakers become the snowflakees. They are the ones who are 'triggered' by the supposed prevalence of trigger warnings. They are hysterical about young people getting hysterical and feel entitled to the things they say that millennials feel entitled to, and so on. They are the ones who use their weekly opinion columns to talk about how they aren't allowed to voice their opinions anymore. They are the American tourists getting mad about their credit cards on holiday in New Zealand.

As tempting as it is, I don't think people should use the term snowflake to make fun of the people who have called them snowflakes. If you do, you are simply making the same point as your detractors: that it's embarrassing to feel things strongly. I think the term snowflake should be aspirational, and not merely tossed back at one's ideological foes. In using snowflake defensively, the negative meaning of snowflake is entrenched ever further, to mean an embarrassing display of emotion or hurt feelings or political anger generally. You could call Donald Trump a snowflake for being a sore loser. Or you could call him an aspiring dictator. One is more accurate and more urgent. The other says the worst thing Trump has done in the wake of the 2020 election is display his hurt feelings. If you call a snowflake-hater a snowflake, you get trapped in a cycle of fighting about the wrong things.

In late 2016, at the end of the year of the snowflake's dramatic entry onto the political stage, several commentators argued that the term had already been reclaimed – or was just about to be. Dana Schwartz wrote in *GQ*: 'The only way to fight back against an insult that doesn't mean anything is to reclaim it, to diminish its power by making that identity a point of pride. This is the life cycle of all identity insults, and "snowflake" is already reaching the end of that cycle.'[37] Schwartz pointed to the appearance of signs at various protests saying 'Yes, I am a snowflake' and 'Winter is coming', in reference to *Game of Thrones*. But a few protest signs do not a reclamation make.

In her November 2016 *Guardian* article calling 'poor little snowflake' the 'defining insult of 2016', Rebecca Nicholson also wrote that the left had 'started to reclaim' the term.[38] This reclamation, as opposed to Schwartz's protest signs, was more about the left repurposing the term for its own uses. 'The left has started to reclaim it,' Nicholson writes, 'throwing it back at the people who were using it against them.' A few years after these predictions, Nicholson's version of the reclamation seems to hold more weight. You see many more people, mostly in internet mud-slinging fights, calling other people snowflakes rather than wearing the label proudly. To weaponise snowflake is not a true reclaiming. Queer people did not reclaim 'queer' by calling straight homophobes 'the real queers', although I'm sure it has happened in jest. Moreover, being a 'snowflake' isn't a real identity. It's not even a specifically defined insult, as we've seen. Snowflakedom doesn't cut to the core of who a person is, but to a wide range of possible political beliefs. It's not a race or sexuality. It means you care about something *too much*.

If you have been called a snowflake for getting upset about something you care deeply about, then you probably wouldn't fight back by saying that you don't actually care at all. A snowflake reclamation won't occur by throwing your core, deeply held political beliefs aside and becoming a real asshole. The true way to reclaim the term is to lean into it: 'Yes, I am offended. Yes, I do feel strongly about this. Yes, for saying the racist thing you have just said, I do think you're a potato.'

People aren't comfortable admitting to strong feelings. But in a utopian snowflake future, you'll be allowed to have feelings and name them without undermining your argument. Does this idea make you cringe? Or is it a relief?

What's missing from all of the above definitions of snowflakes – from the benign, the bemused and the furious – is money. In my travels through the inhospitable lands of snowflake discourse, nobody seems to have decided whether snowflakes have lots of money, and that's why they're so awful, or none at all, and that's why they're so bitter. There is no explicit discussion of class. There is certainly a discussion of elitism, but it's an elitism to do with going to university and getting certain ideas there, not an elitism born of old-fashioned cash and assets. Many critics' vision of a snowflake is one who goes to university and studies things that do not matter to a proper working man. But the high-profile critics of snowflakes are rarely any less elite than their targets. One of the most ardent critics of snowflakes in Britain is Tory MP Jacob Rees-Mogg – a man who has kept his childhood nanny around into his middle age – but who works hard to project a certain toughness online, nanny be damned. Even alleged regular-working-man, loves-a-pint, on-and-off UKIP leader Nigel

Farage is the privately educated son of a stockbroker. And so figures such as Piers Morgan don't talk about a cultural divide between the haves and the have-nots, but about the one between the offended and the not-offended. While the United States has faced levels of inequality not seen since the 1920s, the primary division in both the US and the UK is described as a cultural one, not an economic one. What's dividing these nations is not wealth, income and opportunity. It's attitude.

Plus, the snowflake *can't* be made out to be a rich person, because part of snowflake-hating ideology is an understanding that wealthy people became wealthy due to their superior talents. Since many if not most political and cultural leaders who rail most forcefully against 'elites' are themselves richer than most of us can ever hope to be, they simply cannot critique wealth inequality. (See: one Donald J. Trump and his esteemed children.) If people have less, it's because they deserve less. This is an attitude that does not only belong to the right. Instead of economic inequality, snowflake critics call it something else: people with moral character and people without.

It seems like snowflake critics are missing a trick here. When it comes to entitlement and frailty, where better to find a target than in the spoiled children of the idle rich? Because of course there is a vast divide of inequality in the US and the UK, and of course this has in part produced the politics of Brexit, of Trump, and of whatever Brexit-y, Trump-y thing comes next. I have met rich people in both Britain and America who have so successfully segregated themselves from the working classes of their countries that they have literally no clue what it is to not be rich. There's a scene in *Arrested Development* where the extremely wealthy matriarch of the family, Lucille Bluth, asks casually, 'What could a banana cost? Ten dollars?' These people exist. They don't know anything about life for poor or even middle-class people. But it's not only that they don't know. It's that they don't *know* that they don't know. These extra-segregated rich people are everywhere across the political spectrum, including on the left.

If *this* was the enemy of the snowflake-detractor, I'd be all for it. If they were making an argument about economic hypocrisy, of people who profess progressive politics but hide their wealth in tax havens and send their kids to segregated schools, let's have at them. I'm your gal. If being a snowflake meant being precious about gourmet food or being offended by a waiter who didn't come quickly enough or thinking it's 'gross' to take the bus, then sign me up, Piers Fucking Morgan. Because all these things are a type of irritating weakness – a weakness born of isolated privilege.

But that isn't the conversation we're having.

Instead, the snowflake who comes under such scrutiny is someone who *does* care about disadvantage. Someone who *does* acknowledge their own privileges, and *does* live their ideals. This is the source of so much irritation, of miles of column inches and reams of book pages. The snowflake cares *deeply* about economic, racial and gender inequality, even if they are still learning about the ways that they benefit from those inequalities and privileges. Even if they fail at that, they are trying – and they are disrupting business as usual. This is enough to draw the ire not only of far-right fanatics, but of the well-heeled elites of any political stripe who benefit from business as usual.

This is what 'snowflake' actually means, and what a snowflake actually does – despite what the alt-right ghouls intended when they originated the insult. A snowflake is a person who rattles the people who most need a rattling. It's a courageous person. It's a compassionate person. It's a person unconcerned with whether they appear cool to wankers. A person with good vibes and a clear conscience and a sense of purpose. And, I might add, a wonderfully attractive person.

If this is what a snowflake is, who wouldn't want to be one?

What do snowflakes want?

The ground zero of the culture war is, without a doubt, the university campus. As a gathering place of young people, under the watchful eye of a critical press, universities are a factory production line of snowflake panics. This is the case in both the US, where beginning in 2014 a new generation of racial justice activists embarked on bold new protest movements, and the UK, where even the smallest and silliest signals of political correctness can set off the British press and, unfortunately, its readers. The purpose of these press panics is to generate outrage and attention and therefore sales, all the while diminishing the political possibilities presented by the young. But they have another consequence, too: feeding otherwise compassionate people, who might be curious about the young and their interesting new ideas about the world, with a steady drip of poison until they more or less loathe university students. I know that British people would not hate the younger generation so much if they were not directed to do so by those who turn a profit peddling hatred of difference. But it is very easy to distrust and ridicule young people if you are presented with their alleged outrages every single day in the newspaper you most trust.

In each example of a campus snowflake panic, what we usually find, if we care to look for it, are students and their allies suggesting small moderations in practice and tradition in order to better welcome new kinds of people to universities. We find students doing the kinds of things that students have done for a hundred years. Sometimes we find them doing nothing of note whatsoever. If we look behind the hysterical headlines, what we normally find is a much less sexy, outrageous story than the *Daily Mail* would have us believe.

The snowflakes and their allies often want very simple things. Respect for difference. Opportunity where it was historically denied. An end to the prejudices that limit who can thrive in university and beyond. A chance to practise the kind of activism and journalism and political organising that they may pursue in their careers. These are important, big ideas. But sometimes, the press can brew a campus snowflake panic out of nothing at all.

Take one example. When Oxford University's Somerville College decided in early 2019 that it would not serve octopus in its first week of term, it signalled the impending collapse of civilisation, according to some commentators. Why? Well, the college had thought that when arriving at Oxford, some working-class students might find a formal dinner of octopus right off the bat to be a jarring reminder that they would struggle to fit in among the poshest of the posh. This seems reasonable. When I arrived for a Master's degree at Cambridge, I was told off early on for saying 'no thank you' to a waiter offering me more wine, instead of dismissively placing my hand over my glass. I can't say I would know what to do if faced with an octopus on my plate, and I'm an insufferable member of the rootless cosmopolitan elite. I can see why the college declared octopus would be off.

That could have been that. But it wasn't.

The takes came hot and fast. 'Of course Oxford should serve its students octopus – not a snowflake diet of anti-aspirational mush,' a headline in the *Daily Telegraph* declared.[1] Removing octopus from one dinner, according to the writer, would 'fuel the unwelcome trend of wrapping our young people in cotton wool.' To not have students feast upon an eight-legged, squidgy sea creature was tantamount to 'protecting them from views they don't agree with,' a tactic which is 'silly and short-sighted at best, dangerous and regressive at worst.'

Danger! All who enter here will not be served octopus until perhaps the second week of term.

That could have been that with this particular octopus scandal. But to think that Britain could escape a cephalopod free speech scandal with merely one opinion column is to misunderstand our modern media. Restaurant critic Giles Coren of the *Times* chimed in with his own take, complaining that 'uni is a safe space for alphabetti spaghetti' and that 'arrant snowflakery' had got him disinvited from the *Today* programme to discuss the octopus matter.[2]

Yet another journalist, also in the *Telegraph*, found even more to say and more to fear from octopusgate: 'Take octopus off the menu? What utter cretinous stupidity.'[3]

That journalist was William Sitwell, who was formerly the editor of *Waitrose Magazine*, until he emailed a freelancer about murdering vegans and, with apologies for his 'ill-judged joke', parted ways with the magazine.[4] Sitwell seems to make up the head of a many-tentacled snowflake-panic kraken. After he quit *Waitrose*, a chorus of anguished commentators rose to defend Sitwell as a great literary figure and supermarket magazine editor of our time. The consequences of his resignation threatened us all: 'It's offend of the world as we know it after Waitrose magazine boss William Sitwell QUITS over "killing vegans" joke in email,' screamed a headline in the *Sun*. 'This unseemly fiasco is symptomatic of a wider problem that is changing society for the worse,' wrote *Sun* journalist Tom Slater.

How much worse? 'We live in a culture where "offendedness" is power and big companies are all too willing to listen to those tiny minorities that shout the loudest,' he warned. The result? 'The more we indulge these kinds of shrill voices the more authoritarian and joyless our society will become.' Danger! Vego-fascism looms: they have already crushed one innocent, who can now be read weekly on octopus and other matters in the *Daily Telegraph* (but no longer in *Waitrose Magazine*).

Waitrose aside, the controversies stemming from university campuses and their supposedly fragile students range from the eight-legged and frivolous, to truly depressing reminders of our fundamentally racist society. But the media narrative in reaction to any such event is more or less the same. Students are too sensitive – about an octopus dinner or a swastika graffitied on a dormitory wall – and decide to put up anything from a minor complaint to a large and fiery protest. The backlash that follows makes up the heart of the snowflake-panic industrial complex, led by commentators in reputable and disreputable publications alike, who are *certain* that *this* is what the problem is. Civilisation itself is threatened if we, their readers, are too afraid to shovel working-class students full of octopus on day one of university. And on it goes.

The Great Snowflake Campus Panics of our Time come in many shapes and sizes. Media coverage would have you, even the most sympathetic defender of today's youth, side against the students caught up in these Panics. After all, who can resist a well-turned pun in a tabloid headline? Who doesn't love to feel smugly superior to those who are younger, lither and more collagenous than us? With each Panic, though, if you look past the angry takes of columnists and their bilious commenters, the actual picture tends to be more sympathetic to the students involved. What the media often leaves out of these stories is more important than what they put in.

Behind every outrageous headline, you can learn what snowflakes *really* want, and it's a lot more than a revised menu on a formal dinner.

A clapping crisis in the culture war

Let's stay with Oxford for now, with its cobblestones and its problematic octopi and its silly, billowing robes.

In October 2019, the *Daily Mail* reported on something wild going on at Oxford University. The headline read: 'Snowflake students at Oxford University are latest to demand clapping is banned because applause noise could trigger anxiety as they call for "jazz hands" to be used instead.'[5] If you are a cool, calm, mature individual, this headline may evoke some scorn in your heart, or at least a little eye-rolling. Clapping, really? People are too sensitive for *clapping*? In my day, we clapped each other right on the back *in the trenches of the Somme*.

The *Mail* story described how student union officers including Róisín McCallion, then Oxford Student Union's VP for Welfare and Equal Opportunities, presented a motion to their student government meeting that clapping may exclude students with anxiety disorders. The article reads: 'The use of jazz hands – where students wave their hands in the air – is the British Sign Language expression for applause and is deemed a more inclusive gesture.' The story included several photos taken from Instagram of Róisín gadding about in her Oxford gown.

One commenter on the *Daily Mail* story, 'Normal Girl' from Lincoln, wrote in the comments: 'I will not be told if I can or cannot clap. Clapping/applause is a sign of appreciation. Jazz hands are part of dance. Please someone stand up to these snowflakes.' Another *Daily Mail* reader, one 'Ge0ffrey' in New York City, commented: 'Outrageous. Clapping is free speech.' Piers Morgan tweeted at Róisín, urging her and her fellow student officers to 'grow a pair, you imbeciles', among other things.[6] (We must ask ourselves: what does Piers use to clap?) Over ten thousand people liked the tweet. Enough to fill a socially distanced Wembley stadium, we can imagine, with a person standing and clapping their testicles in every eighth seat. The *Metro* picked up the story, writing that the 'mandate' would 'apply at student union events, and if successful, be rolled out to other societies and events.' Based on the reporting, it would seem that incredibly delicate students had indeed banned clapping from events at Oxford. Snowflakes!

It would be a great story, if it were true. Sadly for Ge0ffrey et al, however, it was not.

I called Róisín to find out what really happened, and why she was such a delicate, pathetic, humourless, spoiled little Oxbridge snow-flake. She told me she was 'a very normal person from the north of England', state-schooled, her parents both teachers. This shouldn't matter – but it does. She had an easy manner and laughed a lot in tell-ing her story, even when recounting the quite scary harassment she had experienced as a result of the media attention. The media had led the trolls to her personal social media pages, and she even received some old-fashioned hate mail through the post.

I asked her what had really happened. She told me she had been approached by the chair of the Student Union's disabilities campaign about seconding a motion not to *ban* clapping, but to *encourage* the use of British Sign Language clapping – what the media had termed 'jazz hands'. The disabilities campaign had said they had heard from students with sensory disabilities about the constant clapping at meetings, and that some students with hearing aids couldn't hear due to ringing after the applause at every motion's passing. As a result, they were not attending the student meetings. Róisín saw this as a disability accessibility measure and agreed to second the motion. 'I didn't really think too much about it,' she told me, 'because my view was, if some of our disabled students don't feel that they can come to council, that's bad. Disabled people are underrepresented within poli-tics, and I want to make our political system at the university as acces-sible as possible. So I just said, "Yeah, I'll put a second out."'

Not a very sexy tabloid story so far, is it?

At the council where the motion was discussed, there was a debate as usual, with only one student who pointed out, with all the smugness a teenager may contain: 'But people without arms can't do jazz hands.' Checkmate! Róisín then noted to him that this was true but would mean they wouldn't be able to clap conventionally, either. The motion passed with seventy-something per cent of the vote. A great rift formed in the universe; the fabric of society was torn asunder. The youth rose up and murdered the Britain their grandparents had fought for. They took Blitz spirit and spat upon it. Sorry, that's the tabloid version.

In real life, Róisín told me, she was baffled by the outcry. 'Ultimately, I really don't understand on a human level,' she said. 'If you can do something that makes someone's life a little bit easier, why wouldn't you do it?' Her only regret was this: 'The main thing that I just kept saying was I really wish our own students cared as much about what happens at student council as people who read the tabloid press seemed to . . .'

Róisín and her colleagues on the Student Union decided not to do any press interviews, since it would only drag them into a round of the British media culture wars for an issue that was not top of anyone's priority list. It was frustrating for Róisín, though, to say nothing. 'That was really difficult,' she told me, 'to just sit silently while I heard people saying things that either weren't true about the story in the first place or were becoming more and more intolerant.' It frustrated her that she was being cast as a spoiled elitist despite her un-elite background. She hated that the *Mail* had taken, without permission, photos from her private social media accounts instead of her professional headshot. But as her communications adviser told her, 'All they want to do with this story is let Piers Morgan sit and call you a snowflake. And it will turn into a debate about whether or not university students are snowflakes.' This made sense, so she sat back and opened the hate mail.

This was not the first snowflake crisis to grip Britain, and it wouldn't be the last. In the midst of the outrage, what got lost was the fact that this was a story that didn't affect anyone who wasn't a student at Oxford. It didn't even really affect those who *were* students at Oxford. So how does a story like this take up so much space in Britain's most prominent media, reaching millions and millions of people?

The Oxford clapping 'ban' was framed in the media as a tale of hysterical students coming up with an outlandish new restriction on human behaviour to protect their sensitive feelings. The real story, though, was about students trying, with all due calmness and respect, to make life easier for disabled students, and to make sure they didn't miss out on student government. It's a story about disabled students asking their peers to consider making a small accommodation to help them. For Róisín and most others – with the exception, perhaps, of clever Mr 'What About People With No Arms?' – it was not a controversial idea. This is what snowflakes do: they learn about a new perspective, and they make adjustments.

But the press and the public they riled up felt enough discomfort at this idea that they responded with derision and vitriol. Those with cultural power saw disenfranchised people organising – even in the smallest possible way – and stepped in to ridicule them into submission. The very suggestion that students were making accommodations for disability was enough to turn the media's full fury upon one university student. Róisín still gets comments on social media requests and even had a troll on LinkedIn. She wonders whether having her name and her face attached to this non-story will hurt her chances at future employment. She has been branded a snowflake, and not only a snowflake, but a ringleader of snowflakes. An ur-snowflake. She had become, at least for a time, the face of 'the problem with kids today.' She had been made into fodder for the snowflake critics – the authors and tweets and comedians who have made careers for themselves trading in fears about young students such as Róisín.

In reality, Róisín is the most mature figure in this story, someone who acted professionally in her role as a disability advocate in student government.

But that's not an article most people would love to click on – at least not the Ge0ffreys of the world.

Don't get me wrong: there are plenty of wonderful reasons to hate Oxford and Cambridge, not least their role in turning out basically all the most noxious cultural and political leaders in Britain. When I attended Cambridge for a Master's degree in 2013–14, I met some of the cleverest *and* the thickest people I've ever come across – thick people with extraordinary confidence that has already launched them to dazzling success.

But there's one thing I can say we don't have to worry about when it comes to Oxbridge students, and that's their alleged left-wing radicalism. Anxious commentators should rest assured that working-class kids will still get bullied while at Oxford, whether they're being served octopus for dinner, or beans on toast.

It's funny to think that Oxford, of all places, can become a symbol of out-of-control progressivism in the national press. It's a place where students wear bow ties to take exams. In my experience at Cambridge, it was considered a bit wild to be a mild feminist. Cambridge was the place that I realised I *had* been in a bubble of progressivism in Berkeley and San Francisco, but that I wasn't anymore.

I sat in classrooms where male professors started their lectures with, 'All right, gentlemen, let's begin.' A student leader once held forth in a room where I was trying to get some work done about how 'women don't make good leaders because it makes them bitchy.' (He then got mad at *me* for quietly leaving the room – it made him feel bad. Sorry, pal.) There were no paintings of women anywhere in my college in my time there – I believe they have added one since, to much self-congratulation. For a Burns Night celebration, someone decided that it would be inappropriate for a man to make the toast to the laddies, and a woman to make the toast to the lassies, because it might be offensive to, well, any homophobes in attendance. It was where terrible, posh white boys called my friends the n-word, 'all in good fun.' In the years after I left, my college was embroiled in a sexual harassment scandal.[7] (The college has now formed a 'Sexual Misconduct Working Group'.[8])

Maybe Oxbridge can be a radicalising force – but not for the reasons the tabloids fear.

The trouble with Oxford and Cambridge is not that it's become somehow hostile to posh white men. The trouble is that Britain's top universities are still so unwelcome to everyone else.[9] These universities have made efforts to admit more black students and students from state schools, but privately educated, white students from London and the south-east of England are still vastly overrepresented at both.[10] Some of the students of these institutions are doing the work to try and improve the experience of marginalised students, and for that work, they face ridicule – not only from their peers, but from a national press whose only aim is to convert general societal malice at transgressive students into page views.

The students who get called snowflakes in the press have had to develop incredibly thick skin. It's a mark of their fortitude that they can withstand being named and shamed so personally, publicly and widely. To be a snowflake like this, in the public eye, requires tremendous strength. It shows what students will put up with to get the positive change they want – public ridicule and bullying on a scale and with a speed that has never been possible before. But that doesn't make it fine to use students as scapegoats for whatever societal ill has crept into the mind of a *Telegraph* columnist each week. It doesn't make it OK for the press to react with such fury and vitriol every time they spot a student who has dared to challenge their world view.

Octopus dinners won't break the spirit of student activists. Nor, I think, can the press. But that doesn't mean they should try.

The Oberlin food court that wasn't

Campus snowflake panics arise from student activism much of the time, but sometimes the press will pounce when students are just trying to complete their assignments – or even when there isn't a story at all.

The Oberlin Food Court Panic is one such invention of the addled minds of conservative media. The world would not really discover that this panic was a non-story until long after the media fallout had done its damage, and shaped views about the fragility of students across the world. So what happened?

Oberlin College is a private liberal arts college in Ohio, known for being the first white college in America to admit black students and grant bachelor's degrees to women. It's also known for producing, among other things, Lena Dunham, who in turn produced the HBO hit show of the 2010s, *Girls*, about entitled white millennials living in New York City.

The non-hysterical version of the food court story is this: in the autumn of 2015, Ferdinand Protzman, a former *New York Times* foreign correspondent who was teaching a journalism class at Oberlin, tasked his students with finding a story on their campus and then writing about it. One student, originally from Vietnam, had noticed that fellow international students would make fun of the cafeteria food for how completely strange it was. The cafeteria had put some pulled pork into a brioche with coleslaw and called it 'bánh mì', the delicious Vietnamese sandwich which looks and tastes nothing like this. Making fun of cafeteria food is a proud tradition of student journalism, and a story like this seems like it would be an easy enough way to practise finding a topic, gathering quotes, writing some clean, crisp copy and securing a firm A-. This is what the student did, and then had her story published in the student paper, the *Oberlin Review*. It contained the hot takes of six different students on the state of Asian food in the cafeteria. The students' opinions on the matter ranged from *I don't care about this* to *This food is an insult to my motherland*. The spiciest take came from one Japanese student's critique of the cafeteria 'sushi', some dismal chicken atop some even more dismal rice. The student said:

> When you're cooking a country's dish for other people, including ones who have never tried the original dish before, you're also representing the meaning of the dish as well as its culture . . . So if people not from that heritage take food, modify it and serve it as 'authentic', it is appropriative.[11]

Now we're talking. We have a student who has identified potential cultural appropriation: in this case, the ways that white Americans have murdered Asian food and then had the nerve to call it Asian food. Is this in fact cultural appropriation? Or merely bad cooking from people ignorant to the delights of true sushi? A range of opinion is certainly possible on this matter. Maybe another student who *loves* the grey chicken on the grey rice could write a response to the paper voicing a vehement defence of said 'sushi'. That is how journalism, and especially student journalism, works.

In this case, this small dabbling in student journalism led to a minor institutional change: Oberlin noticed the article and decided, well, I guess that really isn't sushi. The student newspaper reported that the dishes available in the canteen would no longer be named after things they were not. Journalism really does have the power to change the world. As Protzman, the journalism professor, told the *Chronicle of Higher Education* in a debrief of the whole matter: 'This was a great example of what journalists are supposed to do . . . She identified a news story that affected people's lives in the community, and reported on it in a fair, balanced, and veritable fashion.'[12]

That could have been that. Nobody had died on any hills. Nobody had even been all that offended. A student gave a thoughtful, calm answer to a fellow student's question for her assignment. Everyone could have gone on to live their lives in peace. Maybe one or two people even learned something about sushi and bánh mì along the way. These are the experiences that make up the rich tapestry of student life.

But no. All hell broke loose. The Rupert Murdoch-owned tabloid the *New York Post* got hold of the story six weeks later, presumably after scouring the student press for some outrage fodder and published a story under the headline: 'Students at Lena Dunham's college offended by lack of fried chicken.'[13] The fried chicken part had to do with one Chinese student's take that General Tso's chicken should be fried, not steamed, as the canteen had done. And the Lena Dunham part, well, was meant to let the reader know that Oberlin is a particularly hateable college thanks to its particularly hateable alumna, Lena Dunham.

From the *New York Post*, the non-controversy swelled and travelled to the pages of the wider national press. *The Atlantic* ran a piece titled 'A Food Fight at Oberlin College'. The *New York Times* wrote an article titled 'Oberlin Students Take Culture War to the Dining Hall', and *Newsweek* cried out: 'Oberlin College Students Protest "Culturally Appropriative" Dining Hall Food'. My own paper, the *Washington Post*, wrote about it too: 'Oberlin College Sushi "Disrespectful" to Japanese'. *Seventeen* Magazine had: 'These College Students Claim Their Cafeteria Food Is Racist'. The British press were of course keen to get involved in a campus food controversy, octopus or no, and the *Independent* ran: 'US University Accused of Cultural Appropriation Over "Undercooked" Sushi Rice'. This headline, in particular, actually made it sound like the university had been accused of this by the government, or a commission of some kind, or a UN special tribunal – not a bored student quoted for a journalism class assignment.

Long-time snowflake hater and conservative journalist Conor Friedersdorf wrote of the incident in *The Atlantic* as a prime example of 'students who've been acculturated into a seductive ideology' free of any and all challenge to their beliefs.[14] These are students, Friedersdorf said, at dire risk of missing out on dissenting views 'in anything like the quality and quantity needed to prepare these young people for the enormous complexity of life in a diverse society, where few defer to claims just because they are expressed in the language of social justice.' Thinking sushi is gross will *not* prepare students for the coming climate wars. In order to learn how to deal with dissent, they must not dare to dissent about chicken, rice or any other food from any other food group.

Remember: this was all the product of a student drumming up an assignment for journalism class. Think back to when you were in school or university, if you are not one anymore. Did you approach every one of your assignments with a fiery passion, seeing each piece of homework as a chance to tear down the structures of oppression around you? If you did, you probably had a lot more energy and passion than most students. Good for you! But what was actually happening here was a student trying to do her work, and the people she interviewed trying to come up with thoughtful answers. Everyone had a nice time, and no one got hurt. Those decried by the world's press as dreadful little snowflakes were actually just students engaged in the process of learning about the world.

Unfortunately for the student who wrote the story, Linh Tran, it was a painful lesson, in the end. She wrote in her personal blog in 2017 about the media firestorm which, she notes, took place in the same week as final exams. She described watching the media go on and on about the incident – even long after the issue had been resolved between the university dining services and the Asian students they met with after seeing her article. Linh wrote:

As a result of this inaccurate media portrayal of what was happening on campus, hateful messages that contained racist and xenophobic content started pouring into the inboxes of me and the students quoted in my article. I remember sitting by my bed on the day before Christmas, half a world away from home, receiving Facebook messages from strangers who repeatedly told me to 'go back to [my] country' and 'suck it up you little spoiled brat.' So did other students. On that holiday where families gathered in happiness, we found ourselves stuck in loneliness in a foreign country that wanted so badly to get rid of us. Imagine too, for Asian American students, most of whom were born and raised in this country, for them to be told to 'go back' – where would they go back to?[15]

In her blog, Linh connected her experience with the dining hall incident to the history of discrimination against Asian people in America. She also reflected on the smaller, daily indignities of racism on campus as an Asian student. She continued to think carefully and critically about what had happened to her.

Ironically, it was poor journalism that blew up the work of a careful student journalist into an end-of-the-world story. The original *New York Post* story claimed that 'gastronomically correct' students were 'filling the school newspaper with complaints and demanding meetings with campus dining officials and even the college president.'[16] This did not actually happen. Protzman, the teacher of the Oberlin journalism class, lamented to the *Chronicle of Higher Education* that of all the national and international outlets drumming up clicks and outrage over the Oberlin sushi story, 'No one called. No one.'

Critics of an overly 'politically correct' generation will write frequently about how these days, kids making honest mistakes can have their 'lives ruined forever' by the boundlessness and permanence of the internet. A girl who wears a racist Halloween costume and puts

65

it on Instagram can be hounded by thousands of angry commenters. A teenage dirtbag can post a tweet about boobies and have it come back to haunt him at his first job interview. It's a valid concern that young people today don't get to make their mistakes in private, and that online critics can be overly cruel toward people with much less power than them.

There never seems to be much concern, however, for the students whose innocent forays into political and social justice issues in their college years may have *their* actions picked up by every major outlet in their country and beyond. The lesson these students learn is not that perpetuating injustice will 'ruin their lives forever' – but that discussing injustice may. Even if that discussion is as timid as trying to defend the honour and reputation of your delicious national dish.

Universities are meant to be a place to push boundaries, whether that's finding a way to fire rockets to Mars, or finding new ways to understand and root out racism. At the heart of either of these is a willingness to learn. This is what the Oberlin students were punished for by the international press. We can imagine how boring an accurate headline would have been. 'Oberlin student journalist pens article about disappointing sushi.' This would perhaps not have been as titillating for readers of *The Atlantic*. Evidence, perhaps, that the incident was not worth writing about at all, beyond the pages of the student press.

What makes the whole Oberlin affair all the more sinister is that the students under critique were all students of colour. The original *New York Post* article also criticised black and Indian students for separate incidents criticising the college's food. The students mocked for being 'pampered snowflakes', as Protzman put it to the *Chronicle*, came from a number of marginalised demographics, who more likely than not were already well aware that the 'real world' would not handle them with particular care. In the university setting, they were practising their instincts for justice, making change and building up their muscles for the future fights of their lives, big or small. A student journalist can learn how to tell a story with the subject matter of their dodgy cafeteria food, and a young student activist can practise making change with the subject matter of dodgy cafeteria food.

Is this what people are so afraid of?

A snowstorm in Mizzou

The greatest, most enduring campus snowflake panics tend to arise when students of colour, and particularly black students, fight back against the systemic racism of their universities. This was the case at the University of Missouri, also known as Mizzou.

I had seen references to the 'incident' at Mizzou long before I learned what actually happened there in 2015. In dozens of articles, books and columns, I had seen Mizzou held up as what happens when student protest goes 'too far'. But in each reference, the authors seemed unwilling to provide a full account of what happened, point-ing out a few unflattering details of protestors' behaviour, but never addressing the heart of why they were protesting.

We find a great example in American academic and furious Twitter poster Tom Nichols' book, *The Death of Expertise: The Campaign Against Established Knowledge and Why it Matters*. Setting aside the idea of an uncontested thing called *Established Knowledge*, Nichols describes the protests at Mizzou as a case of an exaggerated reaction 'after a juvenile incident in which a swastika was drawn on a bath-room wall with faeces.'[17] Nichols does not focus his attention on the horror of the swastika, but rather, spends his considerable energy in a critique of the backlash to it, which he saw as too furious, and which resulted in the university losing donations. The University of Missouri still stands, but Nichols takes this example to show the horrors, again, not of resurgent white nationalism, but the attempt at institutional power by student protestors. The problem is not the swastika smeared in shit. It's that 'many colleges have become hostages to students who demand that their feelings override every other consideration.' The feeling, in this case, of horror when a swastika (perhaps the single most abhorrent symbol known to man), was smeared in poop at a university, and the university could potentially do more to protect its students.

Nichols throws up his hands in frustration, asking what could possibly be done about a simple poo swastika:

Exactly what Missouri's flagship public university was supposed to do, other than to wash the wall, was unclear, but the campus erupted anyway. 'Do you know what systemic oppression is?' A student yelled at the flustered Mizzou president. 'Google it!' She hollered. Student journalists were harassed and threatened, in one case by a faculty member with a courtesy appointment, ironically enough, in the journalism school. After a few more days of these theatrics, the university's president resigned.

As a result of this, Nichols notes, the university suffered:

Applications and donations soon took a hit in the wake of the protests and resignations. Some months later, the adjunct journalism professor who had confronted a student was fired. When the smoke cleared, the university was left with fewer faculty, administrators, applicants, and donations, all because a group of students, enabled by an even smaller group of faculty, reversed the roles of teachers and learners at a major public university.

Freshman enrolment at Mizzou did indeed drop following 2015 protests, and unoccupied dormitories were shuttered. Nichols goes on to quote a University of Tennessee law professor, who in reaction to student protests such as those at Mizzou and those about racist Halloween costumes at Yale – which we'll get to next – proposed raising the voting age to twenty-five: 'It's bad enough to have to treat college students like children. But it's intolerable to be *governed* by spoiled children. People who can't discuss Halloween costumes rationally don't deserve to play a role in running a great nation.' Looking at the supposed crisis in maturity on campuses, Nichols writes that he is 'haunted' by the fact that once his students leave his classroom, 'I cannot moderate their arguments forever.' Once students leave the circle of his wisdom and authority, he 'cannot prevent them from dismissing others, from rejecting facts, from denouncing well-intentioned advice, or from demanding that their feelings be accepted in place of truth.'

If we were to draw from Nichols' summary alone, here's what we would assume happened at Mizzou: some spoiled students got very, very upset about a 'juvenile' swastika – a telling word, assuming the childlike innocence of whoever decided that drawing a swastika in paint would not be enough; only poo would do. As a result of this poo swastika, protestors yelled at a 'flustered' university president about 'systemic oppression'. There was nothing the university could reasonably be expected to do in reaction to the poo swastika. And a visiting lecturer harassed a journalism student. Sounds quite bad! A reader is left to wonder: why would these spoiled children overreact like that to one innocent incident? They must be mad snowflakes.

Britain's own Claire Fox also included the Missouri protests in '*I Find that Offensive!*' Her summary goes: 'student activists forced the school's president Tim Wolfe to resign after demanding he "admit to white privilege" and apologise for his alleged failure to address a series of racially tinged incidents.' Presumably, 'racially tinged' is what people say when they don't want to admit something is simply 'racist'. Fox goes on:

> . . . but they were not satisfied with [Wolfe's] scalp and shortly after their victory turned on the press. 'We are calling the police

because you aren't respecting us!' shouted one protestor at a member of the media. Others chanted 'No comment!' holding placards saying: 'No Media, Safe Space' as they pushed and shoved reporters and cameramen. This no-comment approach sums up an attitude that 'we're not answerable to anyone' from those who most persistently demand that others are silenced.

Fox doesn't say any more about what happened at the University of Missouri. She files the incident under the chapter subheading 'ME, ME, ME: the entitled generation', about the 'narcissistic entitlement' inculcated in young people from childhood. Bob's your chapter.

The Atlantic's Conor Friedersdorf, that great snowflake critic of our time, critiqued the ejection of a photojournalist from the activists' encampment because it was a 'safe space'.[18] Video footage shows the protestors walking toward the photographer in order to get him to leave the space. Friedersdorf says that students had 'weaponised' safe spaces. They are made to sound quite unhinged.

How do these events sit with you so far? If this was all you knew about what happened, you might find yourself grimacing at the thought of out-of-control protestors and their aggressive actions against well-intentioned others. The students sound strange, detached from reality, and even violent.

The thing about Nichols' and Fox's descriptions, though – which they decided to include in their respective books to make a point about entitled young people forgetting their place – is you still don't actually know what any of these protests were about. You have the poo swastika, sure, which the authors laugh off as if shit swastikas were a common feature of anyone's youth. You have also a vague sense of 'racially tinged' incidents on campus. You have a vague idea of a misuse of 'safe spaces', and you have a quote from a university professor suggesting people under twenty-five shouldn't be allowed to vote.

The thing these authors leave out is that the students in question, who led protests at Mizzou and elsewhere – the subjects of the fear and their ire – were black. How does it sound if you include a quip about removing voting rights from young people if you know that those young people are black? Does the analysis of entitlement and spoiled narcissism hold up if you knew that the students in question were historically marginalised on their campuses? What does it mean to say that black and working-class students are spoiled – is it that they are forgetting their place?

Here's what actually started the Mizzou protests of 2015: the black student body president, Payton Head, was on his way to a party at a fraternity when a pack of white students in the back of a pickup truck screamed the n-word and other racial slurs at him.[19] This was not an uncommon occurrence on Mizzou's campus, nor was it the first time such a thing had happened to Head. The history of racist abuse at Mizzou stretched back years – all the way back to 1950, when the University of Missouri admitted its first black student. In a Spike Lee documentary about the Mizzou protests, students described dozens of incidents of being called the n-word or otherwise explicitly racially abused.[20] In 2010, two white students had scattered cotton balls across the ground in front of the university's Black Culture Center. The university responded by saying it was 'a childish prank', and the students were charged with littering. Again, racist incidents like the swastika are brushed off as 'childish' and therefore fundamentally innocent.

The Mizzou protests took place only one year after the protests in Ferguson, Missouri, (only a few hours' drive from Mizzou,) which followed the fatal police shooting of the black teenager Michael Brown in 2014. The University of Missouri is the flagship campus of the public university system of a former slave state. Its history is present on campus in the form of buildings and statues of historic slaveholders. Throughout the autumn of 2015, students continued to protest in response to ongoing racist incidents. A drunk white student shouted the n-word at a group of black performers rehearsing for homecoming (an autumn festival, parade and football game which takes place on American university campuses). At the homecoming parade that 10 October, black protestors temporarily blocked the car of the president of the University of Missouri, Tim Wolfe. Wolfe did not speak to them – for which he later apologised – and a group of white people linked arms to block the car from the protestors.[21] One black faculty member commented in Spike Lee's documentary about the protests that 'there's still some people who value homecoming more than they value black lives.'

In response to these incidents and the failure of the administration to address racism on campus, Mizzou student protestors formed a group called Concerned Student 1950 – named for the first year black students were admitted to their university. They issued Wolfe a series of demands ranging from his dismissal to trainings and education about racism on campus and hiring more faculty members of colour. Then, the poo swastika happened. It was not, amazingly, the first swastika graffitied on campus that year – another had been drawn in ashes that April.

One of the Concerned Student 1950 activists, Jonathan Butler, began a hunger strike to put pressure on the administration to address racism on campus. It gained the attention of the black members of Mizzou's football team, who said they would not play their next game unless Wolfe resigned. Although college football players are not paid in the US, their games and ticket sales generate millions in revenue – not to mention a fine the university would have to pay if its players did not turn up. The team's white coach and white players also stood in solidarity with their black teammates and the protestors.

In Nichols' summary of the Mizzou incident, he described with horror and amazement the way that protestors yelled at Wolfe about 'systemic racism'. It turns out, they asked him if he knew what systemic racism was, and his answer was this: 'It's – systematic oppression is because you don't believe that you have the equal opportunity for success.' In Wolfe's telling, systemic oppression is not about systems – it's about your own beliefs. Turn that frown upside down, and you'll be systemically oppressed no more! In reality, systemic racism (Wolfe incorrectly said 'systematic') is one way of referring to to the way that racism is embedded within institutions and societies. It can mean, for example, the way that housing inequality is the result of racist policies of the past and present, or the way that unequal access to education among different races leads to obviously different outcomes in income, health and more. If your grandmother had never heard of this idea that would be one thing. But it's something you'd hope that a university president might intuitively understand. Instead, Wolfe came up with an explanation which implied the problem of racism could be solved by fixing your attitude, as if you could pull yourself up by your bootstraps and away to a magical land of equality and prosperity.

Eventually, with the football players, the protestors and the Missouri Students Association against him, Wolfe resigned. 'I take full responsibility for the inaction that has occurred,' he said in his resignation statement, but added: 'This is not – I repeat, not – the way change should come about,' referring to Jonathan Butler's hunger strike.[22] As news of the protests spread across the state and the nation, a Missouri University of Science and Technology student posted that he was going to come to the campus and 'shoot every black person' he saw. Then-presidential candidate Donald Trump weighed in on the events, saying he thought the protestors were 'disgusting' and that those who resigned were 'weak ineffective people' who had 'set some-thing in motion' that he didn't like one bit.

In the video of students disrupting the progress of Tim Wolfe's car at homecoming, you can see a few of the protestors crying. 'In 2015 the MSA President Payton Head was called a n****r on campus and Tim Wolfe did nothing to change the situation,' one of the demonstrators yells at the car. 'It is our duty to fight for our freedom.'

'We have nothing to lose but our chains.' 'We will not continue to be called n****s on this campus.' You can also see in the video a group of white homecoming visitors forming their own human chain to block the black students from the president.

It's an emotional scene. The stakes were high and the threat of violence was real. The students felt the meaning of their protest, and the perceived lack of concern from their university's president, very deeply. You would have to be black to understand the experience of those students completely. You do not have to be black to understand that their tears were not the result of being 'spoiled' or narcissistic or entitled – or why equating activism with spoiled privilege is a dishonest and manipulative move.

For the snowflake critics, from condescending columnists to Donald Trump himself, the tragedy of Mizzou was not its long history of racism. It was that a group of students tried to do something about it – and could not be stopped. In the wake of the protests, the University of Missouri hired new leaders, including a diversity, equity and inclusion officer.

The power of the Mizzou protestors reaches to this day. Missouri in 2014 and 2015 was one of the crucibles of the Black Lives Matter movement itself, founded by three black women in 2013 in response to the acquittal of George Zimmerman, the man who fatally shot unarmed black teenager Trayvon Martin in Florida. In Missouri following the police killing of Michael Brown in 2014, and then on Mizzou's campus the next year, the movement continued to grow and develop. It would be another five years of constant work and activism in the face of outlandish criticism – including politicians' and police's attempts to brand Black Lives Matter a terrorist organisation – before the summer of 2020, when the brutal killing of George Floyd in Minneapolis, Minnesota, inspired the largest wave of protests in the United States since the civil rights movement of the 1950s and 60s.[23]

The student activists at Mizzou in 2015 were faced with the

impossible task of combatting racism on their campus. They wanted change, but their message and their meaning were twisted by a hostile national press. To those who benefit from the status quo, or are uncomfortable confronting America's racist past and present, their protests were unacceptable.

The work of student activists continues to be mocked, diminished and feared to this day. But the work of committed students is neither silly nor inconsequential – and nor does it herald the collapse of civilisation. This should be a great relief to those snowflake critics who spend their days and their word counts foretelling the doom wrought by student activists, but sadly, it isn't.

Yale's very racist Halloween

In the autumn of 2015, the leaves were changing in New Haven, the air was getting crisp, and the students of Yale University were busy deciding whether their Halloween costumes should be sexy, spooky or racist. But then, controversy came knocking. Students received a polite email asking them to *avoid* racist Halloween costumes, for once.

Then came the backlash, and then the backlash to the backlash, and then the backlash to the backlash to the backlash.

First, the email: White Yale students, like white students everywhere, had shown a tendency each year to find horrifying ways to dress up for Halloween – and not the good, spooky, ghosty type of horrifying. Several Yale students had decided in 2007 that blackface would make a great Halloween get-up, for example. So in 2015, the university's Intercultural Affairs Committee sent an email to avoid 'poor decisions' such as wearing 'feathered headdresses, turbans, wearing "war paint" or modifying skin tone or wearing blackface or redface', which refers to white people dressing up in an imitation of Native American dress.[24] While you're at it, the email requested, don't be racist to Asians or

Latinos either. It wasn't the first time a university had gently requested its students not be racist. But this time, a faculty member took it personally.

This brought the backlash: a lecturer in early childhood education at Yale, Erika Christakis, sent an email to the students at her residential college. The email was nostalgic for a bygone era in which every Halloween, students could be as racist as they liked without consequence. 'Is there no room anymore for a child or young person to be a little bit obnoxious . . . a little bit inappropriate or provocative or, yes, offensive?' she asked. 'American universities were once a safe space not only for maturation but also for a certain regressive, or even transgressive, experience; increasingly, it seems, they have become places of censure and prohibition.'

Ah, the good old days. Back when universities were a safe space for a gal to wear blackface and experiment with the outer limits of her racism. If a student saw a costume she found offensive, Christakis suggested, she could merely look away. This would presumably not work if you were in a party *surrounded* by devil-may-care Halloween racists, everywhere you turned, but Christakis did not clarify where one should turn in such a situation.

Then came the backlash to the backlash: students were not pleased with Christakis's email! Over 700 of them wrote an open letter to her in criticism of her footloose and fancy-free approach to racism on campus. Their letter said: 'To be a student of colour on Yale's campus is to exist in a space that was not created for you. From the Eurocentric courses to the lack of diversity in the faculty, to the names of slave owners and traders that adorn most of the buildings on campus – all are reminders that Yale's history is one of exclusion.' Christakis's husband Nicholas, the head of Silliman College, wrote an apology in response to the letter, saying that he and his wife 'understand that many students feel voiceless in diverse ways'. He and his wife were there, he assured students, to support them.

But then came the backlash to the backlash to the backlash: One student, Jencey Paz, wrote for the student paper that the Christakis' roles as heads of a residential college meant that part of their job was to create 'a safe space that all students can come home to'. Expressing her frustration with constant arguments about the pain of students of colour on campus, she wrote a line that would be ripped by the national press as indicative of everything wrong with students today: 'I don't want to debate. I want to talk about my pain.' And so the Yale story became a shorthand in the national press for students too tender, fragile and feelings-obsessed to take part in disinterested, rational debate about whether it's OK to be racist.

That Halloween at Yale, after all the emails and columns and thought pieces from the national press, a white fraternity student allegedly turned away students of colour from a Halloween party, telling them, 'White girls only'.[25] (Several white girls apparently jumped at the opportunity to get into the party faster after hearing this.) This incident did *not* spark a national firestorm the way the protests against racism had. The fraternity denied it had happened, despite multiple eyewitnesses quoted in the *Washington Post*. The university declined to comment to the *Post*. The incident did not become a household example of what fraternities are like. It did not lead to a national conversation about whether college students nowadays are far too racist. But the protests *against* racism at Yale did fuel a national conversation about how students are too sensitive. The Yale Halloween costume incident was trotted out over and over again as a classic example of how censorious universities and their students have become. American TV host Bill Maher jumped in with his take. *The Simpsons* parodied it. The incident has been discussed in at least twenty books. It has become one of the standard examples of everything wrong with the modern snowflake.

Erika Christakis ended up resigning her teaching job at Yale, and her husband took a sabbatical, though they remained in their college leadership roles. The next year, Nicholas Christakis was promoted to Yale's highest professorial rank. Erika Christakis, meanwhile, has been lionised by those who see her plight as evidence of the threat to free speech on university campuses – and all for saying students should be a little racist if they want to.

In a column for the *Washington Post* a year after the Halloween costume fracas, Christakis wrote about 'the worrying trend of self-censorship on campuses.'[26] She said that in seven years across two colleges, she had observed that 'a growing number of students report avoiding controversial topics – such as the limits of religious tolerance or transgender rights – for fear of uttering "unacceptable" language or otherwise stepping out of line.' She says that the content of her 'albeit imperfect message fell squarely within the parameters of normal discourse and might even have been worth considering on its merits as an adjunct to prevailing campus orthodoxy.'

This, though, is exactly the problem. It is widely accepted by many white people that they will dress up in offensive Halloween costumes and get away with it every time. Christakis also did not consider that the arguments around her email to be an exercise in free speech itself, a discussion of how the parameters of respectable debate are pushed and pulled in different directions by different groups over time. And this is exactly the kind of conversation that *should* happen at universities. But this is not how outside commenters saw it, as they leapt forward to breathlessly say that debates about racism at universities herald the demise of democracy and free speech rights. 'Certain ideas are too dangerous to be heard at Yale,' Christakis wrote. She says that her experience had led to a 'shadow' on the universities 'magnificent motto, "Light and truth".' Those sexy, *dangerous* ideas for which she faced criticism, remember, included: maybe students should wear blackface to parties without consequence, and maybe students of colour should simply pretend not to have seen it.

One moment from the Yale protests has gained particular mileage in the snowflake discourse – when a student confronted Christakis and said, 'It is not about creating an intellectual space! It is not! Do you understand this? It is about creating a home here!' If you took this line on its surface, and if you had no interest in its context, or learning how it might sound to someone unlike yourself, it would be a great headline for the *Daily Mail*: 'SNOWFLAKE students complain university is too INTELLECTUAL!' Kids these days are even afraid of *thinking*.

If this student's words do indeed sound ridiculous to you at first, it may be worth wondering why. Have you ever felt unwelcome in the place that you lived because of who you were and what you looked like? If this statement by a student sounds to you like the product of coddling, could the truth be the opposite? That the student has spent a lifetime dealing with people who do not understand them and make no effort to do so? These are the kinds of questions good snowflakes have to ask themselves – questions that, despite what you may have heard, force you to consider another person's perspective. Students are accused of not being interested in different perspectives. In reality, a snowflakey student spends all day learning about different perspectives. The student who uttered this line was not talking about university *generally*. They were talking about the fact that Christakis and her husband were the leaders of their residential college – quite literally the students' home away from home.

Many snowflake critics have also taken up the Yale racism protests as an example of students who overreact to *nothing* and expect to be held in perfect comfort at all times throughout university. This might feel true if you don't consider that for Yale students of colour, the Halloween email was the last straw, not the first. The students trying to force a conversation about race at Yale were not lazily whining or crying out like the babies that they were characterised to be. Rather, they were deciding on action, and attempting to change attitudes among the most powerful figures on their campus, rather than simply 'looking away' as they had been advised to do. These students were training for a future of political engagement. They were the ones who actually wanted to force a difficult conversation about racism on campus, not avoid it.

Yale's student press documented the perspective of students at the time – a perspective that appeared next to nowhere in national reporting. *Down Magazine* collected the Facebook statuses of black women on Yale's campus at the time, to document the voices of the student movement. The statuses describe racist treatment by their white peers ranging from being mistaken for a custodian or a panhandler to having their hair touched to violent assaults at frat parties.[27]

Once again, a Great Campus Free Speech Panic of Our Time focused its sights not on wealthy, white, spoiled students, but students of colour – though outraged columnists tended not to admit they were critiquing black women, but rather painted an image of an 'entitled' and elite student body. This is never how campus panics are framed: as political action by black and other minority students. And yet that is so often what these incidents are.

Modern student activism has been twisted and misrepresented in the press, but it's also been ripped apart in well-reviewed books of the liberal intelligentsia, albeit with a more concerned, gentler touch. While snowflakes on campus fight for change, these figures tut and sigh and make enormous sums of money pathologising young people.

Such is the case in Greg Lukianoff and Jonathan Haidt's 2018 book, *The Coddling of the American Mind: How Good Intentions and Bad Ideas Are Setting Up a Generation for Failure.*[28] Failure, friends! The generation in question, if there could be any doubt, were millennials and zoomers – members of Generation Z, who were born after millennials and make fun of them on TikTok. Both groups, though, have been prepped and primed for *failure*, and *Coddling* is a book to find out how it all went so wrong – and what happened to previous generations' minds that made *them* turn out so delightfully right. Much of what went wrong, you may be able to guess, went wrong on university campuses.

Unlike many conservative snowflake haters, Lukianoff and Haidt are dignified members of the American centre-left. Their book is wildly popular and very influential. Its blurbs are impeccable. This is a book read and enjoyed by former US President Barack Obama. It was a finalist for the National Book Critics Circle Award for Non-Fiction, a *New York Times* notable book of 2018 and *Financial Times* and *Bloomberg* best book of 2018. Its well-heeled reviewers praised its analysis of 'disturbing' campus trends, revealing both an authoritarian creep and the contemptible weakness of the young. Empire-loving historian Niall Ferguson called the book 'important if disturbing.' David Aaronovitch of the *Times* said that 'some of the campus happenings' since 2015 have 'affrighted old liberals' such as himself, as 'some campus behaviour is absurd and worrying.' Neil deGrasse Tyson called it 'a candid look at the softening of America,' when, I suppose, America is better off getting harder.

One of the two authors, Greg Lukianoff, is the president of FIRE – the Foundation for Individual Rights in Education. This is an organisation that tallies up supposed violations of free speech on campuses – with questionable methodology which we'll get to later. Jonathan Haidt meanwhile is a social psychologist and professor at New York University's business school. The two authors identify themselves politically as lurking in the centre-left and approach their subject matter in the manner of concerned elders worried that younger radicals are making things worse for themselves. They are not supporters of alt-right ideologues who seek to make the university their soapbox, nor of white supremacists who march through the streets. But the target of their book is not these members of the far right, but rather, the apparently 'coddled' students who protest them – but go about it terribly wrong.

This book is crucial to the literature of snowflake criticism, because it shows the way that the language and the targets that originated among the alt-right are shared and reinforced among extremely polite company, such as liberal academics, and former President Obama himself. It's a book that sees modern undergrads as *uniquely* prone to the wrong kinds of protest – quite different from the student protests of the past. It is a book that believes there was a time when everyone got along much better on a university campus and fears the world that today's young protestors might bring about. And it is a gateway drug for those who are suspicious of young students and activists, lubricating the slide towards a full-throttled denunciation of the special snowflake.

Haidt and Lukianoff organise their book around the idea that university students since around 2015 have succumbed to a belief in what they call the three 'Great Untruths'. These are:

1. The Untruth of Fragility: What doesn't kill you makes you weaker.
2. The Untruth of Emotional Reasoning: Always trust your feelings.
3. The Untruth of Us Versus Them: Life is a battle between good people and evil people.

To the authors, these three 'untruths' are types of 'cognitive distortions'. This is a term from the world of psychiatry, specifically from the practice of Cognitive Behavioural Therapy (CBT), a practice often used to address and eliminate specific phobias – like an irrational fear of spiders or flying, for example. To say that someone is experiencing a 'cognitive distortion' is to say that they are perceiving reality inaccurately. This is the framework Haidt and Lukianoff use to judge today's young students:

they are succumbing, tragically, to a distorted perception of reality. Or 'even when students are reacting to real problems,' the authors write, 'they are more likely than previous generations to engage in thought patterns that make those problems seem more threatening, which makes them harder to solve.' With the impeccable logic of a bad boyfriend, the authors tell us: if the problem isn't totally in your mind, then you must just be reacting to it incorrectly. Thanks to the prevalence of the three Great Untruths, the authors tell us, 'many university students are learning to think in distorted ways, and this increases their likelihood of becoming fragile, anxious, and easily hurt.' The authors prescribe the techniques of CBT, which Haidt in particular advocates for 'its close fit with ancient wisdom'. ('Ancient wisdom' is a phrase that turns up all across the anti-snowflake discourse. This sounds nice but let us remember that other ancient wisdoms include: sacrificing virgins and curing syphilis with mercury.) The authors provide a caveat: 'we are not saying that the problems facing students . . . are minor or "all in their heads". We are saying that what people choose to do in their heads will determine how those real problems affect them.' It's an important caveat, but an increasingly unconvincing one as the book progresses to tell young people all the ways that the things causing them pain are actually not a big deal.

Haidt and Lukianoff have taken student politics, particularly the efforts of minority, LGBTQ+ and women students of the past few years, and medicalised them. They have looked at student efforts to protect themselves from an ever more empowered far right and diagnosed their attempts as not only an overreaction – but a misperception of reality. The authors do consider the recent resurgence of far-right visibility, activism and politics, but their book is not telling *those* people that they have misperceived the world as they see it. Their target – for whom they have plenty of pity and concern – are the students who are attempting to fight back against that far right in what they see as misguided ways.

The first 'Great Untruth' that Lukianoff and Haidt identify is the idea that students, or children, are fragile. The authors suggest instead that children are actually 'anti-fragile'. Though the authors call themselves 'ambivalent' about the word 'coddling' in the title of their book, they see it as an accurate descriptor for the problem at hand and refer to a dictionary definition citing coddling: 'to treat with excessive care or kindness.' (When we look back at the Trump era, will we worry: were we too excessively kind to children?) The authors worry that 'neurotically overprotective parents' are doing more damage than good. It's worth mentioning again that the students who lead the most active protests on campus are not the neurotically raised ones. They are usually new entrants to elite spaces, and often come from marginalised communities. But Haidt and Lukianoff conflate spoiled children with the students who tend to be activists. They wonder if childhood safety, such as car seats and childproofing of homes and day care centres, has gone too far. 'As a result, death rates for children have plummeted,' they write. 'This is, of course, a very good thing, although in some other ways, the focus on physical safety may have gone too far.' How many children is the right number of kids to die from accidents? They don't specify.

Yes, let kids run free. Let them fall over and get nails stuck in their legs. That's fine. The problem with Haidt and Lukianoff's argument, though, is their insistence that 'safety' can only be physical. They complain that there has been a 'concept creep' to expand the meaning of safety to the emotional. They cite a 2014 guideline from Oberlin College to its faculty, suggesting the use of 'trigger warnings' in order to 'show students that you care about their safety.' They were also encouraged to use students' preferred gender pronouns. 'Are students in any danger in the classroom if a professor uses the wrong pronoun?' the authors ask, revealing their ignorance about how misgendering trans people does indeed lead to physical violence, let alone psychological harm. But Haidt and

Lukianoff do not subscribe to the idea that harm can be anything other than physical.

Another 'Great Untruth' is the Untruth of Emotional Reasoning. This is the one where you believe that your feelings mean something, like a ninny, and is another of those pesky cognitive distortions. The authors promote CBT in part because 'with CBT, there is no need to spend years talking about one's childhood,' as you might in other kinds of therapy, which is a pretty grim statement. What the hell happened in your childhood that you *don't* want to talk about? In any case, emotional reasoning means 'letting your feelings guide your interpretation of reality.' Feelings, though, *are* real. They are information about reality. But to Haidt and Lukianoff, they are getting in the way of good old-fashioned Enlightenment reasoning. The authors write: 'It is not acceptable for a scholar to say, "You have shown me convincing evidence that my claim is wrong, but I still feel that my claim is right, so I'm sticking with it."' They will be relieved to hear that no scholar has ever said this.

The authors also take aim at professor Kimberlé Williams Crenshaw's theory of intersectionality. Intersectionality is a theory of how power and oppression can work across multiple types of identity. The authors fear this will only serve to increase the 'tribalism' innate in the human mind. They warn: 'The main axes of oppression usually point to one intersectional address: straight white males.' This means that to the intersectional scholar or activist, these are necessarily 'the evil people'. It is a mind-numbingly simplistic interpretation, concerned only with where the authors themselves might be harmed by a theory. And, of course, that being among 'the evil people' means you could fall victim to 'call-out culture' at any moment – meaning you might be critiqued for your speech or your behaviour. 'Life in a call-out culture requires constant vigilance, fear, and self-censorship,' they write. What are the Lukianoff and Haidt so afraid they're going to do should their vigilance lapse for even a moment? Pinch a secretary's bum? Slip a racial slur into daily conversation? No, this is a culture 'in which almost anything one says or does could result in a public shaming.' *Anything*, really? You can't search your mind for a way to spend a day without doing anything that might be called out?

The authors also see protest itself as poor behaviour from students nowadays. Because, they say, if you 'claim that injustice is being done,' you produce a narrative 'about what is wrong, who is to blame, and what must be done to make things right.' Indeed. The problem, they believe, is that 'reality is always more complicated than the narrative.'

What would the authors say to the protestors of previous generations? The authors note that Martin Luther King Jr, was a good kind of protestor, because 'King's approach made it clear that his movement would not destroy America; it would repair and reunite it.' This is certainly not how most white people – even liberal ones – saw King's work at the time.[29] Sixty per cent of respondents to a Gallup poll in 1963 had an unfavourable view of the March on Washington, when King made his 'I have a dream' speech.[30] The numbers were worse for views of other civil rights actions such as the freedom rides and sit-ins at segregated lunch counters. Haidt and Lukianoff point to the American fight for marriage equality as espousing an 'ennobling common-humanity approach' to protest. This is a naive understanding of not only the gay rights movement, but the backlash against it, which produced narratives claiming that gay people marrying would lead to the destruction of marriage itself – which wasn't that long ago, and which continues in many corners. Just as bigoted people don't mark themselves out as bigots, civil rights and social justice protestors never believe themselves to be *tearing* the country apart. There is no such thing as a fuzzy, warm protest movement which unites the country without disturbing the social order whatsoever. You don't get gay marriage without the Stonewall riots, and you don't get black liberation without the Black Panthers. You don't get women's suffrage without militant feminism. The only purely warm and fuzzy, non-divisive protest in history was the one depicted in a baffling television ad in 2017, in which model Kendall Jenner inexplicably hands a police officer a cool, refreshing can of Pepsi.[31]

Haidt and Lukianoff also believe that student protests have been accommodated by 'irresolute' university administrations. I am not sure that universities which occasionally pepper-spray their student protestors directly in the face, as University of California, Davis police did in 2011, can be thought of as overly accommodating. (The cop who pepper-sprayed the students was fired but ended up getting $38,000 from the university for psychiatric injuries.)[32] But more than anything, university administrations fear disruption. They fear lawsuits – not least those brought about by conservative political groups seeking to enforce a free speech absolutism on college campuses. Haidt and Lukianoff believe that universities are on a slippery slope. 'Universities have an important moral and legal duty to prevent harassment on campus,' they write. 'What counts as harassment, however, has changed quite a lot in recent years.' (You can't even tell your secretary she's really filling out that blouse anymore!) The authors are more afraid of overreach of anti-harassment policies than of harassment itself. They are likely to be affected by the former but not the latter. The authors decry a 2013 rule from the US Department of Education which defined harassment as 'unwelcome conduct of a sexual nature' including 'verbal, nonverbal, or physical conduct.' This, by their measure, is much too broad – and turns the 'emotional reasoning' of thinking you are being harassed 'into a federal regulation.' They believe that issues should be sorted out person-to-person, as if this is how rights were won for women, black people or LGBTQ+ people across history – without recourse to the crafting of new laws. The authors see the use of anti-sexual harassment laws and policies as disempowering, rather than empowering to the students who make the difficult choice to fight back against their harassment.

And they believe that 'young people have come to believe that danger lurks everywhere, even in the classroom, and even in private conversations.' Perhaps the authors have never spoken to a suburban boomer father who senses danger in every unexpected ring of the doorbell.

Throughout *The Coddling of the American Mind*, Haidt and Lukianoff seem to fear students calling people white supremacists more than they fear white supremacy itself. They do not believe that words can be violence, which is wrong in an intellectual sense, in a historic sense and in a psychological sense. Speech is what delivers the idea to commit violence. And yet Haidt and Lukianoff believe that it is students, since the 2017 anti-Milo Yiannopoulos protests at UC Berkeley particularly, who have become newly and uniquely violent (overlooking the near constant violence of the 1970s, when student protests were literally *blowing things up* and universities were killing students). They see it as unreasonable that students at Middlebury College in Vermont said that anyone who makes the white supremacist claims of the discredited race scientist Charles Murray is a white supremacist. They believe that not giving controversial speakers the chance to say horrible things is the result of 'fortune-telling', as it would be unreasonable to predict what nasty things nasty speakers will say in advance. They believe that an 'us versus them' attitude is always inappropriate – even in the wake of Nazi rallies at Charlottesville. And on and on and on it goes, as Haidt and Lukianoff cite times that students got out of control with their protests, using tactics that 'alienate many people who might otherwise support them' – as if this hasn't been the case in every student protest in history. They literally compare modern campus protestors to the enactors of the Chinese Cultural Revolution of the 1960s, and to the Salem Witch Trials (in modern times, the witches are men in power). Wrap your puny lizard brain around this one:

Does Bergesen's Durkheimian analysis of the Cultural Revolution help to explain the dramatic events that have been happening on campus since 2015, some of which we described in the previous chapter? As historical events, the two movements are radically different, most notably in that the Red Guards were supported by a totalitarian dictator who encouraged them to use violence, while American college students have been self-organised and almost entirely non-violent.

It is a quick and sly concession, one that skirts over the fact that unlike the creators and enforcers of the Cultural Revolution, students don't have much totalitarian power when it comes down to it. But that doesn't make them any less terrifying to the authors. (They go on to say, 'Yet there are similarities, too.' While we apparently weren't supposed to focus on intent, both campus protestors and the Cultural Revolution had the same intent in mind: 'the remaking of society along egalitarian lines.')

Like other snowflake critics, Haidt and Lukianoff see students as extremists, but waste very few pages of their books on the far right. They funnily enough fail to heed their own warning about the cognitive distortion of catastrophising. The authors long for mid-century gentility, 'a period of unusually low political polarisation and cross-party animosity,' when 'American politics was about as centrist and bipartisan as it has ever been,' perhaps eased along by the fact that only one type of person was allowed to hold power – or attend universities at all. Their concessions to minority groups are weak and mealy-mouthed ('members of some identity groups surely face more frequent insults to their dignity than do straight white males, on average'). They believe that the best response to a speaker like Milo Yiannopoulos is to be unmoved. They believe you can 'make yourself immune to trolls.' They believe that the actions of neo-Nazis and left-wing students are part of a 'polarisation cycle' for which each party is equally responsible. They believe that 'even as we work to lessen hatred and heal divisions, all of us must learn to ignore some of the things we see and just carry on with our day.'

This is not the point of a university – to ignore things. It is not the way to make positive social change – by looking the other way. It is certainly an easy path, and a comfortable one. But it is explicitly what Martin Luther King Jr, and others, have warned us about. In critiquing what they call 'safetyism', Haidt and Lukianoff draw a line from saying 'kids should ride the subway' to 'kids should not object to microaggressions'. But the most radical kids I went to college with were perfectly street-smart; it was the coddled kids who were apolitical. University is a time for those groups to meet.

Anti-snowflake authors tend to combine the idea of a spoiled childhood with the creation of the politics they don't like. For Haidt and Lukianoff, their analysis of where childhoods go wrong is very reasonable: middle-class children have too much screen time, not enough free time, and are locked from kindergarten in an arms race to get into university by anxious parents. Ivy League universities have more students from the top one per cent of wealthy families than the bottom sixty per cent. Rates of teen suicide are skyrocketing in the United States and Britain. Young people are almost certainly too stressed, but this cannot be explained by overbearing parents alone. You have to consider the fault of a modern winner-take-all economy marked by a chasm of inequality. What Haidt and Lukianoff and other snowflake critics tend to do is see this type of stressed, middle- and upper-class childhood as producing a type of politics and a type of protest they are uncomfortable with. True, even well-off young people may be drawn to more left-leaning politics in the face of instability and the potential for their own downward social mobility. But the incidents on college campuses that most tend to lead to snowflake panics are about, for, and led by working-class students and students of colour.

So why does this incredibly popular book and its well-respected, left-leaning authors matter to the debate around snowflakes? Their manner, their argumentative style, and their reception by critics may vastly differ from Trump-supporting cartoonists such as Ben Garrison. But on one thing they fundamentally agree: today's students are weak, and overly sensitive, and censorious, and extreme. In dressing up this argument in a book palatable to Barack Obama, they make disdain for young people more acceptable and more mainstream.

They may not like to admit it, but Lukianoff and Haidt are in perfect agreement with the far right when it comes to one thing at least: snowflakes.

If you were to pick up today's copy of the *Daily Mail*, you may find a fresh campus snowflake panic to mull over. But the next time you read an article or a book about students who have supposedly gone wild, it's helpful to ask yourself the following questions before believing that university students these days are indeed irreparably spoiled, terrifying and awful.

First of all: is the incident real? Does the author, columnist or angry tweeter refer to any evidence leading to their outrage? Have students indeed kicked off about cafeteria food? Have they in fact banned clapping? Is there any evidence whatsoever that students are behaving the way that a furious, dish-faced columnist has said they are behaving?

Secondly: what additional context could help explain the seemingly outrageous thing that students have done? Are Oxford students indeed terrified of clapping, or are they making an attempt to accommodate their peers with disabilities? Can you do a quick Google to find the perspective of the students themselves?

Next: what details are missing about the students who have led to such cause for concern? Is it possible that they are not spoiled, rich and terrible? Have the students complaining about racism dealt with racism themselves? Would you be comfortable saying that young people should be stripped of their right to vote once you know more about them?

And finally, unclench your sphincter and ask yourself: is this a real problem? Even if students *were* furious about cafeteria sushi and octopus and clapping and Halloween and emails, is that such a bad thing?

Ask yourself: what do these students actually want? And would it be so terrible if they got it?

University students are faced with student fees, massive debt, sexual assault, racism, a mental health crisis, a diminishing job market and, in the US, the threat of mass shootings. Those at university in 2020 and 2021 also faced a pandemic that has confined them to tiny dormitories or prevented them from enjoying the beginning of their independent, adult lives. In the face of an unprecedented economic fallout, many will lose the chance to go to university at all.

After everything, if you still believe in your heart of hearts that university students are tiresome troublemakers, perhaps the only question you should ask yourself is: so what?

What is young adulthood for, if not a time to make trouble?

3

Free speech and the snowflakes

I have lived, studied and worked in both Britain and America, I'm a citizen of both places, and I have been embarrassed on the national stage by the foolish and/or destructive electoral decisions of each country. As a result, I spend a lot of time comparing cultural and political differences between the two 'special' friends and wondering where I should ultimately end up someday to raise the least terrible children I possibly can. The answer is probably New Zealand.

In any case, I have come to understand that the chasms between legal systems, cultural understandings and pronunciations of the word 'yoghurt' are more vast than you might expect from two countries that used to share a king. The laws governing free speech rights form one such rift between my two countries, such that an American's right to a neo-Nazi parade might shock a British person, and a British person's inability to slag off the Queen on television would shock an American.

But while this divide in legal rights and regulations governing speech persists into the twenty-first century, outrage over supposed threats to free speech bestrides the Atlantic like a colossus. The primary threat to freedom of speech in Britain and America is, according to some, none other than the special, censorious, sensitive little snowflakes who we've come to know and hate.

There are those in the US who think that Americans should adopt European-style laws barring hate speech, and there are those in the UK who advocate for an American-style broad protection of speech in all its ugliest forms. But among those who hate them, 'snowflakes' have once again become a shorthand, this time for threatening our rights to free speech in either place.

Even within the context of wildly different legal and political systems, free speech arguments in both countries borrow from each other's examples. They share not only the English language, but the language of the culture war. They speak of being muzzled, censored and cancelled. They speak of students who are afraid – nay, terrified! – of hearing words they don't like. They tell their large readerships and television audiences that young people don't believe in the freedom of speech, and therefore they have been silenced. Silenced by *the mob*. These fears, I'm happy to say, are unfounded. A December 2019 study from King's College London found that seventy-one per cent of students surveyed in the summer of 2019 thought that the freedom of speech was not very or not at all threatened at their university.[1] Only forty-three per cent, by comparison, thought free speech was not threatened in the UK more generally. Whether or not you care to trust university studies (and you should!) more of them believe that free speech is better protected on campus than in the 'real world'. And eighty-one per cent agreed with the following statement, inspired by the 'Chicago Principles' which were formulated by the University of Chicago and have been implemented by many American universities to protect free speech:

> Intellectual enquiry necessarily involves ideas that are in dispute, that may cause controversy, that may cause offence and that may provoke a reaction amongst audiences in the university community and beyond.
>
> Universities should be committed to a safe and civil environment for the exchange of ideas and the cultivation of knowledge.

This commitment will at times see universities serving as places in which intellectual, moral or political disputes come to the fore. At such times, the role of a university is to ensure that all parties feel confident and safe in expressing their views except when this speech discriminates based on race, class, disability, sex, age, gender, identity, transgender status, religion or sexual orientation.[2]

This very wide support for such a statement contradicts the arguments we hear daily from those who decry the censorious student snowflake.

As historian Charlotte Lydia Riley notes in *The Free Speech Wars*, 'some of the key spaces and concepts around which British freedom of speech arguments have coalesced – "safe spaces", "trigger warnings" and "no-platforming" – are seen as newly central to university life.'[3] But in her ten years as an academic, she has seen the way each of these things has actually served to increase speech, not limit it, at universities. Safe spaces and trigger warnings are in fact 'policies aimed at being as inclusive as possible and allowing as many people as possible to participate in conversations,' while not inviting an offensive speaker is hardly controversial. They can always go speak in Hyde Park – as members of the far right actually do. 'There are absolutely limits and threats to free speech in British academia,' Riley writes, 'but they are not the tabloid spectres haunting campuses; right-wing journalists digging up academics' personal opinions, university administrators monitoring their lecturers' tweets, and the Prevent duty turning academics into Home Office police are far more pernicious.' The Prevent programme, meant to save vulnerable students from the clutches of terrorism, ends up policing what students – particularly Muslim students – can read or say in the course of their education. As my friend and former colleague, the journalist Siraj Datoo, tweeted in reaction to news that the government was preparing to create a new law to 'strengthen free speech' at universities: 'The irony of this is that by my first year at university, the British government had enacted a policy that meant any Muslim who said anything that criticised government policy could be subject to scrutiny and have their names passed on to authorities.'[4] This should be exactly the type of censorship that rattles the British tabloid press. It is not.

Nevertheless, a certain strain of conservative British soothsayer has taken up the cause of defending free speech, especially from university students. In early 2020, right-wing British journalist Toby Young created the Free Speech Union, an effort to fight back against those who would trample upon British free speech rights through such measures as getting angry at people on Twitter and quoting liberally from George Orwell. The FSU's homepage boasts of its many strategies for protecting free speech wherever it may be in peril, promising to, quite ironically, 'mobilise an army of supporters' for anyone who has found themselves 'targeted by a digital outrage mob on social media for having exercised your legal right to free speech.'[5] Membership in the Free Speech Union is, alas, not free, and will run you anywhere from £2.49 a month to £22.95 a month for 'Gold' membership – a small price to pay to mobilise an army. In any case, they may want to investigate the Free Speech Youth Advisory Board, a student campaign to promote free speech which was eventually disbanded when many of its student leaders quit, claiming their political views were being silenced by the involvement of the Free Speech Union.[6] An FSU director told the *Guardian*: 'No doubt the students who have contacted you see themselves as supporting free speech, but the Free Speech Champions project is unequivocal that it is an indivisible right and a fundamental civic virtue.' Speaking of civic virtues, the Free Speech Union also took up the cause of 'COVID dissidents' during the pandemic, that is, people who didn't think the illness was all that bad.

While Britain's moral outrage over its young people is of course homegrown, thriving in the furious minds and Twitter feeds of figures such as Toby Young, those in Britain who would critique British students' 'censorious' treatment of unpopular speakers at their own universities craft very American-sounding arguments. Even in a place that suppresses many types of speech, the gravest threat to speech, from the point of view of snowflake critics, is whenever they feel their opinions have fallen out of fashion or have been disinvited from a talk at a student union. British people do not get to assemble and rally and worship and rabble-rouse under a First Amendment, but British snowflake critics argue like they do. For that reason, it's worth figuring out what free speech really means in the United States – and what it doesn't.

Though wistful American patriots like to speak about free speech as something born with the ratification of the Bill of Rights in 1791, our current interpretation of the First Amendment is a much more recent invention. This is thanks to a number of Supreme Court rulings, as well as the work of activists such as those of the Free Speech Movement at UC Berkeley in the 1960s.

The actual text of the First Amendment, for those who missed out on a mediocre American state school education, is this:

> Congress shall make no law respecting an establishment of religion or prohibiting the free exercise thereof; or abridging the freedom of speech, or of the press; or the right of the people peaceably to assemble, and to petition the Government for a redress of grievances.

By reading the text alone, you may already be able to guess at a key problem with many contemporary arguments about free speech. That is: a public figure who has tweeted something noxious, and has been told to fuck off by a teenager online as a result, has not had his free speech rights abridged. Firstly, Congress did not make a law telling him to fuck off. Secondly, the teenager has not prohibited their free exercise of religion, speech or assembly, nor is the teenager a government agency. Nor has the noxious commentator been prevented from petitioning his government for a redress of grievances. He has simply been told to fuck off.

Many of those who decry a modern threat to free speech rights from snowflakes are, if we were to be exceedingly generous, often making a cultural argument, not a legal one. They do not literally think, I have to hope and believe, that their First Amendment rights are being trampled upon. Nevertheless, there is an alarming amount of crossover into claims of *legal* free speech rights being trampled on in the United States. So what can an American actually say?

Central to the American understanding of free speech is the idea of 'viewpoint neutrality'. This is the idea, more strictly enforced since the second half of the twentieth century, that speech cannot be restricted because of its content. You cannot rule against someone's freedom of expression simply because they are expressing that they are a communist, or an abolitionist, or gay or a civil rights activist – though all of these groups have had their free speech curtailed throughout US history due to the feared 'danger' it might bring. You also can't restrict someone's speech in the United States simply because they are a huge Nazi – as many court rulings have found. In the US, unlike in, say, modern Germany, you can be an *enormous* Nazi and live comfortably within your free speech rights. The Supreme Court has affirmed the viewpoint neutrality principle as 'the bedrock' of freedom of speech in the United States.

This is not to say that free speech is *never* restricted in the US. There are plenty of things you can't say in America. Among the types of *not* constitutionally protected speech, we find obscenity (you can't always say swears), commercial advertising (you can't say that crystals will protect you from measles in a TV ad) and defamation (you can't purposefully spread lies to the press that your neighbour killed your guinea pig, if they did not; if they *did* kill your guinea pig however, and you can prove it, you're golden). Having worked in both countries as a journalist and writer of occasionally very silly satirical pieces, I should add that it's a lot easier to get sued for libel in the UK than the US. (Please don't sue me if I've critiqued you in these pages. It was all my honest opinion. Also I don't have any money.)

Another type of non-protected speech is the delightfully named category of 'fighting words'.[7] 'Fighting words' can mean an incitement to riot. For example, you can say you think an election is stolen, but you may not be allowed to say it to an angry mob with the full intention of setting them on the United States Capitol building to kill and harm lawmakers. (I say 'may' because it turns out, maybe you can. Any future consequences for that riot are pending.) Over the years, the Supreme Court has narrowed the definition of 'fighting words'. In 1989, it defined 'fighting words' to be 'a direct personal insult or an invitation to exchange fisticuffs.' In the same ruling, the court decided it was *not* considered 'fighting words' to simply burn the US flag. In a 1992 decision, the Supreme Court also reiterated that 'fighting words' could not be restricted if the reason for restricting the speech was viewpoint discrimination – that is, you can't just say something is 'fighting words' because you don't like *why* a person is uttering them.

Speech can also be restricted under what is known as the 'emergency test'. This is the idea that if speech is *not* suppressed, it will lead to enormous calamity. In her book *Hate: Why We Should Resist it with Free Speech, not Censorship*, the former long-time president of the American Civil Liberties Union (ACLU) Nadine Strossen argues for a broad protection of so-called 'hate speech'. She doesn't like the term hate speech and is a big critic of campus efforts to restrict controversial speakers, as we'll see. Here's how she explains the emergency test:

Under this test, the government may punish speech about public issues only when, in context, it poses an emergency: only when it directly, demonstrably, and imminently causes certain specific, objectively ascertainable serious harms that cannot be averted by non-censorial measures, the most important of which are counter speech and law enforcement.[8]

If you can't stop the harm speech is about to produce, and you can't simply make a better argument against the harmful speech ('counter speech'), and not even the cops and their billy clubs can stop the bad thing happening, the government is allowed under the emergency test to censor speech. As ever with the idea of an 'objective' assessment, this measure has been applied selectively and politically. For example, the Patriot Act, passed in the wake of the 11 September 2001 terrorist attacks, prohibited 'expert assistance or advice' to terrorist organisations – a vague term that was wielded against civil rights lawyers, charities, and Muslim and Arab Americans.[9]

Before the days of viewpoint neutrality and the emergency test, there lived another idea: the bad tendency test, or harmful tendency test, which has fallen out of favour with the Supreme Court. Strossen explains that the bad tendency test permitted government 'to suppress speech whenever it maintained that the speech might cause harm at some future point.' It was by this principle that the Supreme Court in 1919 upheld the right of the government to jail those who had spoken against US entry into World War I. The feared 'future harm' was that people might not want to sign up for military service as a result of hearing such speech, and that would harm the national interest. The Socialist Party leader Eugene V. Debs gave one such spicy speech against the draft and was called a 'traitor to his country' by President Woodrow Wilson. He was sentenced to ten years in prison, then ran for president in 1920 from the Atlanta Federal Penitentiary, winning 3.4 per cent of the national vote. Wilson hated him too much to pardon him during his presidency, but President Harding eventually commuted his sentence to time served. Harding did not pardon him, however, believing him still to be a dangerous and guilty man – guilty of having made a speech against the war.

Labour activists in the 1910s were great proponents of free speech rights for workers, and from 1912 to 1913, Industrial Workers of the World members, also known as 'wobblies', fought a street battle against police in San Diego, California, over their right to soapbox – that is, their right to stand on soapboxes and rail against their bosses and capitalism generally. The famous anarchist Emma Goldman was among those who ventured to San Diego to get involved in the fight. She and her ilk were frequently at the wrong end of the government's speech-suppressing laws. For the politicians of their time, it was unquestionable that socialist and anarchist speechmaking constituted an imminent threat, fostering the type of harm that necessitated the suppression of speech.

As with every part of the Constitution and the Bill of Rights, free speech rights were not born, automatically, with the Republic. As a document promising freedom for all happily legitimised the fact of American slavery, the rights enshrined in the Constitution have continued to be defined, narrowed or broadened. Free speech rights have changed over time, generally in the direction of removing limitations – but the government has frequently restricted speech throughout history, particularly in the name of protecting the national interest, and usually to the detriment of marginalised people and workers.

Some who invoke their free speech rights when being told to fuck off by a teenager on the internet, will do so as if it is a concept that came to us perfectly defined and fully self-enforcing.

It is not, and never has been. Freedom of speech exists, as all rights do, in the midst of great political battles.

Imagine the scene: a police car rolls through a university campus, where it has been called to arrest someone who has broken the law. As the car attempts to drive away, hundreds upon hundreds of students surround the vehicle and block its path, chanting, 'Release him! Release him!' The students continue to defy the police and block the car for thirty-six hours. They give food and water to the arrestee through the back of the car's window. One student climbs on top of the police car to make a speech calling on the university to change its rules and release the activist. The crowd swells to around 7,000 protestors. By the end of the stand-off, the university has conceded to student demands to release the activist and change their laws.

Now imagine how this incident would be covered in the press. The headline in the *Sun* would blare: 'Snowflake students DETAIN police car and BLOCK officers from ARRESTING lawbreaker!' The YouTube videos that would be uploaded would have titles like: 'TRIGGERED college students throw hissy fit and waste TAXPAYER DOLLARS!' *Breitbart* would have multiple columns about spoiled students and the cowardly administrators who bent to the demands of coddled children. Columnists in the *New York Times* would write that they admire the students' passion, but there are better ways to participate in democracy than obstructing a police vehicle. Why not write a letter to the university administration instead? Why not simply *vote*?

This isn't a scene from recent years, but it is a true story. It was a critical moment in Berkeley's Free Speech Movement. The fight erupted in 1964 over a somewhat absurd misunderstanding. At the southern entrance to UC Berkeley's campus, on the corner of Bancroft Way and Telegraph Ave, students used to set up tables to share information about political causes. These tables were a place where students could learn about how to get involved in off-campus activism, like those Berkeley students who travelled to the South to take part in the civil rights movement's summer freedom rides. The university at the time didn't allow political advocacy on campus (though the sharing of 'information' without advocacy was allowed). The university believed, however, that this area was indeed outside the university, so people were allowed to have their tables there. But then one day they discovered that the street corner actually *did* belong to the university, and so in September 1964 the Dean of Students sent a letter to student organisations saying that tables would no longer be permitted at Bancroft and Telegraph. What's more, fundraising and recruiting for political activities such as off-campus protests would no longer be allowed. When a group of eight students continued to table in the area on behalf of a civil rights organisation, the Congress of Racial Equality (CORE), they were called in for a disciplinary hearing. Outraged at their punishment, over five hundred supporters joined the students on the steps of the administration building, Sproul Hall, for the first of many sit-ins. They stayed until two in the morning. The students were suspended.

Things only escalated from there. CORE activist and former Berkeley grad student Jack Weinberg set up his table in defiance of the ban and was arrested. Demonstrators gathered around the police car where he was being held. After thirty-six hours of protest and speech-making, the Free Speech Movement's most iconic speaker, Mario Savio – who did not like to be thought of as a leader of the movement – announced that the administration had agreed to release Weinberg and set up a committee of students and administrators, if only the students would stop their demonstration. The protest came to an end, but the fight was far from over. Under the leadership of Chancellor Edward Strong and University of California President Clark Kerr, the university administration remained adamant that students should not be allowed to engage in political advocacy on campus or take part in off-campus activities including 'illegal' demonstrations. Students were going to protest in the Jim Crow South, after all, where it was then illegal to defy segregation.

In November 1964, students decided to resume political advocacy on Sproul Plaza, as they put it, to 'exercise our constitutional rights' – or what the administration would call 'illegal advocacy'. Thousands of students protested the administration's ongoing defiance in a huge rally at Sproul Hall. In a famous photo of this rally, a group of smartly dressed male students in suits and ties, and women students in elegant skirt suits, marched across campus with a banner reading 'FREE SPEECH'. Mario Savio and a fellow FSM activist, Art Goldberg, faced new disciplinary action for their advocacy. By December, tensions had reached a boiling point. Mario Savio gave a speech from the steps of Sproul Hall on 2 December 1964, and spoke his most famous line:

> There is a time when the operation of the machine becomes too odious, makes you so sick at heart, that you can't take part, you can't even passively take part, and you've got to put your bodies upon the gears and upon the wheels, upon the levers, upon all the apparatus, and you've got to indicate to the people who run it, to the people who own it, that unless you're free, the machine will be prevented from working at all.[10]

Over eight hundred of the students entered Sproul Hall and occupied the building, where they held classes and study sessions (because, at the end of the day, they were still nerds there to learn). Students outside passed food and information to those inside through a window, until police entered the building and took control of it violently. It took police twelve hours to arrest all of the students inside.

In response to the arrests, teaching assistants led a strike, cancelling many classes and joining picket lines on Sproul Plaza. A few days later, on 7 December 1964, 16,000 students gathered at the university's large outdoor amphitheatre, the Greek Theater, to hear whether and how the administration would respond to protestor demands. Clark Kerr, the university president, announced amnesty for arrested students, but maintained the campus ban on political advocacy where it may lead to lawbreaking off-campus. Mario Savio climbed on stage to address the crowd. He was pulled away by police officers, but then allowed to speak, and called for another rally. The next day, the university's

Academic Senate, which comprised the university's faculty, voted to back the demands of the FSM. It was huge show of support from the professors, and a victory for the students. University leadership eventually relented that speech and advocacy were protected by the Constitution and ought to be allowed on campus. After a bit more administrative turmoil, a new chancellor announced new rules allowing for more protest in certain areas on campus. Other universities across the country followed suit and also began to allow political advocacy and free speech by students.

Allow me to make a wild and unprovable claim, but one that I feel in my bones: the very people who today loathe university students, including those who most profess to care about free speech, and seek to carry the mantle of Mario Savio, would have hated him in 1964. They would have hated him and all his radical, ungrateful hippie friends. They would have called them ridiculous snowflakes. How could these coddled students overreact to a simple campus rule? Why must they travel and break the laws of the South? How spoiled must they be not to simply appreciate the privilege of attending university, when their parents had fought in a World War? Why don't they just write a nice letter to their administrators? Why don't they just *vote*? (Well, at the time you couldn't vote until you were 21. But *still*. They should have aged and *then* voted.)

The fact is, the Free Speech Movement, though its leaders were largely white and largely male, was a fight for the right to advocate for racial justice and civil rights. Its members were arrested and disciplined repeatedly. They were rule breakers, and even law breakers – of some pretty morally repugnant laws. The FSM completely disrupted a semester's learning with strikes and demonstrations and sit-ins. It would be totally outrageous to commentators today. Like today's Black Lives Matter protestors, they would be called terrorists. Like today's student activists, they would be called spoiled, tyrannical and overly sensitive. They would be called Marxists and communists and rioters – as they were in the press back then, too. They may, ironically, be called a threat to free speech rights.

Of course, many people *were* outraged by the free speech movement at the time – including Ronald Reagan himself, who ran for governor in 1966 on a promise to 'clean up the mess in Berkeley.' He won in a landslide, not least by playing off conservative fears of the mayhem taking place at a publicly funded university. Our current culture war may be particular to our time, but its historical roots in grievance-fuelled politics run deep. At one press conference, Reagan waved around a 'secret' security report with the following, scandalous scene, as detailed by historian Robert Cohen in *The Free Speech Movement: Reflections on Berkeley in the 1960s* (in this passage, the 'VDC' stands for an anti-Vietnam War student society, the Vietnam Day Committee):

> [Reagan] claimed that it revealed that the University had condoned a VDC-sponsored dance on campus at which strobe lights projected pictures of nude bodies while students gyrated in shocking positions amid clouds of marijuana smoke. Declaring the material too obscene to be quoted, Reagan conflated radicalism and the counterculture, condemned both as immoral and abnormal, blamed the University, and thereby created an effective conservative moral issue.[11]

Obviously, this party sounds great. But Reagan used the visceral image of gyrating, high, sexually active anti-Vietnam war protestors and their shocking beliefs to propel himself to the highest political office in California – and then the country. Once Reagan took charge of the state, he did indeed do his best to 'clean up' campus protest, working with the FBI and CIA to infiltrate and undermine the VDC and other protest groups. In 1966, FBI director J. Edgar Hoover complained that 'agitators on other campuses take their lead from activities which occur at Berkeley.'

Following the events of 1964, and making use of the rights gained by the FSM, students at UC Berkeley have continued to demonstrate over different causes – though not all protests are memorialised with such care as the Free Speech Movement, which produced such handsome images of well-dressed white men. In the years after students gained the right to political advocacy on campus, they clashed frequently with police and even the Hells Angels motorcycle gang, marching on and off campus against the Vietnam War and the draft. In the late sixties, Berkeley students joined those at nearby San Francisco State University and launched the Third World Liberation Front, which sought to create Ethnic Studies programmes at their campuses. After a strike in 1969 which caused then-governor Ronald Reagan to declare a 'state of extreme emergency' and send state police to campus, the university indeed created a Department of Ethnic Studies which exists to this day. Students worked with the Black Panthers and Student Non-violent Coordinating Committee on civil rights issues. Women began to organise for their own liberation after experiencing marginalisation in the biggest anti-war student activist groups. Black and Latina women's groups tried to push a burgeoning women's movement away from the singular concerns of middle-class white women. And on it went.

In 1969, students fought with the university over attempting to create a new public gathering space in what became known as People's Park – a place known for radical speechmaking much like London's Hyde Park Corner. The university had wanted to build a dormitory on the land. On 15 May 1969, police began removing the park's advocates. Students led a mass demonstration, clashing with police. Thirty-two people were injured, and one person died. Governor Reagan sent 2,700 National Guardsmen to Berkeley and banned all meetings of more than three people. A helicopter sprayed tear gas across the campus. Reagan justified these violent tactics, saying that 'whether that was a tactical mistake or not, once the dogs of war are released, you must expect that things will happen.' The violence against students echoed across the country: in 1970, police killed student anti-war demonstrators at both Kent State in Ohio and Jackson State in Mississippi.

Student protest would not die down as a result of violent repression. Berkeley students had won their free speech and were not going to stop using it. In 1984, a small group of UC Berkeley students demanded a meeting with the University of California's chancellor and president to convince them to withdraw billions of dollars of the university's investments from companies doing business with South Africa's apartheid government.[12] At the time, the University of California system invested $4.6 billion in South Africa – more than any other university. In March 1985, activists began a sit-in outside Sproul Hall – on the same spot where Free Speech activists had sat in more than two decades prior. They slept in tents and sleeping bags for a week before police arrested 158 protestors. Ten thousand students boycotted their classes in reaction to the arrests. When the Bishop Desmond Tutu visited Berkeley's Greek Theatre that Spring, he asked his audience: 'As God looks down on you today, he's saying, hey, hey, have you seen my children in Berkeley? Eh? Don't you think that they're something else?' By July of 1986, the regents of the University of California voted to divest $3.1 billion from South Africa. When he was released from prison in 1990, Nelson Mandela visited nearby Oakland and said that the student protestors' actions had helped end apartheid rule.

On Berkeley's campus today, there is a cafe dedicated to the FSM. In its entryway is an image of Mario Savio and his words exhorting students to put their bodies into the gears of the machine. In my years at Berkeley and since, multiple police forces have been called to campus to remove student protestors by force. In one such confrontation in November 2009, in a year of student protests against enormous fee hikes, police beat back students with batons. The university's then-chancellor released a statement saying that it was 'truly regrettable' that 'a few members of our campus community may have found themselves in conflict with law enforcement officers.'[13] The university later issued an in-depth report with recommendations for 'police training, policy and practice designed to reduce the severity of confrontations.'[14]

Student protest has never stopped, and nor has its criticism, even as minds may change about the struggles of previous decades. Those who critique the actions of student protestors today accuse them of betraying the legacy of Mario Savio and the Free Speech Movement. Among those who did so were the alt-right extremist Milo Yiannopoulos, who came to Berkeley's campus in 2017, sparking a new wave of protests, a new set of claims about the radicalism of Berkeley students, and a new talking point in the war over snowflakes and free speech rights at universities.

When the now-defunct British alt-right 'provocateur' Milo Yiannopoulos came to speak at UC Berkeley in February 2017, he was met by thousands of peaceful protestors, and a few hundred less-than-peaceful ones who shot fireworks at a venue, set things on fire and smashed windows. Yiannopoulos had said he planned to out a list of transgender students, as he had done previously at another university. Shortly after the violence started, but before Milo could speak, the university cancelled the event citing safety concerns.[15] The university and surrounding city ended up with thousands of dollars in property damages, and the resulting media attention made UC Berkeley, the home of the Free Speech Movement, once again the focus of all the world's angst about students and free speech. Even President Trump got involved, saying that the University of California didn't deserve its (already paltry) federal funds.

As I watched images from the protests appear on Twitter, I saw one image shared by a reporter of students chanting 'This is what community looks like' beside a raging fire. As an alumnus, fond of Berkeley's tendency to mayhem, I quote-tweeted the image, simply adding, 'lmao berkeley'. As a result of my tweet, an alt-right figure with a massive following set hundreds of trolls on me, telling me to die and/or be fired and/or be raped and/or all of the above, because I 'found violence funny'. (I then pitched *BuzzFeed* an 'If Disney princesses were telling me to die on Twitter' article. My editor said no, in an egregious assault on my free speech rights.)

After the February chaos, Yiannopoulos planned to return that fall for a 'Free Speech Week'. He told the *Washington Post*: 'I'll bring an army if I have to. I have the money to do it. And if the university refuses to actively help us in planning it or tries to block us, we will make it even longer, a month-long rally, not just one week.'[16] He planned to spend each day of the week attacking a different group, among them feminists, Black Lives Matter activists and Muslims. He also told the *Washington Post* he would bring his own private security: 'I'll bring a whole truckload of Blackwater contractors if that's what it takes to occupy Sproul Plaza,' the site of so many free speech protests over time. Indeed, Yiannopoulos had planned to create a free speech award named after Mario Savio and give the first award to the American conservative extremist Ann Coulter (America's Katie Hopkins, if you like). Mario Savio's son called the award 'some kind of sick joke'. In the end, the student group planning to hold the free speech week did end up cancelling it, citing pressure from the university administration. (The university had actually claimed it was prepared to support the events and would spend over a million dollars in campus security.)

It was shortly after this star-crossed attempt at a month-long military occupation on Berkeley's campus in the name of free speech that videos surfaced in which Yiannopoulos appeared to endorse paedophilia. It transpired that this was an 'edgy' opinion too far, and he lost his platforms both on social media and at universities across the US. Today, he has lost his money and his relevance. The rest is history.

In the wake of Yiannopoulos's 2017 cancellations, some former members of the Free Speech Movement disowned the young protestors who had resisted him. One former 1960s anti-war activist, Paul Glusman, told the *Daily Californian* that protests against Yiannopoulos may have been justified due to Yiannopoulos's apparent advocacy of child abuse – but of the protestors, he said that 'Revolution has to be deeper than a tantrum.'[17] Another former anti-war activist, David Horowitz, has since become a conservative firebrand – and a sponsor of Yiannopoulos's college speaking tour. Horowitz told the *Daily Cal*: 'I would characterise today's student left as fascist. They want to shut down everyone who disagrees with them. In the 60s, the left still had some democratic aspirations. I don't see that today. Berkeley is a national disgrace.'

Perhaps today's student protestors will also grow up to be their own fiercest critics. Or maybe we'll all be too busy with the climate apocalypse.

The former Berkeley radicals-turned-conservative-boomers are not the only ones who saw Berkeley's protests as a disgrace or a threat to democracy, though. The Foundation for Individual Rights in Education is an organisation which tracks the number of speakers who have been disinvited from speaking at American universities. The organisation hopes this work will protect First Amendment rights on college campuses. The group counted a record forty-three such 'disinvitations' in 2016, out of hundreds of thousands of university-speaking invitations across the country. The *LA Times*' Michael Hiltzik, however, found that of those forty-three, just twenty-four were true 'disinvitations', while the other incidents were just protests against speeches which happened regardless.[18] For example, FIRE recorded as a 'disinvitation' a letter from eighty-nine Notre Dame students (out of thousands) expressing that they were 'disappointed and discouraged' that then-Vice President Joe Biden had been invited to speak because they were offended by his support for abortion. (Notre Dame students also objected to then-President Obama giving a commencement address in 2009 for the same reason.) And of those forty-three incidents recorded by FIRE, eleven were events with Milo Yiannopoulos, four of which were cancelled – one by Yiannopoulos himself. The next year, 2017, FIRE recorded thirty-six 'disinvitations' of speakers, while the *LA Times* reported that only nine were true cancellations.

Is this the epidemic of censorship we're meant to be so afraid of? Out of hundreds of thousands of speakers speaking at hundreds of thousands of events?

It may be that Yiannopoulos's right to free speech would be more limited in parts of Europe compared to America – though judging by his frequent appearances in the mid-2010s on every major news programme in Britain, he would still find a way to be heard. But in the United States, hate speech, as long as it does not directly incite violence, is a fiercely defended right. Most free speech absolutists, as we could think of them, believe that the only true way to fight against hate speech is with more speech to counter it.

Former ACLU president Nadine Strossen argues forcefully that hate speech must be protected. It cannot be restricted, she says, without threatening the principle of viewpoint neutrality – which you'll recall is the idea in American law that you can't limit speech simply because you don't like its content. Strossen's broad argument is that constitutionally protected hate speech does not cause real harm. Moreover, even if it did, laws restricting hate speech would make things worse, not better. And even if hate speech laws such as those that exist across Europe really *did* help the bad effects of hate speech, if those bad effects did exist, they *still* wouldn't be worth implementing, because they would still undermine Americans' freedom of speech under the First Amendment.

What troubles me about arguments over speech in both the US and the UK, though, is the way that high-minded freedom of speech arguments are wielded against students specifically. Claims about students destroying free speech principles are applied unequally and out of proportion. Sure, when you are nineteen you may feel impossibly powerful at times, even invincible. But I do not think that student activists wield powers of censorship akin to governments, who have armies and police forces and make laws and punish whom they like. Those who harshly critiqued the protests at UC Berkeley in 2017 against a planned speech by Milo Yiannopoulos do not tend to also worry that Berkeley's administration threatened the sanctity of the First Amendment when, over and over, it oversaw the violent removal and suppression of student protestors by multiple police forces several times in the same years. They are not particularly concerned with new laws and rules at universities which seek to punish disruptive students with expulsion. Instead, they are mainly worried that students are too fragile to hear what Yiannopoulos has to say about trans people.

Strossen writes that hate speech laws are often, in practice, turned against the very people they were supposed to protect. Hate speech laws can give governments the ability to suppress the speech that they do not like, giving them 'largely unfettered censorial power'. This is indeed a terrifying idea, and one that has played out time and time again for most of American history. But why do people take this real fear and project it with such passion and regularity onto students who would shout down a speaker for his racist ideas?

The problem is, I don't think campus critics of snowflakedom, even liberal ones, are motivated by the same concerns as an eminent ACLU lawyer, most of the time. While it may feel very noble to say the source of your discomfort with a student protest can be found in the Constitution of the United States of America, I unfortunately believe that discomfort with campus snowflakes arrives from a place a little less hallowed. Too frequently, with white critics of black protestors in particular, the source is white people's discomfort with criticism of racism.

Snowflake critics will argue that not only is it a suppression of free speech for a university to cancel a planned campus visit, but that it's the students *themselves*, in protesting, who are censoring speech in disregard of the First Amendment. But what happens in a campus protest is not an example of state power being used to censor free expression. To put it frankly, more often than not, those who would decry campus activists for shutting down speech are in fact taking issue with the activists exercising their own free speech rights. Again, this happens most frequently when the activists are not white and upper class – at Mizzou and at Yale and at Oxford alike.

Snowflake critics will also often suggest that rather than, say, shouting down or disinviting a speaker, their odious theories should instead be debated in a 'marketplace of ideas'. This phrase was once used by Supreme Court Justice William Brennan in a 1989 ruling which found that Americans were allowed to burn the nation's flag. Brennan wrote of the neutrality principle as the 'bedrock' of the First Amendment and added that even such 'sacred' concepts 'as the principle that discrimination on the basis of race is odious and destructive' could be questioned and argued in the 'marketplace of ideas'. Strossen argues that even private universities not subject to the First Amendment should take care to mind constitutionally protected hate speech on their campuses, as public universities must. 'Encountering 'unwelcome' ideas, including those that are hateful and discriminatory,' she writes, 'is essential for honing our abilities to analyse, criticise and refute them.' Strossen quotes the former president of Brown University, and first black president of an Ivy League school, Ruth Simmons, who said: 'I believe that learning at its best is the antithesis of comfort.'

But is racial abuse a form of learning? Is it one that students of colour are unlikely to learn before or after their time at university?

Students who 'can't handle' unwelcome views when they seek out or are offered counselling after visits from troubling speakers will be criticised as snowflakes. But student measures to protect themselves from all manner of hate speech are not the same thing as 'censorship'. Telling a racist speaker to fuck off is not, in the end, the same as sending someone to prison for their speech. Telling a racist speaker to fuck off, to their face, or before they have been invited to campus, is in fact speech itself.

People throw the term 'censorship' around these days with wild abandon, and often in hilarious contexts. An ironic example could be found at Donald Trump's second impeachment vote, shortly after rioters stormed the US Capitol, when one Republican congresswoman wore a mask which read 'censored' while speaking on the floor of the House of Representatives. Such bad-faith claims of censorship confuse criticism with censorship's true meaning: the government restricting, suppressing or removing speech. If we believed that censorship was a purely cultural problem, we could even say that calling someone a 'snowflake' is a way to delegitimise and thereby censor their views. But that isn't censorship either, though it is deeply annoying.

Strossen argues that 'counter speech' is more effective than anti-hate speech codes to battle hateful ideas. I don't doubt that in an ideal world, you really could debate each and every racist out of their hateful views. I believe that there are people whose minds can be changed about their deep prejudices. But it's naive to think that students marginalised for their race, sexuality or gender are not engaged in this work every single day.

What if universities were, instead, a respite? What if the university offered a few small places where students could, for a few years, focus *not* on debating racists, but on figuring out how to get to Mars, or writing poems, or solving climate change? What if those who really couldn't be bothered, for just part of the year for a few short years, didn't *have* to face the agents of their dehumanisation? Those who *are* up and ready for that fight would always be able to go and find it, in their real lives and relationships and at council meetings and in the media. Millennials and Gen Z are not afraid of the 'marketplace of ideas' – they have seen what a true, unfettered marketplace of ideas actually looks like. It's called the internet, and it's a total shit show. If a student ever feels like they are missing out on an ideas marketplace, they can always find someone online who's ready for a tedious, circular, racist argument.

What if university was a time when you really could enjoy a good coddling? Would that be such a bad thing?

Despite what the Toby Youngs of the world might contend, it isn't really the job of a university to invite *any* old windbag to speak to its students.

This is the subject of a 2019 book by New York University professor of comparative literature Ulrich Baer: *What Snowflakes Get Right: Free Speech, Truth, and Equality on Campus*.[19] Baer's central point is that it's actually the role of universities to limit speech under certain circumstances. In fact, this is something the university does all the time. It is the role of the university to draw boundaries and confer upon certain knowledge the sanctity of accepted truth. It is for this reason that universities do not, for example, invite mermaid scientists to discuss their findings in the same forums that would host a marine biologist who studies real creatures. (Sorry to mermaids.)

A university does not entertain speakers on debunked subjects. It does not invite anti-vaxxers (hopefully) or 9/11 conspiracists to speak to its students. There are all kinds of people who would like to speak at universities, and thus bask in the glow of academia and respectable discourse. They would love to change their profile pictures on social media to impressive photos of themselves speaking to a rapt audience of Harvard students. Most of them, though, would not make the cut

– and nobody would kick up a free speech fuss on behalf of a 9/11 conspiracist unless they were a 9/11 conspiracist themselves. When it comes to debunked science about racial inferiority, though, this has not been the case – as when Charles Murray was invited to speak at Middlebury College in Vermont. The Southern Poverty Law Center (SPLC), an American civil rights organisation, describes Murray as a white supremacist.[20] He is the co-author of the 1994 book *The Bell Curve*, a book based on the racist pseudo-science of Nazi sympathisers and eugenicists which, unsurprisingly, said that white men are biologically superior in intellect to other races and to women. He believes that disadvantaged groups are disadvantaged due to their genes. (Murray has denied that he is a white supremacist.[21]) The SPLC summarises Murray's beliefs:

> According to Murray, disadvantaged groups are disadvantaged because, on average, they cannot compete with white men, who are intellectually, psychologically and morally superior. Murray advocates the total elimination of the welfare state, affirmative action and the Department of Education, arguing that public policy cannot overcome the innate deficiencies that cause unequal social and educational outcomes.

Murray's work is not based in good science. It is not cutting-edge. It is debunked. It is embarrassing. But when students forcefully protested his invitation to speak on their campus, their protest was denounced by snowflake critics as yet another example of college students suppressing free speech. The Middlebury incident is the opening scene of Johns Hopkins English professor William Eggington's book, *The Splintering of the American Mind*, in which he sets out the horrors of students shouting over Murray despite the fact that 'Murray had come to speak on another topic entirely.'[22] That is, he wasn't there to talk about the *Bell Curve* on that particular day. Eggington asks his reader:

'How much braver and more dignified would it have been, if the students . . . had come prepared with arguments and hard-driving questions and engaged Murray?' Instead, the manner of their protest 'was so easily co-opted into the long-established narrative of privileged, left-wing intolerance on college campuses.'

If a notorious anti-vaxxer came to speak at Middlebury, about something other than vaccines, would the right take the ensuing student protest as evidence of the left's disdain for free speech? And would liberals like Eggington chastise those students for playing into the right's hands? Probably not, although I'm less sure of that these days.

The trouble is, even if students did come to Charles Murray talks with their diligent notes about why race science is not only racist, but bad science, it wouldn't remove any of the influence of his incredibly famous, bestselling book. Instead, Murray's repeated invitations to speak at universities have indeed added a shine to his once-defunct reputation. His book, his ideas and his presence have re-entered the mainstream, disguised in a bad-faith argument about free speech. If some students yelling is more alarming to you than a book which claims that 'Latino and black immigrants are, at least in the short run, putting some downward pressure on the distribution of intelligence,' you are likely not only a fellow racist, but an exceptionally bad social scientist.[23]

Baer writes that campus free speech controversies are not actually about speech, or hurt feelings, or offence-taking, but about power. They centre on the power of the university to determine what is studied, discussed and understood. The university is not the same as a soapbox in a public park. A public park, more likely than not, does not confer legitimacy to whatever is being said upon the soapbox. It may even have the opposite effect, as speakers in Hyde Park are often today met with an awkward grimace and not a halo of respectability. And so controversial speakers, Baer writes, 'seek out the university because that is where some of the rules are made about what counts as legitimately established knowledge, and what ideas are simply bunk.'

They take a selfie in front of an esteemed university's front gates. They write on their websites that they have spoken at prestigious institutions. They get invited to a 'debate' on *Newsnight*, where your uncles and aunts and mothers and fathers listen in and ask you at your next dinner whether you think an egregious argument might have some truth to it. Political candidates listen and learn new ways to drum up their voters' passions. Their bigoted talking points are legitimised – you can hear them at the Oxford Union, after all.

American public universities are bound by law to protect not only the free speech but also the equal participation of their students, according to Title VI of the Civil Rights Act of 1964, and Title IX of 1972. The Supreme Court also ruled between 1972 and 1981 that universities are permitted to exclude First Amendment activities which interfere with education. When a speaker comes to campus to debate the humanity of black people, you can argue that white and black students do not face the same access to education. Frederick Douglass, the nineteenth-century, once-enslaved abolitionist was a champion of free speech and is often held up by bad-faith free speech warriors to prove a point. But Douglass was also not interested in debating his equality as a human being. 'Would you have me argue that man is entitled to liberty?' he once asked in a speech. 'That he is the rightful owner of his own body? . . . To do so, would be to make myself ridiculous, and to offer insult to your understanding.' Douglass also said: 'Is it not astonishing. . . we are called upon to prove that we are men!'[24]

No one would call Douglass a delicate snowflake too afraid to debate difficult topics in a marketplace of ideas – no one nowadays, anyway. What he understood, rather, is that some topics were beyond the grasp of academic debate. Some debates were incompatible with humanity.

The thing is, you don't actually have to invite a bona fide white supremacist to learn about, debate or challenge white supremacy on a university campus. But in inviting a white supremacist and his supporters to campus, you ensure that all of your non-white students are faced with either risking bodily harm, having to defend their own humanity, or sheltering in their dorms until those that would eradicate them have left campus. You don't need Richard Spencer in the US or Tommy Robinson in the UK to speak to you face to face to learn about racism and how to challenge it. You don't even need to hear from Richard Spencer and Tommy Robinson directly to learn everything you need to know about Richard Spencer and Tommy Robinson. Students already do have these conversations about the most difficult topics of our day – often more respectfully than, say, boomers on Facebook do. My husband led a seminar of undergraduates at Columbia University in New York in the lead-up to the 2016 US presidential election, which included both supporters of Donald Trump and Hillary Clinton. His students were better at having conversations that cut to the core of their values than the older, whiter pundits who fight viciously on cable television about the same topics. Students of colour who feel their worth discounted as a result of racism spend *every day* treading lightly about the feelings of those they would debate with – if they debate with them at all.

The purpose of a university is to educate. Far-right speakers, including the neo-Nazis who rallied on the University of Virginia campus in 2017, do not come to further the university's educational mission. To think otherwise is to wilfully, naively misunderstand the motivations of the far right.

Students and young people are not the world's gravest threat to free speech, but if you are genuinely worried about protecting free speech, now is not the time to relax, I'm afraid. The truth is the very people who attack students for their alleged censoriousness are the same ones who seek to prevent and punish speech they do not like. Demonising snowflakes is a deliberate tactic which opens up the possibility of legislating against their enemies.

It's often conservative activists in the US and UK who most frequently claim their free speech rights are being abridged, despite belonging to a political movement responsible for the most egregious attempts to curb First Amendment rights. Conservatives in politics and media engage in regular, coordinated action to punish the speech of their political adversaries, both in law and through informal methods of harassment. And the targets of this harassment are frequently women and people of colour, particularly black people.

Adam Serwer wrote in *The Atlantic* in September 2017 about the way that conservatives in the US 'deploy public humiliation to deprive speakers of their livelihoods or bully them into submission.'[25] He added that the 'strain of conservatism that insists those on the left are sensitive snowflakes who cannot sustain a dissenting view . . . simultaneously angrily demands that the state and society sanction the left for the expression of political views it finds distasteful.' These are the supposed free speech warriors of our times.

Steve Bannon's *Breitbart* and other right-wing media remain committed to naming and shaming left-wing academics whose views they do not like. In one such case, a black philosophy professor at Texas A&M, Tommy Curry, was forced to flee his university after a conservative blogger's criticism of his academic work on historic armed struggles of black people led to violent threats and racist harassment against his family. The Palestinian professor Steven Salaita had a job offer rescinded from the University of Illinois Urbana-Champaign when conservative bloggers attacked his tweets about Israel's bombardment of Gaza during the summer of 2014. Indeed, criticism of Israel can lead to blacklisting by organisations such as Canary Mission, who maintain a database of thousands of students, professors and other individuals who support Palestinian rights – so that when they are Googled, searchers will find their picture and the claim that they support 'terrorism', which creates obvious economic and political harm.[26] Speech about Israel is also limited not only in practice but in law: many state governments have limited not just the right to boycott Israel, but to speak about doing so.

Meanwhile, Tory and Republican politicians have sought to ban the teaching of 'critical race theory' in British and American schools – borrowing from and wildly misunderstanding an academic field which studies systemic racism. Tory equalities minister Kemi Badenoch warned parliament in October 2020 that teachers who 'teach their white pupils about white privilege' and other 'elements of critical race theory' would be breaking the law.[27] Laws banning teaching of 'critical race theory' have been proposed or passed in various states across the US, leading to a situation in which a government would police a teacher's ability to mention, for example, the ways that white people might benefit from an unequal criminal justice system. This is a wild abridgement of free speech, and just one chapter in an ongoing attempt by Tory leaders to prevent such speech as would 'rewrite history' (i.e. better understand it) or critique modern Britain.

But conservatives do not live by the free speech principles that they tout when it comes to their own ideological foes. They called liberal lawmakers who voted against the Iraq War in 2003 traitors. They paint Black Lives Matters activists not as free speech defenders, but as threats to free speech. The Milwaukee, Wisconsin county sheriff David A. Clarke Jr, an ardent supporter of Donald Trump, has called the Black Lives Matter movement a 'hate group' and a 'terrorist organisation'. (He also frequently refers to them as 'Black Lies Matter'.) During his term as President, Trump joked about killing journalists, and journalists were killed. The White House itself once called for sports network ESPN to fire one of its hosts, Jemele Hill, for calling Trump a white supremacist.

History provides many examples of conservative silencing of speech. During the civil rights movement, legislatures in the South tried to ban civil rights groups and protests. And a century and a half before, in the 1830s, southern states suppressed speech about abolition, fearing it would inspire slave revolts. Enslaved people themselves could not read or write, let alone speak. The staunch pro-slavery southern senator and later Vice President John C. Calhoun complained that abolitionists 'libelled the South and inflicted emotional injury' for their criticism of southern slavery. ('Emotional injury' sounds like something the *Daily Mail* would mock modern students for. And when women picketed the White House during World War I demanding the right to vote, they were arrested, imprisoned and tortured for their protest.

Conservative suppression of speech is often enshrined in law and governs the most personal and private of matters. Since President Ronald Reagan declared the so-called 'Mexico City policy' in 1984, he and all subsequent Republican presidents have upheld a policy which forbids non-governmental organisations with federal funding from using any language on or about abortion. Doctors are not allowed to discuss even the existence of abortion with their patients under this rule.

Republican-held state governments have also sought, successfully and unsuccessfully, to limit First Amendment rights to protest across the country. In February 2017, the *Washington Post* reported that Republican lawmakers in at least eighteen states had introduced legislation limiting protests, one of the rights explicitly protected by the First Amendment.[28] A bill passed by the Arizona state senate would have allowed the government to criminally prosecute and seize the assets of anyone who helped plan or merely participated in a protest that later turned violent. It also would have subjected protestors to anti-racketeering charges – the same laws used to fight the mob. The anti-protest bill was not taken up by the Arizona state house, so it didn't become law.

State senates in Colorado, Oklahoma and North Dakota – the site of long-term protests against the expropriation of sovereign Native American land to construct the Keystone XL Pipeline – have proposed laws against trespassing or tampering with oil and gas pipelines, intended as a way to suppress such protests. The North Dakota bill was also defeated in its state house. A proposed Florida bill would make it fine, under some circumstances, for drivers to strike protestors with their cars. An Iowa law, in response to an incident when anti-Trump protestors shut down part of an interstate, would make intentionally blocking highways punishable with up to five years in prison. A Minnesota measure considered making it possible to charge protestors for the security costs of their protests. An Oregon measure required public community colleges and universities to expel students convicted of participating in violent riots.

As of January 2021, the International Center for Not-for-Profit Law's (ICNL) US Protest Law Tracker counted 172 such bills that had been considered in forty-three states.[29] While most had been defeated or expired, twenty-six had been enacted, and forty were pending. Those enacted include heightened penalties and restrictions for protesting near gas and oil pipelines. Others, such as HB 1413 in Missouri, limit the right of public employees to picket – though a judge found it unconstitutional and has prevented its enforcement. In North Dakota, participating in a protest that turns into a 'riot' can lead to ten years in prison. Obstructing a highway or street in Tennessee can send you to jail for thirty days. A West Virginia law eliminates police liability for killing people while dispersing a riot or unlawful assembly. The law was passed during a teachers' strike which included large protests across the state. And in Tennessee, in the wake of protests which followed the killing of George Floyd in the summer of 2020, Republican Governor Bill Lee signed a law increasing punishments for protests, stipulating that anyone who camped on state property or blocked highway access would face felony charges – and, if convicted, lose their right to vote forever.[30]

Some of the above bills were proposed by Republican lawmakers who claimed they were intended to crack down on the protests of 'paid' and 'professional' protestors – a conspiracy frequently touted by Donald Trump. Critics of the bills were not only concerned at the abridgment of protestors' First Amendment rights, but worried that making it legally less dodgy to hit a protestor with your car might, in fact, encourage people to strike protestors with their cars. What's more, most of the proposed laws were useless – it is already illegal to block traffic, for instance. Their goal was not to clear highways and run over protestors (one hopes). Rather, they were meant to make people think twice before exercising their speech rights. (Or collect that big, juicy cheque for paid protesting, as the Republicans would have it.) Many of these bills echo the UK's own Police, Crime, Sentencing and Court Bill, introduced to Parliament in March 2021. This bill, covering England and Wales, would extend police powers to break up and punish protesters they deemed a 'public nuisance'. It would also make it possible to imprison those who damaged a public memorial – such as a statue of a famous enslaver – for up to ten years. (The bill's status was pending as of October 2021.)[31]

Another way that conservative groups in America seek to suppress free speech is through lawsuits against universities. The conservative publication the *National Review* has published a guide to suing liberal arts colleges for attempts to regulate speech on their campuses. Codes of conduct in workplaces and expectations of what employees in a business may or may not say online rarely draw such ire. Meanwhile the right-wing Goldwater Institute proposed a model 'Campus Free-Speech Act' which includes provisions to suspend or expel 'any student who has twice been found guilty of infringing the expressive rights of others.'[32] Remember: a student does not censor free speech the way that a government does. A student does not have the institutional capability of true censorship. Under such a policy, though, a university could judge in what circumstances a student has 'infringed' another student's speech rights. That would be a very fraught process, without a clear guideline of where to place the line of 'infringement'. But with the threat of exclusion, a student who has racked up tens of thousands of dollars of debt might not want to get anywhere near that line. USC law professor Michael Simkovic described the Goldwater proposal to the *Los Angeles Times* business columnist Michael Hiltzik as 'stripping universities of any autonomy or editorial discretion and empowering outside groups to decide who gets to speak on campus.'[33] Under the terms of such legislation, not only can those who claim their speech has been 'infringed' get the peers expelled, but they can also sue their university for damages. Under the states that have adopted such laws, a student who feels he has been 'silenced', perhaps because he has been called a dickhead for his views, wields unsettling legal power.

In practice, the Goldwater proposal's implementation has been highly partisan. Goldwater-backed-and-inspired legislation and university policies have been proposed and passed largely in Republican-controlled states and at public universities with Republican-appointed regents. A report by the non-profit American Association of University Professors noted that Goldwater-style measures 'are tailored specifically to respond to the kinds of incidents that have affected conservative speakers. The legislation rarely addresses other constraints on campus free speech, such as the recording of professors in classrooms or professor watch lists.'[34]

Princeton professor and author Eddie S. Glaude Jr wrote a piece in September 2017 for *Time* magazine titled 'The Real "Special Snowflakes" In Campus Free-Speech Debates'.[35] This is a classic case of lobbing the snowflake hot potato back from whence it came. In any case, Glaude argues that universities are facing real free speech threats from the legislation of conservative state governments, not left-leaning students. Glaude writes:

Some conservatives want to proselytise without pushback. They want to exact judgement without being judged. When others reasonably call them racist or sexist or homophobic, they clutch their pearls and cry foul. One wonders who the real snowflakes in this drama are.

Glaude was writing in response to a policy approved by the University of Wisconsin in October 2017 which called for students who disrupt campus speakers and events to be suspended or expelled. Under this law, a student who had twice disrupted a speech would be suspended, and expelled after three such disruptions. The President of the University of Wisconsin system Ray Cross explained the law's purpose: 'Perhaps the most important thing we can do as a university is to teach students how to engage and listen to those with whom they differ.'[36] The previous year, students had disputed a speaking event with conservative columnist Ben Shapiro. 'If we don't show students how to do this, who will?' Cross asked. 'Without civil discourse and a willingness to listen and engage with different voices, all we are doing is reinforcing our existing values.'

The Republican State Assembly also drafted similar legislation at the state level. The university's administrative board is appointed mostly by then-Republican Governor Scott Walker. The only dissenting vote, a Democrat, said that the policy would ironically 'chill and suppress free speech on this campus and all campuses.' A Democratic state representative asked, 'Who's going to show up to a protest if they think they could be potentially expelled?' Certainly not a student taking on debt to attend university. (Again, we see echoes of this policy in the white paper put forward by then-Education Secretary Gavin Williamson in February 2021 – which would allow 'deplatformed' speakers to sue universities which cancelled their events in the face of student protests.)[37]

While the Supreme Court affirms that speech must not be restricted due to its content, both liberals and conservatives will frequently find that some topics, in their eyes, are beyond the pale. A free speech watchdog does not jump to defend the rights of a YouTube conspiracy theorist who doesn't get invited to discuss his closely held belief that the world is flat. Nor would such a person get a fair chance to join the 'marketplace of ideas' in the opinion pages of a national newspaper.

Which ideas a society deems to be beyond the pale changes over time. It is the work of snowflakes to exclude outdated opinions about race and gender from acceptable conversation. For this, they are understood to be suppressing free speech. But true 'censorship' does not come from an angry student – even one who relentlessly heckles a speaker. Censorship comes from those with real, institutional authority. It is not delicate little snowflake students who are proposing laws to state governments or Parliament to punish protest with prison time and the loss of voting rights, after all.

I believe that the students and activists and various outraged snowflakes of UC Berkeley today are not harming free speech rights, but continuing the work of the Free Speech Movement. I think that today's British universities could also learn a thing or two from the wild abandon of Sproul Plaza, site of decades of protests, and discomfort, and learning, and attacks by law enforcement. It is a strange and magical place.

I went to UC Berkeley because they admitted me, because they offered me some scholarships, because it was cheaper than private universities, because I had been rejected elsewhere, and because it was close enough to home that I could do my laundry for free in the splendour of my parents' 1980s appliances.

Growing up in the Bay Area, I was familiar with Berkeley's reputation as a hotbed of activism, past and present. My parents would take me to protests across the Bay Area against the Iraq War when I was an uncool thirteen-year-old, painfully embarrassed that my mother had brought a ziplock bag with some cold sausages to a demonstration, 'in case we got hungry.' ('You can't bring sausages to a protest,' I angrily told her through my braces.) The university itself would often make the local Bay Area news, with images of people protecting trees from the chop across Berkeley's campus by living in them for weeks on end. I knew the Berkeley deal, and I was interested in it. I visited once as a pre-teen on a school field trip, on a day in spring which the campus celebrates each year as 'Cal Day', luring prospective students to its glorious, sunshiny fields and pathways. A student handed me a daffodil, and I thought, 'This place is wondrous. Maybe I'll live in a tree someday.'

In reality, UC Berkeley can be a gruelling experience for an undergrad. While the university may be thought of as a protective bubble for snowflake sensibilities, Berkeley can also chew you up and spit you out just as viciously as the 'real world'. There are over 40,000 students at Berkeley. It is possible to go an entire four years there without ever speaking one-on-one with a professor. You must find your way in a huge metropolitan area. For the most part you had to figure out how to cobble together a degree, you had to fight to get into popular courses, and you had to make sure you were actually going to graduate with the credits you'd accrued. (I know someone who thought he had graduated, but it wasn't until he tried to request his degree years later that it turned out he *hadn't*.) Nobody helps you get a job afterwards. Nobody helps you with anything unless you seek out that help very actively. And it's certainly not easy to feel unique or special amid thousands of your peers who also did very well in high school and had a 'promising future'. UC Berkeley is a public university, and twenty-nine per cent of its student body are the first in their families to attend college. There's a lot to figure out, and it can be overwhelming even if you *aren't* the first in your family to go to university. If there are people there to mollycoddle you, I never found them.

What I did find was exposure to Californians from all walks of life. I made friends with people of different social classes, races and religions. I lived for the second half of my undergraduate career in student co-operative houses, where you had to clean and cook and occasionally build a cement wall as part of your keep. The co-op houses were unclean, graffitied, occasionally contentious, often very loving and a pretty wonderful place to live. In finals week each year, many of the co-op students run naked through the libraries in joyous abandon. I cannot comment as to whether I did this, too.

But while there was always some kind of activism happening or about to happen on campus, and a very intense student politics scene, most students were only really interested in their own grades, their own social worlds, and their own chances of getting a job in an economic recession after graduation. Berkeley was, and still is, a big fat entry into the real world, whether you're ready or not. Students at Berkeley, as at all universities, are most interested in gaining the grades and the credentials to attempt to stay afloat in an uncertain world, under the burden of student debt, often with the expectation that they will in future have to support their extended families. These aren't the conditions that produce whiny, self-entitled outrage machines, devoted only to the cause of eradicating free speech.

I worked for all four undergrad years writing for Berkeley's excellent student newspaper, the *Daily Californian*. I wrote primarily on the arts desk, laying out my important nineteen-year-old's opinions on all the culture the Bay Area had to offer, as well as a few weekly columns. At the time, our offices were at the top of a building so structurally unsound that it has since been knocked down. (It's better to knock your buildings down before an earthquake does in California.)

One day, I remember standing on our perilous balcony, watching a protest move down Bancroft Way, the street skirting the university's southern edge. I do not remember what the protest was about, but it was likely to have been one of the many at Berkeley protesting the sharp increase of student fees – which went up by thirty-two per cent in 2009. What I do remember vividly is two senior editors of the paper laughing at the protestors below, and one of them saying, 'protests have never changed anything.' A few weeks later, another friend from the paper said the same to me, with a knowing look. *He* knew that the students' protests were actually pointless, just as protests had always been and always would be. This made him very cool, in his mind. (I don't blame him for this. It's better to get your smugness out of the way in your late teens than to inflict it on wider society later. He's less smug now.)

As a writer for our newspaper, even though I mostly covered the arts, I was not allowed to take part in protest activity, in the name of protecting the image of our paper's objectivity. Instead I observed. I once ate a sandwich while watching rather unfit police officers attempt to remove a long-term resident of a central tree on campus. He was much nimbler than the cops, though, who eventually gave up. I don't remember what he was protesting. But I do remember the general attitude to protests for any reason on campus – that it was a bit embarrassing to care enough to protest.

But when people did protest, or get in arguments, or write fiery denunciations of each other in the *Daily Cal*, or stage a takeover of a campus building, I always felt: *Now this is some free fuckin' speech*.

Speech never feels truer than when someone is screaming something from a tree at a cop. For me, this is free speech at its finest – pushing the boundaries of what is actually legally allowed. I associate free speech with the kinds of students people today decry as delicate, offended snowflakes. I learned from these people, friends and classmates, the courage it took to call out injustice wherever you saw it. Most people did not have that courage. I don't think I really did either. But I respected it. If I was not ready to live in a tree, I understood it was a good thing that other people did.

How did activism come to be seen as weakness? How did the exercise of First Amendment protest rights come to be seen as the very thing tearing at the heart of the First Amendment? In the story of Berkeley student activism, from the FSM to the burning dumpsters of the Milo protests, we see how the practice and criticism of free speech on college campuses has changed. But why do we feel differently about the same university's protests in the 1960s and now?

One reason the university and free speech advocates so tenderly memorialise the Free Speech protestors may be the safety and the distance of time. But protestors of the 1960s were seen at the time as equally destructive as those today. Another reason, I believe, is the image of suited, white and distinguished-looking activists of the Free Speech Movement. And yet another reason is the fact that the modern university can agree more comfortably on the right to free speech than it can to other movements – and it can place the Free Speech Movement at a discrete moment in time, one we no longer have to worry about. Anti-Vietnam War protests led to violent clashes with state government and police. The Third World Liberation Front won a department, but it challenged the whiteness of the university and the curriculum and isn't as celebrated by the university as the FSM is. Modern protests against fees were shut down with enormous police force, and protests against alt-right speakers are seen to shame the university in the eyes of the national press – not to mention the then-president.

In 1976, eight-four per cent of American college students were white, and fifty-three per cent were men. Nowadays, just under sixty per cent are white, and a majority of students are women. With new students representing new backgrounds gaining access to elite universities in large numbers for the first time in American history, this will of course inspire a reckoning of what the university is for, who it serves and how. It will mean new types of protest, by new types of college student. It will mean new types of speech challenging new symbols of authority. It will mean that young activists challenge even the causes that previous generations of activists fought for.

Perhaps universities, commentators and the press are happy for students to have free speech *in theory* but are deeply uncomfortable whenever students choose to use it, particularly when those students challenge racial and gender hierarchies.

In any case, critics of campus snowflakes agree on one thing: students protest about far too much nowadays – and those protests are a threat to a healthy debate in the marketplace of ideas, and to the foundational right to free speech itself.

What if the opposite was true? What if students aren't protesting enough?

Malcolm Harris writes in *Kids These Days: Human Capital and the Making of Millennials* that young people are not made rebellious by the modern world. Rather, an unequal economy makes us 'servile, anxious, [and] afraid'.[38] As a perfectly average millennial, I like to think I balance my servility, anxiety and fear with a healthy dose of rebellion when required. Still, this sentiment squares with my experience of my generation.

An old professor and mentor of mine who had taught at Berkeley for decades – and who prefers to remain anonymous here so as not to sound like a shit-talker – drove this point home to me recently. He had started working at Berkeley in the 1960s during the years of widespread student protests and told stories of how students would devour even the dullest of ancient history in search of tips for how to be revolutionary. Students would ask to speak to the class and deliver passionate speeches about politics. He says it was an exciting time to be a teacher. Indeed, it should be every teacher's dream to lead a classroom of fiery students whose main problem is that they're a little *too* engaged with the material. In 1970, though, he noticed a change in his students. After a decade of unrest and revolt, suddenly a fresh crop of students were interested, primarily, in getting good grades that would allow them to get good jobs and make good money. I asked my professor if the students of the following decades ever returned to their 1960s fury. He said they didn't.

It seems that most students nowadays are quite the opposite of disruptive. They work with the fear of an unstable economic future, amid the rising tides of climate change. They may be interested in changing the world, but few are interested in getting in trouble. It's a simple point, but one missed by those who decry a generation of hysterical, violent, out-of-control student protestors. While a few incidents surface to the national conversation – always without much context or sympathy for the causes of student protest – most campus speaking events, even controversial ones, come and go without much notice. Princeton professor Eddie S. Glaude Jr wrote in *Time* magazine in September 2017, in reaction to campus protests of lectures from Charles Murray (the *Bell Curve* man), former Ambassador to the UN Susan Rice, and conservative commentator Ben Shapiro:

> Thousands of lectures across the ideological spectrum happen on campuses. Students go to classes, participate in various organisations and attend lectures without incident. Imagine how many times Murray or Rice or Ben Shapiro have actually spoken on campuses without it becoming a national spectacle. The protests we have witnessed recently are not the norm, but conservatives and even some liberal columnists would have us believe otherwise.[39]

Glaude captures a sort of base rate fallacy that commentators fall victim to when they speak of a supposed plague of shutdowns and protests. Universities in fact host an exhausting number of talks, lectures and debates, all trying to bribe attendees with free food. The number of newsworthy 'incidents' pales in comparison to the sheer volume of lectures which happen each term.

I am convinced that students are better at encountering, debating, and changing their minds in the face of new ideas than many older people. The truth is, the university is, and will remain, a cauldron of free speech, and not a damper. When else in your life will it be your job to favour argument over polite accommodation? The university is among a person's only chances to educate and even yell at each other.

It's a chance to sort out people's objectionable biases and assumptions before they enter that 'real world' we've heard so much about. It is a chance for a white person who has never seriously considered racism to do so before entrenching themselves into a lifetime of defensiveness. What are students *supposed* to be doing at university? Are they meant to be becoming app developers and doctors, or terrifying political activists, or both? Are they meant to absorb the wisdoms of a bygone age, or challenge them? Are they supposed to be studying conscientiously in the library, or revelling in orgiastic, youthful, drug-fuelled abandon at parties? Why not all of the above?

The university is a place where the children of once-disenfranchised people can figure out how to use the laws and policies available to them to carve out space for themselves. (Yes – this includes 'safe spaces'.) It is a time in which young people lucky enough to get to further their education can try on new ideas and political identities. It is a time to get in fights, while you're young enough and have the energy to fight for what you believe in. It's a time to expand your perception of what is possible of the world. It's a time to look at 'ancient wisdom' and rethink whether it was really so wise, as uncomfortable as that may be to consider. It is indeed a time in which people should encounter views that make them uncomfortable – but for some reason, snowflake critics always tend to think this means students of colour should come face to face with the same racism they encounter out there in the 'real world', or that trans students should continue to encounter the kind of devil's advocacy or outright hostility over their humanity that the world has in store for them. Funnily enough, it is never white people who are meant to face the 'uncomfortable' ideas about their own position in society when it's asserted that young people today are *unable* to face difficult speech and difficult ideas. Indeed, this is the kind of educational encounter that Tories and Republicans are hoping to eradicate by legislating against the teaching of 'critical race theory'. What could be a more difficult idea for a white person to consider than that many of their comforts in life are a result of their race?

The assumption underlying a lot of snowflake critique is that without exposure to it at university, students could not possibly learn how to combat vile -isms or hate speech in real life. But the only people who could in fact turn up to university without any prior exposure to hate speech are young white students who grew up in very segregated schools, neighbourhoods and friendship circles. This is doubly true in Britain, which has such vast, monoracial swathes of the country. For those white students, hate speech is simply something to study when you learn about the civil rights movement. They are unlikely to have considered their own racism, let alone that of their communities. For white students, the opportunity to learn about the nastiness of the 'real world' comes not from campus speaking tours of alt-right figures, but from their peers with first-hand experience of racism. This was exactly how I learned about racism. And it was how my friends of colour at university took their personal histories and struggles and placed them in historic context, and understood their pain as part of wider systems. In doing so we all expanded our understandings of the world. And when we protested, whether or not we 'changed anything', we managed to change ourselves.

It should not shock observers to see sometimes raucous demonstrations taking place on university campuses. It should surprise us how few protests there are, not how many.

4

I hope to never hear the phrase 'cancel culture' again, thanks so much

Closely related to debates over free speech, and even more ludicrous, are arguments over so-called 'cancel culture', that is, the idea put forth by some commentators and politicians that your career can be destroyed, and you can be forever banished from public life, for simply uttering the wrong thing. This is not the original meaning of this phrase, as we'll see. But if you were to shout it in a supermarket, this is what the guy buying cornflakes would think you were on about.

It is not only conservatives who fixate on the idea of cancellation. Indeed, as we have seen, it is many elite liberals who most fear the snowflakes and their cancelling tendencies. Cancellation is, at the end of the day, something feared by powerful people. You can only really be 'cancelled' if people know who you are to begin with. I will remove the quotation marks from 'cancel' now, but I beg you to see enormous, neon quotation marks around this term whenever and wherever you encounter it.

This argument over cancel culture reached a fever pitch in 2020, of all years. As millions of people died in a pandemic, politicians in Britain and America answered questions from an acquiescent press about the supposed scourge of wokeness. ('Woke' is a term originally taken from black American slang, to mean awareness of injustices and systemic racism, which is now frequently co-opted by pathetic old racists and recast as a supposedly bad thing to be.) As Britain's death toll from the coronavirus pandemic passed 100,000, the highest number of COVID casualties in Europe at the time, the Tories introduced new legal penalties against those who would do harm to statues, citing the existential threat of the 'baying mob'.[1]

A week after an actual violent mob stormed the US Capitol, Republican congressman Jim Jordan stood on the floor of the House of Representatives during President Trump's second impeachment and declared that he would bravely stand against 'the cancel culture that only allows one side to talk.'[2]

Claims of cancellation were constant throughout 2020 and 2021, forming a sort of background drone to life. Each supposed victim claimed that they had been effectively removed from public life, over and over again, like a preacher on a street corner who has to keep updating his predicted date for the end of the world when it doesn't come to pass.

When the National Trust announced in August 2020 that it would study its landmarks' historic connections to slavery, it faced a wave of accusations that it, too, had fallen foul of tradition because of the cancel-culture-woke-mob. The Chair of the UK's Charity Commission said in a front page interview with the *Daily Telegraph* that she would investigate whether the National Trust had lost sight of its job in preserving historic sites.[3] (The investigation eventually found that it had not, in fact, broken charity law.[4]) Twenty-two Tory MPs from the so-called 'Common Sense Group', who claim to 'speak for the silent majority of voters tired of being patronised by elitist bourgeois liberals,' signed a letter in the *Telegraph* saying that the National Trust ought not be led astray by 'cultural Marxist dogma, colloquially known as the "woke agenda".'[5] Some National Trust members were so distraught that they might have to learn about slavery that they threatened to cancel their memberships (clearly not seeing the irony there).[6] These members, so bravely willing to sacrifice their right to a cream tea at a stately country home on a fine spring day, accused the Trust of trying to 'erase history' – by further studying its history. This took place in October 2020, when coronavirus cases in Britain were once again on the rise, foreshadowing a catastrophic death toll to come.

Even so, many of Britain's leaders and publications remained focused on the real threat to Britain: the woke. 'If COVID doesn't kill us, woke will,' wrote television presenter Neil Oliver in the *Sunday Times*.[7] 'Everything is so serious now, we're afraid to laugh, afraid to make the joke in case we end up in jail, or as social pariah,' he added. (Neil has not been imprisoned for laughter – yet.)

Ed West, the deputy editor of *UnHerd*, wrote for *Conservative Home* in August that 'When the Coronavirus hit, politics seemed irrelevant but then, after the death of George Floyd and the general insanity that followed, it seemed to have returned, more depressing than ever.'[8] What was so depressing, to Ed? That 'the left now controls almost every institution in Britain,' he contended, writing under an eighty-seat Tory majority. 'It doesn't matter who's in government, because the generation growing up – including my children – will be bombarded with progressive messages and signals,' he lamented. The ability to cancel has nothing to do with hard power, to Ed and his ilk, and the most terrifying form of censorship is a random internet stranger calling you a bigot.

'It's not an exaggeration to compare the methods used by the new "woke movement" to those of Mao's Red Guards,' screamed a headline from retired LSE professor John Gray in the *Mail on Sunday* in July.[9] These methods, according to Gray, include diversity training at corporations, adding non-white thinkers and writers to school curricula, and being mean on Twitter. 'In some ways, today's Twitter Maoism is worse than the original Chinese version,' Gray clarifies, noting that 'Mao's Cultural Revolution was unleashed by a communist dictator,' while 'in Britain and America today, our leading institutions have shamefully surrendered their own authority to a destructive ideology.' This, he writes, threatens 'British civilisation' itself. Of course, Mao's Red Guards were more known for imprisoning, torturing and murdering their enemies. To Gray, though – a professor who laments the passing of the 1970s, when things just weren't so bad – this is a fair comparison to modern justice movements and their activities on social media.

Journalist Janice Turner wrote in the *Times*, also in July, an article titled 'The Woke Left is the new Ministry of Truth' which compared the actions of a 'tyrannical minority' and the 'angry throng' of career-threatening woke 'mobs' to George Orwell's *1984*, that favourite book of snowflake critics.[10] Turner decried her own various cancellations due to her frequent transphobic statements. (Turner denies she is transphobic, but writes outrageous, scaremongering columns with headlines reminiscent of homophobic media coverage from the 1980s and 1990s, such as 'Children Sacrificed to Appease Trans Lobby'.[11]) Those who object to her writing, Turner said, are silencing her. Or at least, that's the kind of thing she frequently writes about in her weekly column in the *Times*. 'Social media pile-ons' by 'censorious peers' are, to Turner, exactly what Orwell sought to warn us about. In any case, Turner has not yet been so cancelled as to prevent her from receiving the prestigious Orwell Prize for politics writing in 2020. The very journalists who claim to be most censored are rewarded again and again by a British media class which sees itself as a threatened minority.

And in January 2021, as British hospitals were crushed under a crippling wave of coronavirus hospitalisations, the Tories introduced a new plan to name roads after wartime heroes and Victoria Cross recipients in what the *Telegraph* called the 'latest Tory plan for "war on woke".'[12] The plan was in reaction to a Birmingham City Council initiative to create new street names such as 'Equality Road' and 'Diversity Grove', for which they were accused of 'virtue signalling'.

This is a term which, much like 'snowflake', finds its origins in online far-right media. It's meant to imply that people who do virtuous things – whether standing up for an important cause, publicly supporting a vulnerable population or donating to charity – only do so to impress others with their righteousness. It's a term which clearly says more about the person using it than the 'virtue signaller' herself. (In October of 2020, the BBC banned its journalists from 'virtue signalling' in their official social media rules, showing how far the term has travelled from fringe discourse to the mainstream.[13])

On and on the conversation went, as British politicians and journalists and columnists looked upon the horrific year that was 2020 and diagnosed us all with incurable wokeness. They were joined enthusiastically by American leaders and commentators across the political spectrum.

Perhaps the most bewildering example of a cancel culture panic was an open letter to *Harper's Magazine* published in July 2020, during the heart of the racial justice protests which followed the murder of George Floyd by police. While nodding to the existence of 'powerful protests', the letter went on to condemn the 'new set of moral attitudes and political commitments that tend to weaken our norms of open debate and toleration of differences in favour of ideological conformity.'[14] This conformity, according to the letter, had been 'intensified' by the civil rights protests. While, yes, Donald Trump had brought his own illiberalism to the world, the letter explained, 'the democratic inclusion we want can be achieved only if we speak out against the intolerant climate that has set in on all sides.' In the eyes of the letter, your society is equally likely to succumb to fascism at the hands of the 'intolerant' woke as it is to Donald Trump. All sides bear responsibility.

The signatories to the *Harper's* letter made up a collection of the richest, most pre-eminent and widely published writers and academics in the English-speaking world, from Noam Chomsky to J.K.

Rowling to Steven Pinker to Malcolm Gladwell to Salman Rushdie to Gloria Steinem. After the letter was published, several signatories sought to distance themselves from it, uncomfortable with the strange bedfellows they had found their names cuddled up to. Others who had been approached to support the letter announced they had declined to sign it in the first place, including former US Labour Secretary and UC Berkeley professor Robert Reich. Reich wrote on Twitter: 'I declined to sign the *Harper's* letter because Trumpism, racism, xenophobia and sexism have had such free rein and baleful influence in recent years that we should honour and respect the expressions of anger and heartache finally being heard.'[15] For Reich – as for many who read it that summer – the letter's timing could not be separated from the moment of civil rights reckoning in which it was published. A collection of around 150 people had added their names to a document which loudly declared, in so many words, that they would not cede their own cultural power to those who would seek to share in it.

Or, as a *HuffPo* director and former editor of the *Nation* Richard Kim put it: 'I did not sign THE LETTER when I was asked nine days ago because I could see in ninety seconds that it was fatuous, self-important drivel that would only troll the people it allegedly was trying to reach.'[16]

The great irony of the *Harper's* letter, beyond the obvious irony of 150 eminent, wealthy writers announcing their fear of being silenced in the pages of a famous magazine, was that *not everyone's ideas* were in fact welcome at the 'we love the free exchange of ideas' party. In fact, the letter's organiser, Thomas Chatterton Williams, admitted in an interview that he was 'outvoted' on the issue of inviting independent journalist Glenn Greenwald to sign it. Greenwald is a free speech absolutist who would have been an obvious choice to sign – but has enough unpopular opinions, and a trolly presence on Twitter to get him cancelled from the anti-cancellation letter. Greenwald tweeted that the letter signatories were 'frauds' for not including him, using principles of free speech only to protect 'honoured elites from criticism.'[17]

In the midst of civil rights protests and a raging pandemic, those mostly liberal 'honoured elites' found themselves using the same language and arguments as an increasingly authoritarian Republican party. Republicans running for election or re-election in 2020, from the president down to local races, incessantly referenced cancel culture, declaring that they would *not* be cancelled, protestors be damned. The speeches at the Republican National Convention contained dozens of references to cancellation – including a strong implication from a nun that Jesus Christ himself was cancelled for 'political incorrectness'.[18]

Conservative Supreme Court Justice Samuel Alito even found the time in November 2020 to claim that protections of LGBTQ+ people were in themselves a threat to free speech. He said those who believed that marriage should only be between a man and a woman risked being 'labelled as bigots' and said the freedom of speech was 'falling out of favour in some circles.'[19]

And Marjorie Taylor Greene, one of the new 2020 Republican House members from the outer edges of the fringe, who once said the House Speaker Nancy Pelosi should be shot in the head, claimed that she had been cancelled when she was removed from her committee assignments.

As a majority of Republicans did not believe that Donald Trump had actually lost the 2020 presidential election, they cried cancel at any attempt at censure. As far-right websites which hosted domestic terrorists were kicked off app stores and booted from their web service providers, they cried cancel. As Donald Trump's second impeachment trial took place in the US Senate, his defenders argued that he would not have his free speech (to incitement) abridged; he would not be cancelled. As people in Britain and America were asked to wear masks, they called them 'muzzles' and cried cancel.

Everybody cried cancel in the year in which two million people died in a pandemic.

As we've learned by now, free speech isn't a golden ticket that allows you to express vile opinions without someone calling you, as a result of said vile opinions, a prick. The ability of people to say that you are bad and wrong is yet another beautiful expression of free speech, not its suppression. A teenager calling you a boomer for something you have said or done is not the same as a government censor busting down your front door and arresting you for your boomer activities. Sure, it may be hurtful, and potentially rude. It may feel really bad. It may even be wrong. But you have almost certainly not been 'silenced by the mob'.

And yet a wide variety of well-connected commentators with large platforms believe themselves to be on the cusp of something fearful: being cancelled. The fear of cancellation haunts public figures like a spectre. It is the fear that if they say or do anything 'problematic' or 'politically incorrect', an unruly mob of 'social justice warriors' will not only persecute them and call them horrid names but will *ruin their careers and their lives.*

Sure, sometimes people do have their careers affected by an outpouring of loathing for their 'politically incorrect' behaviour. Many of those felled by the #MeToo movement, for instance, were fired from their jobs or had their television and movie projects literally cancelled. And yet even those who have supposedly been *most* cancelled, have faced *actual* legal action for their bad behaviour and really *should* be banished from polite society, are usually very wealthy and often just *fine.* Louis C.K., the once-much-loved comedian whose show and films were cancelled after revelations of his repeated harassment of female comedians, is already making a comeback. After a brief silence and little to no public reflection beyond an initial apology, he returned with a warm welcome to his usual comedy club, the Comedy Cellar in

New York City, where he continues to make jokes about masturbating in front of unwilling women.[20] He was, of course, not 'cancelled' for his jokes – he was 'cancelled' for his behaviour, harassing women comedians who then, as the *New York Times* reported, feared career repercussions from his manager for talking about it.[21] (Louis C.K.'s manager told the *New York Times* that he 'never threatened anyone'.)

Of course, a social media mob can also be just that: a lot of people yelling at someone *without* much power for sport. In *So You've Been Publicly Shamed*, Jon Ronson paints a compelling and very sympathetic portrait of those who have been 'cancelled' (or 'destroyed', as he would have it) for minor misunderstandings and transgressions.[22] Of course people online can be cruel and punishing and can launch an unsuspecting rando unwittingly into the public eye. This can indeed be very gross behaviour. But these aren't the people leading the moral panic about cancel culture. The people who cry cancel are, more often than not, people with extraordinary cultural capital, like those who signed the *Harper's* letter. And many of the people whose careers did in fact suffer from a 'cancelling' are criminally liable, or have expressed support for, say, white supremacy. Even then, though, cancel-ees will sometimes successfully launder their reputation as a politically incorrect or 'dangerous' speaker or thinker into a new career. Often, the people who are 'cancelled' for a dodgy tweet are doing just fine, if not better than they were before. If this weren't true, we would never have heard of Katie Hopkins.

One prime example of a cancellation spun into an improved career can be found once again with our old friend, William Sitwell, the erstwhile editor of *Waitrose Magazine* who was fired for telling a reader that he'd like to murder vegans. A flurry of devastating columns followed heralding the end of civilised discourse and a world in which even 'big companies' will cower before the will of the mob. Outraged media painted a picture of a shrill horde of snowflakes ruining a man's life because he joked about killing vegans. But in the end, Sitwell ended up with a much more prominent job writing for the *Daily Telegraph*, where he continues to rail against the fascist power of snowflakes alongside many a like-minded columnist, having gained the credibility of a cancelled figure. Who better to hold forth on cancel culture than one who has been cancelled himself, and lived to tell the tale?

Nevertheless, for some commentators, being 'cancelled' is spoken of as something akin to being murdered. After controversy over his book deal following multiple allegations of sexual harassment, the American political journalist Mark Halperin's publisher critiqued 'this guilty-until-proven-innocent cancel culture where everyone is condemned to death or to a lifetime of unemployment based on an accusation that's twelve years old.'[23] (Halpern denied some of the allegations, but apologised for his conduct.[24]) As far as I know, though, nobody has been murdered by the #MeToo hashtag – nor are people actually condemned to obscurity and/or career death. Many of the men named in #MeToo accusations have since quietly returned to their careers in media, for example – a little quieter, but already enjoying the short memories of their fans and employers. The same cannot always be said for the victims of sexual harassers and abusers.

The idea that there exists such a thing as a coherent, organised 'cancel culture' persists among snowflake critiques and in countless articles fearing the end of free speech as we know it in Britain, America and around the world. The phrase has become a catch-all term, as journalist Sarah Hagi wrote for *Time* magazine, 'for when people in power face consequences for their actions or receive any type of criticism, something that they're not used to.'[25] In the age of social media, criticism for any type of work, statement or behaviour can be delivered directly from the consumer of that work to its producer. Of course this can be difficult to hear from time to time, and some kinds of criticism are more valid than others. But people in power have come to believe that criticism from the masses is not only hurtful but threatening to their careers. Hagi writes for *Time* that as a black, Muslim woman, she and other marginalised people have for the first time in history an unprecedented ability thanks to social media to not only express themselves, but to be heard. 'That means racist, sexist, and bigoted behaviour or remarks don't fly like they used to,' Hagi writes. The term 'cancel culture' is a way for powerful and privileged people to delegitimise criticism – just like the term 'snowflake' is meant to shut down debate and discount people's feelings and experiences.

The phrase 'cancel culture' did not first emerge from the mouths of powerful people. In fact, the opposite is true. Dr Meredith D. Clark is a professor of media studies at the University of Virginia. After the absurd *Harper's* letter came out, she wrote a short paper on the etymology of the term, tracings its origins from black American vernacular, particularly on Twitter, to white media elites who have wielded it like a cudgel against those that would threaten their power. Clark provides a thoughtful definition:

'Cancelling' is an expression of agency, a choice to withdraw one's attention from someone or something whose values, (in) action, or speech are so offensive, one no longer wishes to grace them with their presence, time and money.[26]

Now, though, the meaning of cancellation has been twisted into 'a tool for silencing marginalised people', seized upon by outsiders to the culture from which it first emerged, where once it was a tongue-in-cheek meme or an effort to draw attention to various injustices that *weren't* being covered by the media. Dr Clark traces how in 2013 hashtags brought the attention of mainstream media to racist incidents, including celebrity chef Paula Deen's use of the n-word. It was a long journey from there to where we are now, as we watch, for example, New York's Governor Andrew Cuomo saying that he was a victim of cancellation – because multiple women had accused him of sexual harassment. (Cuomo apologised and said he didn't know he was making women 'uncomfortable'.[27]) Alleged cancellings, says Dr Clark, 'should be read as a last-ditch appeal for justice.' Cancellings happen when justice has *not* been served.

The phrase 'cancel culture' emerged into even more popular usage in 2016, when Kim Kardashian called Taylor Swift a liar for saying she had not been warned that her name would appear in an unflattering light in a Kanye West song. Kardashian shared evidence of a phone call in which Swift thanked West for letting her know about the upcoming song, and the hashtag #TaylorSwiftIsCancelled swept the internet. Yes, this targeting was doubtless stressful and upsetting for Swift. But you don't need to be very pop-culture savvy to know that not only was Swift not cancelled, but she is thriving in her career.

Nevertheless, cancellation is framed as something that destroys a career or even a life. And as snowflakes are critiqued for being 'overly sensitive' without naming what they are actually sensitive *about*, critics of cancel culture strongly suggest that the 'mob' overreacts purely to incidents that don't matter very much. One of the main problems with critiques of cancel culture as a term is that it lumps together allegations such as sexual harassment with smaller mistakes. You cannot look at the backlash to a cheeky joke about vegans, and also to the backlash against the serial sexual predation of a powerful man, and say, 'this is the same.' Critics of cancel culture accuse the 'mob' of lacking nuance; but their own arguments against cancelling are themselves dangerously nuance-free.

The sad truth is, often those who have claimed themselves to be victims of cancel culture have, with their own behaviour, 'cancelled' the careers and opportunities of others. This is certainly the case in the many stories of the men felled by #MeToo scandals. While some apologists for harassing behaviour worry that the great work of these men would be lost to the world as result of their cancellation, they spare no regrets for the people, usually women, who never got the chance to create their genius work. We will never experience the work of women who left the entertainment industry, for example, because of their harassment and dehumanisation. What classic films and television shows and books from women have we missed out on because of the hellish behaviour of abusers? How many brilliant women decided that it just wasn't worth the daily degradation? The premise of cancellation, as put forward by our culture's most hysterical culture-war town criers, is that it can ruin an entire life. They do not tend to ask, though, what ruin the cancellable behaviour itself can bring.

The harm done by cancellable behaviour extends beyond careers. As we'll take a closer look at in the next chapter, intense psychological stress and trauma can have devastating effects on the body and lead to physical illness. But even smaller, sustained stresses can take their physical toll on bodies, as studies of microaggressions from the past decade show. The 'microaggression' is a much-derided term by snowflake critics. It refers to the small offensive comments and behaviours experienced repeatedly and frequently by members of marginalised groups – whether the offence was intentional or not. The term was coined in the 1970s by Harvard University psychiatrist Chester Pierce, and resurfaced after an influential paper from Columbia psychologist Derald Wing Sue and his co-authors in 2007, which laid out the hidden messages behind seemingly innocuous phrases like, 'you're so articulate,' and how therapists and counsellors could work to avoid them.[28] (The hidden message behind 'you're so articulate,' according to the article, is that 'it is unusual for someone of your race to be intelligent.')

It's never too late to learn how to spot a microaggression in the wild. I was amazed and delighted when my dad, on a tour of my workplace years ago, asked me if it had been a 'microaggression' when a male colleague made a weird comment to him implying that I was attractive. (To my awkward British father!) It was like being briefly transported to 1955. I laughed awkwardly and we moved on, as those on the receiving end of microaggressions usually do. But my dad had just had a workplace diversity training, and he asked me seriously after the tour if that had been an example of a microaggression. In asking me this, which was both hilarious and great, it did not crumple his sense of well-being to have spotted and named a microaggression. For so many snowflake critics, though, the idea of microaggressions as a concept is deeply threatening – and being accused of one can come as a fatal emotional blow. It is a slippery slope in their minds from accusations of microaggressions to full-scale cancellation and career ruin.

It is not, however, the microaggressor who actually suffers from microaggressions. (My colleague who said the weird sexist thing to me is employed and thriving.) Intentional or not, a microaggression reinforces who does and does not belong to a society's dominant culture. It should be enough for a person to hope not to do this for its own sake, and when we do make mistakes, to react with learning and apology rather than reflexive denial or defensiveness. If this is not a convincing enough case to learn about or avoid perpetrating microaggressions, though, recent studies have shown that there are harmful *physical* effects of a lifetime of small but repeated stresses. The way that human beings treat each other takes a toll on the body, no matter how 'tough' someone seems, or how innocent and small a racist statement.

A 2010 study published in *Human Nature* presented the theory that black women experience accelerated ageing compared to their white peers due to 'repeated or prolonged adaptation to subjective and objective stressors.'[29] It was the first-ever study focusing on telomere length, a way to measure someone's biological age, in black versus white populations. Telomeres are 'the stabilising caps on chromosomes,' and every time a cell divides over the years, they get a little shorter until the cell dies or stops dividing. (Can you hear that? That's the sound of your telomeres shortening as you march steadily on towards death.) Anyway, the length of telomeres on certain cells can serve as a stand-in for how biologically old you are – as opposed to how many trips you've taken around the sun. The researchers at the University of Michigan and Virginia Commonwealth University found from their research that 'at ages 49–55, black women are 7.5 years biologically "older" than white women' on average.

In the United States, life expectancy and prevalence of chronic disease is tied to your socio-economic status and your race. The gap is not steadily improving as we enter a more enlightened future. Rather, there is some evidence cited in the telomere study that 'black health disadvantages worsened after the early 1990s, especially among women.' Black people in the United States may suffer worse health than whites as a result of what can be called 'biological weathering'. A biological age can be more advanced than a chronological age 'due to the cumulative impact of repeated exposure to and high-effort coping with stressors.' Stress hormones take a toll on the human body – and chronic stress is even more detrimental, leading to inflammation, obesity, diabetes, immune and cardiovascular disease, among other health troubles. Studies comparing black and white people in America show black populations to have less well-functioning stress response systems. It is even worse for poor, black women, because it is they who 'often bear central responsibility for the social and economic survival of their families and communities.' These problems are a result of stressors both 'subjective and objective' – that is, intent doesn't matter, if you feel you have been threatened or harmed in some way. Perceived stress affects telomere length as well. (The study's authors advise their readers to take their findings as 'suggestive'. There is more work to be done in this field.)

Another such study, focused on discrimination and racial bias and telomere length in black American men, published in 2014. The study found that men who reported higher levels of racial discrimination – and who harboured anti-black bias themselves – had the shortest telomeres of the 92 men who took part in the study. Poverty also accounted for shorter telomeres. The report laid out a clear conclusion:

> Results suggest that multiple levels of racism, including interpersonal experiences of racial discrimination and the internalisation of negative racial bias, operate jointly to accelerate biological ageing among African American men.[30]

Black men in America have a life expectancy of just 69.7 years, compared to white men who live on average to 75.7 years. This difference, say the study's authors, 'may be traced to disproportionately greater psychosocial stressors experienced by African American men.' What snowflake critics think are bad-faith accusations by black people looking for reasons to get offended – microaggressions – are the kinds of daily stressors that may actually shorten life expectancy.

Those who deny that we live in an unequal society, in Britain or in America, tend to categorise such arguments as emotional, and not grounded in a supposed 'rational, unbiased' fact. Studies of the way that racial stresses – from trauma to smaller daily microaggressions – are exactly the kind of proof they are supposedly after. Studies like these shouldn't be necessary to feel deeply that racism is bad. Yet they are a forceful response to the favourite cliche of snowflake critics that 'sticks and stones may break my bones, but words can never hurt me.' It is perhaps the most core belief of a snowflake critic anywhere on the political spectrum – but particularly on the far right. When you think about your own privilege if you are a white person, consider the ways that your race may help you avoid biological weathering and live longer. As a white person, you may have the privilege of cells that will continue to thrive in your body for a long time to come. If you are a black person, you may not.

Snowflake critics would have you believe that even acknowledging microaggressions as a concept is threatening to society. They believe that being accused of microaggressions would be a threat to their well-being, their careers and their happiness. But the real problem isn't that it's uncomfortable to be accused of a microaggression. (And most of the time, based on my experience and those of my friends, microaggressions are quietly and generously ignored.) The real problem is that every day people of colour, and particularly black people, and particularly black women, are faced with reminders large and small of their lesser status in society. The toll of this is real. The answer is not for marginalised people to tug on their bootstraps a little harder. You can't pull up your bootstraps when you've died an early death. The solution is for white women and men to make peace with the fact that they might feel slightly uncomfortable every now and then when someone comments on their poor behaviour.

If being cancelled is your biggest fear, and your biggest source of stress, consider yourself lucky.

Another public figure who has done a lot of the work of spreading hatred of snowflakes and moral panics about cancel culture is, I'm afraid, the red-faced town fool, the squealing gammon of television, the perennial turd on Britain's shoe, Piers Morgan. Piers, unfortunately, has an audience on both sides of the Atlantic, from his recent job as a *Good Morning Britain* presenter to his former role as an *America's Got Talent* judge and CNN journalist. I can't believe I am repeatedly writing his name in this book, but he has made such a life-consuming project of hating snowflakes he can't be ignored.

In August 2019, Piers appeared on an episode of American conservative commentator Ben Shapiro's podcast, the *Ben Shapiro Show*. (These two had previously met to have an argument about gun control on Piers Morgan's show on CNN in 2013. It helped to launch Ben Shapiro's notoriety as a conservative thinker in the US, so thanks for that, Piers.) I decided to listen to the meeting of these minds, because I'm very strong and brave.

Piers rants throughout the podcast about the 'illiberal' liberal snowflakes he thinks are not only responsible for ruining lives – but for causing the rise of far-right populism across the world. 'Populism's rising because people are fed up with the PC culture,' Piers contends. 'They're fed up with snowflakery. They're fed up with everyone being offended by everything.' This is, of course, an ass-backwards argument. It is an almost heroic feat of projection. It is an argument, though, that Ben and Piers agree on enthusiastically, despite what they see as their political differences. To cancel someone is not only to foster fascism but is a fascist act in itself. What's more, everyone is offended by everything, according to the pair. Piers explains:

> . . . No one's allowed to say a joke. If you said a joke ten years ago that offended somebody you can never host the Oscars, you know? So now there's no hosts for anything. The Emmys now just said they're not going to have a host either. The hosts have gone. And soon every award winner will go. Because everyone's a human and they're all flawed. So no one can win awards anymore because they will be no-platformed before they even get on the podium. So then, no hosts, no stars, then no one can make any movies because we're all flawed so no actors, and suddenly, where are we? The liberals get what they want, which is a humourless void where nothing happens. Where no one dare do anything or laugh about anything or behave in any way that doesn't suit their rigid way of leading a life. No thanks![31]

Things are looking grim at this point for jokes, awards shows, actors, celebrities and the art form of cinema itself. Piers' mention of the Oscars is a reference to a 2019 incident when Kevin Hart stepped down as host of the upcoming Academy Awards after public anger about his old homophobic comments. For Piers, this is evidence of a budding authoritarianism. For Kevin Hart, well . . . his career is fine.

The world is not a humourless void as a result of his un-booking as host of the Oscars. He made $59 million in 2019 – more than any other comedian, according to Forbes.[32]

Piers continues to critique the fascism of cancel-happy snowflakes with the crazed, threatening speech of the snowflake of his imagination:

'You don't lead the life the way I'm telling you to, then I'm going to ruin your life. I'm going to scream abuse at you, I'm gonna get you fired from your job, I'm gonna get you hounded by your family and friends. I'm gonna make you the most disgusting human being in the world, because you said a joke ten years ago.' And that's the attitude we're now operating in. And it takes forceful personalities to rise above it. Donald Trump rose above and went like Godzilla, 'OK, you want a fight? I'm here.' And guess what? Millions of people in middle America went, that's our guy! That's our guy. He's the one who's gonna help us. Same thing happening across Europe.

To Piers' mind, fascist snowflakes have caused all that is wrong with the world and everyone in it. At the end, we arrive at Donald Trump, Italy's Five Star Movement, France's Front National, Greece's Golden Dawn, Germany's Alternative für Deutschland, and they're all ready for the 'fight' against all their countries' fascist snowflakes on behalf of their countries' alienated average Joes. Rather than searching for actual causes for the rise of the far right – politicians who manipulate their countries' worst demons to drum up votes and power and money – it is so much easier, and generates more views and listens and clicks, to blame it on the dreadful young.

It's hard to say if Piers really believes this. To become a media celebrity requires the formation of a brand. Even those media figures you love are hard at this brand-building work. Piers, we must remember, cut his teeth as the editor of the *News of the World* and *Daily Mirror*, building an audience as all British tabloids do by stirring up conflict in order to sell papers while maintaining the current political system. But it also doesn't matter if Piers believes the things he says or not. It matters that he says them. He articulates something that others can then believe, which affects everything about their cultural and political participation. He says these things over and over again, week in and week out, to an audience of millions across many different platforms. Ben Shapiro's podcast is one of the most popular podcasts in America – and it's also carried on hundreds of radio stations. If only a fraction of his listeners agree with what Piers has to say about snowflakes and the descent from political correctness to outright fascism by way of cancel culture, that's still a lot of people, and a lot of voters.

What are people actually saying when they claim that they've been cancelled by the mob?

Often, a person who cries cancel can be diagnosed with one of two problems. On the one hand, the cancel-ee may just be absolutely incapable of accepting criticism, particularly when accused of bigotry or racism, regardless of who is doing the criticising. The second problem, though, is much simpler: the cancel-ee may no longer be relevant and is lashing out at the tide of their own gathering inconsequence. And while sensitivity to criticism may be an inescapable human feeling, as may be grumpiness about losing touch with the times, our reactions to these situations are entirely within our control and can make all the difference between contentedness and outrage.

Among those who tend to decry cancel culture due to their impending obsolescence are male comedians, and especially male comedians of a certain age.

Indeed, a common reason people cite when critiquing snowflakes is their alleged humourlessness, as outlined so beautifully by our friend Piers. Search the comments on an opinion piece about a social justice issue, or the replies to a tweet, and you will find the rejoinder: 'Bet you're fun at a party.' It's a particularly annoying cliché. First of all, one doesn't need to be in a party spirit at all hours of the day. Sometimes you're taking shots of tequila with your pals on a Thursday night, and sometimes you're writing about how the prime minister has a shocking history of racist statements. Human beings come with many different settings. You can both be very pissed off about something at one moment in time, and very fun at a party a few short hours later. And secondly, the people who say 'bet you're fun at a party' are *guaranteed* not to be fun at parties. They're the ones who corner you in the kitchen of a house party to tell you how, actually, they don't subscribe to any ideologies. They just look at the *facts*.

People who hate snowflakes also like to hate them for not being able to *take* a joke – this is where our jilted, obsolete comedians come in. They believe the snowflake to be a sour-faced, prudish and unfunny scold. The snowflake, in the mind of a snowflake hater, has rarely if ever laughed. Nary a chuckle nor a guffaw has escaped her lips. Famed humourist and MP for North East Somerset Jacob Rees-Mogg once complained on Twitter, while sharing an episode of his 'Moggcast' podcast, that 'snowflakes have no sense of humour.' (An actual comedy writer, James Felton replied to the MP's tweet: 'There's a huge difference between "no one laughed at my shit joke" and "snowflakes have no sense of humour" you fucking potato.')[33]

The world of formerly beloved comedians is a rich seam of snow-flake discourse. Ricky Gervais, rather than remain a much-loved crea-tor of *The Office* and *Extras*, has used his enormous online platform to complain that people are too sensitive for no longer laughing at his jokes. Gervais reaches far and wide for the subjects of his ire. 'The earth is 4.6 billion years old. Suck it up, snowflake,' he tweets in response to nothing, presumably for the benefit of religious ears. In another tweet, he calls *himself* the snowflake, in order to complain about the extremist left *and* right, who it sounds are even more snowflakey than he is: 'I'm an old-fashioned lefty liberal snowflake but I've noticed the new breed is really aggressive, intolerant authoritarian. It's like the far left and right have gone full circle and overlapped.' In this, he draws a line between the old-school snowflakes and the new, bad ones. In another tweet, he casts the snowflakes as his critics: 'I love that whenever I make a joke about politics, some thick offended cunt snowflake always says, "stay out of politics and stick to jokes".' In yet another tweet, which includes a dramatic black and white image of himself, glowering and uncorking two champagne bottles in what he may believe to be a sexy pose, Gervais writes: 'I'm an old-fashioned liberal lefty, champagne socialist type of guy. A pro-equality, opportunity-for-all, welfare-state snowflake. But, if I ever defend freedom of speech on here, I'm suddenly an alt-right Nazi. How did that happen?' Ricky, perhaps you'd enjoy this book?

The snowflake attacks Gervais from all sides, and from within. Everything about his career, his Twitter presence, and his own self can be defined and blighted by snowflakery. Those who hate snowflakes see them *everywhere*. Snowflake criticism is so attractive because it can provide what we all secretly want: a single unified theory of everything. Why has the world gone to shit? Snowflakes. Why are young people so particularly loathsome? They're pathetic little snowflakes, that's why. Why don't I get to say the slurs I once used with abandon? Because snowflakes took them away. What's wrong with the economy? Snowflakes are too lazy to work hard enough to be able to buy houses. What's wrong with political discourse? Fear of offending snowflakes. Why has my career lost its lustre? Snowflakes cancelled me. Why am I so unhappy? Because the snowflakes have caused me to spend eight hours a day yelling at them on Facebook. Why did my wife leave me for her personal trainer? Was it snowflakes? Probably.

Despite his outrage that people don't find him funny anymore, when it comes to the topic of cancel culture, Gervais is surprisingly sceptical. He has said that he enjoys the pushback he receives and understands that it doesn't actually negatively hurt his career. He both hates snowflakes, and also identifies as one. He thinks the system of hearing from your audience directly works. In September 2019, he tweeted:

> Please stop saying 'You can't joke about anything anymore.' You can. You can joke about whatever the fuck you like. And some people won't like it and they will tell you they don't like it. And then it's up to you whether you give a fuck or not. And so on. It's a good system.[34]

This is a rare admission from the anti-snowflake brigade. It's a simple defence of the right of people to criticise a comedian. Gervais says he doesn't mind – as long as he gets to keep calling his critics snowflakes themselves. Perhaps he would change his mind about cancel culture, though, if he did face repercussions for his often bigoted jokes, especially about trans people. He hasn't so far. Ricky Gervais knows that he probably won't. It is a surprisingly honest position.

There is in fact a long and proud history of pushing the boundaries of acceptable discourse in comedy, and of expanding the right to free speech. From the late 1940s to 1960s, the American comedian Lenny Bruce was repeatedly arrested for breaking obscenity laws in his comedy. He was barred from entering the UK because of his risqué bits which included naughty words, references to body parts and sex jokes. Bruce was someone who used his work to push society forward from a conservative, fearful prudishness, and for that he was punished repeatedly by the government. As a result, he was jailed, and eventually died of a morphine overdose. In a book about Lenny Bruce's travails, his attorney Martin Garbus quotes one of the Assistant District Attorneys of New York who had prosecuted him: 'We drove him into poverty and bankruptcy and then murdered him. We all knew what we were doing. We used the law to kill him.'[35]

This is the mantle that some comedians today who face criticism for their work believe themselves to have taken up. In their telling, though, angry, overly politically correct youths stand in for the government. They see themselves, being told to fuck off on Twitter by teenagers, as following in Bruce's footsteps, as he continued to perform comedy in the face of relentless persecution by the state.

When *Saturday Night Live* announced they had hired the comedian Shane Gillis in 2019, videos surfaced of him making racist jokes and impressions of Asian people and Muslims, repeatedly using racial slurs. In response to the outrage, Gillis initially made a statement apologising to anyone 'actually offended by anything I've said' and explained that he was a 'comedian that pushes boundaries.'[36] When he was fired, comedians and commentators across the political spectrum came to his defence. Sarah Silverman described our current moment as a 'mutated McCarthy era, where any comic better watch anything they say.' In any culture, at any particular moment in time, there are indeed invisible boundaries demarcating what is considered acceptable conversation, comedy and entertainment. Lenny Bruce pushed the boundaries in a progressive direction, boldly dragging his audiences toward a less suppressed future. What comics like Gillis do is not that. The boundaries they claim to break are not boundaries of politeness, but boundaries created by people of colour, or gay people or trans people or anyone else to protect their humanity. A racist impression is not boundary-breaking. It is not new or innovative. It is not funny, and not finding racist jokes funny doesn't mean you don't have a sense of humour. I promise.

Many of the highest-paid comedians in the world, however, have decided that in 2019, 'punching up' doesn't mean making fun of authority or powerful people. It means complaining about young people and how annoying they are these days. At the 2019 MTV Video Music Awards, host Sebastian Maniscalco's opening comedic monologue railed against the supposed sensitivity of young people: 'If you feel triggered or you feel offended by anything I'm saying here or anything the musical artists are doing, they're providing a safe space backstage where you'll get some stress balls and a blankie and also Lil Nas X brought his horse which will double as an emotional support animal.'[37] The audience laughed. Laughing at this kind of humour is a way to signal that you are *not* fragile, you are *not* sensitive, you *get* the jokes and don't think it's reasonable that anyone should get offended by comedy. I understand the temptation of wanting to come off this way. It reminds me of wanting to be 'one of the guys' as a teenager, which required smiling and laughing at whatever terrible thing was said about girls.

But the comedians who complain most of the threat of being 'cancelled' are the very ones, as with their political counterparts, who directly benefit from the cachet that being cancelled brings to their brands. Figures who have built their careers on the idea that they are 'politically incorrect' and 'not afraid to say what they mean' get talk shows and columns and TV presenter jobs and comedy specials. Maniscalco was one of the top ten highest paid comedians in the world in 2018. Osita Nwanevu wrote in the *New Republic* that many of the comics on the highest-paid list, like Chris Rock and Jerry Seinfeld, are among those who most frequently joke about cancel culture, about oversensitivity and the censorious sensibilities of the young. They are, despite the 'mutated McCarthy era' of Sarah Silverman's imaginary, doing just fine. They are still incredibly rich, even if audiences may nowadays find their comedy more tiresome than ground-breaking. As Nwanevu writes, ' "cancel culture" seems to be the name mediocrities and legends on their way to mediocrity have given their own waning relevance.'[38]

A social media mob, it transpires, can rarely compete with cultural power or political power. If it were possible to cancel people, we would not hear and see and read them wailing about their cancellation every day of the year. The truth is, the most cancellable people, the ones who claim their free speech is most under threat from censorious snowflakes, are also the ones who become prime ministers and presidents. Even as Trump was removed kicking and screaming from the Oval Office, his legacy of performative culture-war politics has remained and thrived among those who would seek to be his successors. Stoking the ire of young people and progressives on Twitter isn't a ticket to a ruined life, it's a ticket to media celebrity and institutional power. At the very least, getting cancelled is a ticket to continue doing what you have been doing all along. Cancelled people rarely actually disappear. Cancelled people rarely face lasting consequences. Cancelled people spin their cancellation into political power.

To be cancelled, then, is merely to be criticised – often by voices who until now have not previously been heard by prominent figures in prominent circles. These voices are heard unfiltered and over the internet, breaking down the middlemen of agents and journalists who create a buffer between the creator or the politician and his audience. With the phrase 'cancel culture', snowflake critics can comfortably declare that the cancel-happy mob is *always* wrong, that there is no difference in being cancelled for an alleged rape and being cancelled for a single off-colour comment, and that the real victims of our modern age are the public figures who may have to think twice before making a racist joke.

Famous figures, though, aren't the only ones who fear cancellation, and they aren't the only ones who are sensitive to accusations of racism, sexism or other bigotries. Regular people, too, may believe that they are under the threat of a cancel culture. Let me tell you about one of them.

Shortly after graduating college, I had an encounter with the everyman's fear of cancellation which was so absurd, I think about it regularly nearly a decade later. Without giving too many details, because this person may still be as mad as he was back then, the incident was a brief conversation with a young man a few years older than me, who was the proud owner of an adorable little dog. The dog was white. This is key. I don't remember the exact circumstances, but the dog had just done something bad, because he was a puppy and that's what puppies do most of the time, adorably. It might have been the time he chewed up my nicest pair of shoes. Or maybe it was one of the many times he shat indoors. Whatever it was, the three of us – dog, man and woman – were standing in my kitchen.

I made a joke to the dog's owner that the puppy was displaying white privilege, in doing something obviously bad with impunity. His bad behaviour, whether it was chewing or pooping or whatever else, would probably go unpunished. (The owner did not train the puppy well, but that's a whole other conversation about the responsibilities of dog ownership.) This was, to my mind, a mildly witty joke. It could be taken one of two ways: in saying a puppy displayed white privilege, I could be making a comment on the ways that being white and male can lead a creature to a sense of entitlement, in this case, to poop on the kitchen floor. Or my joke could be taken another way: I was taking on the heightened character of the recent Berkeley grad, looking to apply my new knowledge of structures of power to everything and anything around me. Whichever way you look at it, the joke was middling, and – this is crucial – it was about a dog.

What has seared this middling joke in my mind for the previous decade, though, was the reaction of the dog's owner. He was a friend or, at least, the boyfriend of my friend, who I knew well enough. He knew that I make basically meaningless jokes all the time. But his reaction in this case was outright fury. He was livid. He was defensive. He told me *it wasn't true* that his dog – who was a dog, let's remember – had white male privilege. What's more, white male privilege wasn't a thing. He told me that when he went to university, one of his fellow students was a black guy, and that black guy's family had a *helicopter*. I remember this clearly. The black student with access to a helicopter was on the very tippimost tip of the white owner of the white dog's tongue, in a discussion of white male privilege. He would not let it go. How can there be *white male privilege* when he knew a *black man* with a fucking *helicopter*?! I was so profoundly annoyed by the encounter that I ended up taking a walk around the block, despite the fact that *he* was in *my* house, where his racist dog had just shat on the floor, or chewed up my shoe, or something.

I am sure this was not the first time I had encountered this kind of defensive behaviour in a discussion of privilege – white, straight, male, able-bodied or otherwise. But this was such a beautiful, absurd display of the defensive tendency of white dudes in particular that it has come to define for me what it means to misunderstand white privilege. It was a *dog*. (A few years later, when applying to work at *BuzzFeed UK*, and still irritated by this encounter, I wrote a test post titled '15 Dogs Who Need To Check Their White Male Privilege'. I got the job. I bought new shoes.)

What I learned from this outrage, though, is the simmering rage that lies beneath the idea that one can be *cancelled*, wiped from the earth, made irrelevant, deemed unworthy and wholly threatened by an accusation of racism. And let's be clear – I wasn't accusing anyone of racism in my joke. I was saying a dog was white. But that was enough. It is the same instinct that leads so many white people in or out of the public eye to claim they have been cancelled by a mob, if they are so much as reminded of the existence of racism in the world.

I have seen this dynamic play out in scenarios more serious than an argument about a white dog. I have seen black colleagues forced to apologise to white men for making them 'uncomfortable' by pointing out their racist language. I myself have been asked to apologise to those with more power than me for getting angry about their sexism toward me. I have seen, over and over, in educational settings and professional ones, how people who stand up for themselves face repercussions both subtle and overt.

Who is the cancelled one in these scenarios? It's rarely the person who has revealed their bigotry. In the summer of 2020, as Black Lives Matter racial justice protests swept the United States, Britain and the world, a few public figures did face public criticism and consequences for their histories of racism, as dozens of prominent, abusive men had during the #MeToo movement of 2017 and beyond. The people and institutions who faced this reckoning over racism flailed for a way to recast themselves as victims. They said their critics were authoritarian scolds. They said their freedom of speech had been curtailed. They wrote letters warning that activists had 'gone too far' in their fight against racism. They called their enemies snowflakes. They said they had been cancelled.

While the term cancel culture may be relatively new, similar arguments can be found across history in moments of social upheaval and progressive change – and they are particularly common in times of racial justice protests. In a commencement address in 1991, just a few months after riots swept Los Angeles following the police beating of Rodney King, then-President George H.W. Bush remarked that a movement of 'political correctness', while steeped in a 'laudable desire to sweep away the debris of racism, sexism and hatred,' instead served to 'replace old prejudices with new ones.'[39] Bush described the tendency of political correctness as 'Orwellian', leading to censorship and conflict. And those who espoused 'politically correct' ideas, he said, were known for 'getting their foes punished or expelled.' If he had had the term cancel culture, Bush would have used it here. And decades before Bush and his politically correct Orwellian soldiers, similar arguments were wielded against the leaders and participants of the civil rights movement of the 1950s and 60s.

Modern critics of snowflakes and cancel culture will ironically and inevitably invoke Dr Martin Luther King Jr as an example of how one *ought* to go about making social change when it comes to racism. (Although even that may be a step too far – most snowflake critics tend to believe that all necessary social progress has been achieved.)

Many white liberals and conservatives alike selected from Dr King's quotes to imply that he would have *opposed* the historic protests of 2020. Joe Biden, on the campaign trail for the presidency, denounced what he called 'rioting' and 'looting', and saying that 'it's not what Dr King or John Lewis taught.'[40] (Lewis was a congressman and another civil rights leader from King's time, who had recently passed away.) But King's son, Martin Luther King III, tweeted in May: 'As my father explained during his lifetime, a riot is the language of the unheard.'[41] This was from a quote that King gave in 1965. In 1967, King also explained that the riots of that time were directed not at people, but property – and therefore did not break the code of non-violence. Meena Krishnamurthy, an academic who studies King's non-violence, writes that in his view, 'looting was a physical critique of capitalism,' whether done by black or white people. But in the summer of 2020, prominent white conservatives and liberals alike reached for King's words to denounce protestors, reacting to images of smashed windows and looted Targets with more horror than images of police brutality against black people. (And in January 2021, the same conservatives who condemned Black Lives Matter protestors defended and downplayed those who attacked the US Capitol, whose aim was not to destroy property – though they certainly also did that – but to kidnap and kill lawmakers.)

At the March on Washington for Jobs and Freedom in 1963, Dr King uttered his most famous line, one that has also found a home in the mouths of bad-faith actors ever since:

> I have a dream that my four children will one day live in a nation where they will not be judged by the colour of their skin, but by the content of their character.[42]

This is a comforting line for a modern white liberal in particular. If you misread it and believe that MLK Jr had a vision of social justice based on colour blindness (he did not), then you may comfortably decide that ignoring everything to do with race is what the great civil rights leader would have wanted. It may also be a favourite line because, as it was uttered fifty years ago, you may be tempted to assume that the world he wished for has arrived. It hasn't. In manipulating this line, though, white people can attempt to defend themselves from critiques of their own whiteness. You cannot be judged for being white, and the benefits that flow through whiteness, if the goal is to never think about race at all.

Those who scaremonger about cancel culture often claim that what society needs is more 'moderate', calm and respectful views. They look at the racial justice protests of 2020 and wonder, would it not be better to seek compromise and debate? Many of those who attempt to weaponise King's legacy against modern protestors paint him as not only non-violent, but unintimidating, gentle, persuasive, kindly and non-disruptive. The truth is, Dr King was defamed and denounced by white America in his day – including white liberals. Indeed, these are the people Dr King was talking about when he said another famous line, less open to misinterpretation than his 'dream' speech:

> I must confess that over the past few years I have been gravely disappointed with the white moderate. I have almost reached the regrettable conclusion that the Negro's great stumbling block in his stride toward freedom is not the White Citizen's Councillor or the Ku Klux Klanner, but the white moderate, who is more devoted to 'order' than to justice; who prefers a negative peace which is the absence of tension to a positive peace which is the presence of justice . . .[43]

A 1961 Gallup poll found that sixty-one per cent of Americans disapproved of the Freedom Riders. The poll also asked whether they thought that 'sit-ins' at lunch counters, 'freedom buses' and other demonstrations by black people would hurt or help the black person's chances of being integrated in the South. Fifty-seven per cent thought these demonstrations would hurt, twenty-eight per cent thought they would help, and sixteen per cent had no opinion. By 1966, a Gallup poll found that nearly two-thirds of Americans disapproved of MLK Jr.[44]

If today's Black Lives Matter protests had played out identically to the civil rights protests of the 1950s and 1960s – the same marches, in the same places, wearing the same clothes and saying the same things – modern critics would still find reasons why today's protestors are going about things all wrong. They would paint civil rights protestors as violent, threatening and single-minded, and threatening to free speech. This is, after all, how they were depicted in their time.

An anti-racist protestor may deliver her message any number of ways – by taking to the streets, by posting to social media, by breaking a window, by running for office – but the method hardly matters. Those made uncomfortable by those seeking to fix a racist society will reach for the same complaints time and time again. 'Cancel culture' is merely the latest way to dress up an old, predictable argument which seeks to make victims out of perpetrators.

What critics of snowflakes tend to do in discussions of privilege is cast anti-racist work as unnecessarily divisive or mean. Anti-racist work is framed as an attempt at cancellation. They see the work of students and political leaders who name and challenge white suprem-acy as an effort to tear society apart – society that, to their mind, was working just fine as it was.

Racism, as with other -isms, is not the product of the active choices of a few bad people. It is not mere dislike of another race. It is, as Michigan Schools Superintendent Patricia Biol wrote in her 1972 social studies curriculum *Developing New Perspectives on Race*: 'prejudice plus institutional power.'[45]

Being racist is not the same as being mean – something you do on purpose. A person can be perfectly nice and also perfectly racist. But to admit that you have had greater opportunities and better safety in your life because you are white is, to fragile whites, to say that you are a bad person. This is what made that dog's owner so furious. I said his dog had white privilege, and therefore he, too, the human, must have white privilege, and therefore they must both be bad people. This is ridiculous because the dog was, despite his entitled misbehaviour, a very good boy.

But there are options available to the cancel-ee. There is a way to remove yourself gracefully from a minor cancellation.

Facing the uncomfortable truths of your own privileges and biases is a lifelong task. As it is painful to learn how to do long division, it is painful to learn how not to be a prejudiced prig. It's work that snow-flakes know they must do. A white snowflake shouldn't get upset at the slightest racial discomfort. It is through that discomfort that learning and evolution occurs. White people in Britain, America and other European and European-colonised nations have lived the advantage of being seen as a universal actor, as someone who belongs in elite environments, and have seen themselves represented in media and culture, and have had the psychological freedom from thinking about their race. While all of this might seem natural to white people, it is an exception to the human experience granted because of our race. We get to see ourselves as individuals first and foremost. We are not held accountable for the crimes of other white people.

Racism will not fade naturally from society without work. Young people are not exempt from racism by virtue of being young. One study found that forty-one per cent of white millennials 'believe that the government pays too much attention to minorities' in the United States, while forty-eight per cent 'believe that discrimination against whites is as big a problem as discrimination against people of colour.'[46] Another study conducted in 2017 by NPR, the Robert Wood Johnson Foundation and the Harvard T.H. Chan School of Public Health found that fifty-five per cent of white Americans said white people face discrimination in America today.[47] In Britain, a 2018 study by YouGov found that up to forty per cent of British people didn't think black and ethnic minority people faced more discrimination than whites in such areas as education and jobs.[48] The poll also found fourteen to twenty per cent of Britons thought white people face *more* discrimination. Around twenty per cent, meanwhile, thought there wasn't very much racism in the UK at all. And thirty-one per cent didn't think it was racist to object to people speaking languages other than English in public. Overall, people tended to be more willing to believe that racism occurred in interpersonal interactions, especially between strangers, than institutionally. A large majority of Britons at sixty-seven per cent, however, believed that people were either 'fairly uncomfortable' or 'not comfortable at all' talking about race.

These attitudes cannot be challenged if a person is unwilling to learn about the hard facts of continued racism against people of colour in America and Britain, or even listen to the anecdotal experiences of individual people of colour. That learning can be extremely uncomfortable, as it is to learn about any injustice in history or the present day – particularly one from which you, as a white person, have benefited. You can either shut down when confronted with your racism, and claim that you have been cancelled, or you can shut up and learn.

What I want to shout into the face of every snowflake critic is this: the very people thought to be overly sensitive and fragile – students of colour getting mad about racism – are usually the most resilient people when it comes to dealing with difference. It's the people who don't think about race and racism and privilege who need to build up their resilience for these discussions. For progressive white people especially, being called racist or problematic is a deep-seated fear. It is a challenge to the assumption that a white person is objective, innocent, meritocratic, boot-strappy and individualistic. That she has already done enough learning for a lifetime. That she is not the centre of the universe. If someone tells you that you have been racist, it's not a sign that you've been cancelled. It can be a sign, sometimes, that whoever corrected you doesn't think you're a lost cause.

What, then, is a better way to react to being 'called out' than defensiveness, rage, changing the subject or victim-blaming? If you have made a mistake, what may matter more is how you either repair it or make things worse. First, lean into the discomfort. What does it tell you? Are you angry? Then your next step, friend, is to calm the fuck down. Next, reflect on your action, actually listen, and do your own research into why what you have done was offensive. Make any appropriate apologies, but not in a way that is more of a performative demand for forgiveness than actual contrition. Do not ever use the turn of phrase, '*if* I have offended you,' because in those two little letters you have suggested that it is unreasonable for the person you have offended to be offended. You have made this about how *they* are oversensitive, and that is what you having to apologise for. Believe what you have learned. Your perspective is not universal: you cannot hope to fully understand, ever, what a person of colour has experienced if you are not one. If that is an agonising threat to your sense of centrality, universality and connectedness to all of humankind, run a bath and light a scented candle.

But whatever happens, do not say that you have been cancelled. Do not be that person. This will not kill you; it will not even come close. Instead, let the experience bring you a step closer to that elusive thing that snowflakes supposedly lack: resilience. And please, dear God, help lead us to a world where we never hear the phrase 'cancel culture' used seriously again.

Let it be done. Let it die a miserable death, screaming in agony. Let us cancel it.

The 'resilience' of past generations is not what we want

Content warning: this chapter deals with awful and potentially triggering things like sexual assault, rape, war, suicide, mass shootings and abuse. Skip to page 209 if you so wish.

Cast your mind back, dear reader, to the tales of my grandma's troubled early life. At the heart of the snowflake panic is the assumption that younger generations are not as resilient as those that came before. But in learning more about my grandma's story, I have come to wonder how much that 'resilience' has been a way for older people to cope with the traumas of their childhoods and young adulthoods. Of course, I cannot diagnose my grandma, and I certainly can't frame her as a victim of anything, much less trauma, without risking a good old-fashioned haunting. But I can slowly grow more empathy not only for her, but for all older people. If more people did this, I think we would put less pressure on young people to build the type of 'resilience' which is actually a stifling oppression of all feelings. I think we'd be less afraid of snowflakes if we knew more about the way that trauma affects individuals and entire societies.

Much of the culture war plays out on the battlefield of trauma science. When snowflake critics speak of too-sensitive students, they say they are easily *triggered*. Those groups most readily criticised for their sensitivity are those most likely to have experienced trauma in their lives. When snowflake critics long for the way things used to be, in a supposedly more resilient past, they long for a time before trauma was understood, or treated, at all.

Knowingly or not, many of the strategies that the snowflakes use to protect themselves, whether safe spaces or clearly defined boundaries, are strategies for coping with trauma. A utopian society of snowflakes may not be able to eliminate all forms of trauma – terrible accidents happen, after all. But what snowflakes can do is create a society that is trauma-aware, that is empathetic to the pain that others carry, and takes efforts not to re-traumatise people, but to help them heal.

Understanding trauma science can be a bleak task, but it matters in a book about snowflakes because of the way that human misery has been celebrated in books, articles and political speeches about the 'good old days'. The history of trauma science is a controversial one and a highly political one, fought between those who expose wrongdoing and those who fear being exposed. One of the ways that generations hurt each other is denying the suffering of those that follow or thinking 'they should suffer as we did'. The history of trauma science tells this tale.

So please, come with me on a rather bleak journey into the science of suffering, and as you read, hold the stories of your grandparents in your mind, as I will mine. If you never knew yours, you can think about my grandma and her endless cigarettes.

In 1992, Judith L. Herman published *Trauma and Recovery: The Aftermath of Violence – From Domestic Abuse to Political Terror*.[1] It linked the modern re-emergence of interest in trauma science to the women's liberation movement of the 1970s, and its public reckoning with the traumas of womanhood, including new awareness in the 1980s and 1990s of the prevalence and scale of childhood sexual abuse. (Today, we see echoes of a public reckoning with mental health in the #MeToo movement – bringing legal and political consequences to the traumatising of mostly women at the hands of mostly men.) At the same time as the women's movement in the 1970s, veterans of the Vietnam War were agitating for help with debilitating rates of post-traumatic stress disorder PTSD. As a result of their lobbying, PTSD entered the American Psychiatric Association's Diagnostic and Statistical Manual of Mental Disorders, or DSM, in 1980. But the effects of trauma had first been studied a century prior.

The first person to study what was then called *hysteria* seriously was Jean-Martin Charcot in the late nineteenth century, a French neurologist and the founder of a vast asylum in Paris, the Salpêtrière, dedicated to the scientific study of mental disease. Hysteria was a catch-all term for any combination of strange symptoms that could not otherwise be explained. Charcot's visitors at the Salpêtrière included Pierre Janet and Sigmund Freud himself. Charcot hosted lectures on Tuesdays open to the public, in which well-heeled Parisians would come to watch Charcot demonstrate his patients' hysteria on stage, as well as the potential therapeutic power of hypnosis. While it may seem a bit iffy by modern standards to put a mental patient on a stage, Charcot's investigations and lectures on hysteria were the first instance of this strange mental condition being taken seriously— along with an attempt to discover and demonstrate a potential cura-tive agent in hypnosis. According to Herman, Charcot meant to show that hysteria was a disease, and was not something women simply made up for attention, as the prevailing medical wisdom claimed at the time.

Following Charcot's lead, Janet and Freud, working with Josef Breuer in the 1890s began to explore further the hypothesis that hyste-ria was the result of psychological trauma. Its treatment? Freud and Breuer also experimented with hypnosis, but they also developed a dialogue with their patients, and one, a young woman who went by the pseudonym Anna O., coined the term the 'talking cure' – that is, therapy. Freud came to realise that it didn't seem to be hypnosis in itself that was effective, but the conversation around the act of hypnotising. Freud worked with his patients to uncover traumatic roots to their maladies, and noted the way that more recent, banal events had triggered their hysteria. In 1896, Freud published *The Aetiology of Hysteria*, in which he proposed a radical theory: 'I therefore put forward the thesis that at the bottom of every case of hysteria there are *one or more occurrences of premature sexual experience*, occurrences which belong to the earliest years of childhood, but which can be reproduced through the work of psychoanalysis in spite of the intervening decades.' Hysteria was not the result of a haywire uterus. It was the result of childhood sexual abuse.

Dr Herman traces how within a year of publishing his work on hysteria, though, Freud repudiated his claim:

> Hysteria was so common among women that if his patients' stories were true, and if his theory were correct, he would be forced to conclude that what he called 'perverted acts against children' were endemic, not only among the proletariat of Paris, where he had first studied hysteria, but also among the respectable bourgeois families of Vienna, where he had established his practice. This idea was simply unacceptable. It was beyond credibility.

Freud abandoned his theory. Instead, he contended that not only were his patients' claims of abuse false, but that they actually received pleasure from abusive sexual contact.

And so the psychological effects of trauma faded from scientific study and popular understanding until the scope of human trauma became unavoidable with the return of soldiers from World War I. 'Under conditions of unremitting exposure to the horrors of trench warfare,' Dr Herman writes, 'men began to break down in shocking numbers.' At first it was believed the symptoms of Great War veterans could be attributed to concussions brought on by proximity to bomb explosions – which led to the condition's name, 'shell shock'. But even men who had not been caught up in explosions were suffering the same symptoms. This finding was not without controversy, once again. In the first place, the British did not want to lose men who could fight and even at one point issued an order forbidding the use of the term 'shell shock'. Instead, soldiers suffering psychiatric problems would be deemed 'NYDN' or 'Not Yet Diagnosed, Nervous'. Dr Herman notes that as a psychological source of the World War I soldiers' suffering grew more apparent, 'medical controversy, as in the earlier debate on hysteria, centred upon the moral character of the patient. In the view of traditionalists, a normal soldier should glory in war and betray no sign of emotion.' This is a romantic image of a soldier that persists in pop culture and political speech to this day.

It's almost funny to look back on nowadays: the parents and grandparents of the generation who fought amid unfathomable horrors in the trenches of World War I once considered them absolute pansies. The generation now known for exceptional, tragic bravery were judged harshly by their elders for their supposed weakness. And those who suffered from this new 'shell shock' as a result of their experiences at war were criticised for their lack of character. According to Dr Herman, medical writers referred to their traumatised patients as 'moral invalids'. As for traumatised German veterans of World War I, they were 'treated' with electroshock therapy, and when the Nazis later came to power, they banned the 'degenerate' book by Erich Maria Remarque *All Quiet on the Western Front* for its recounting of the psychological suffering of soldiers at war. In that book, published in 1929, the narrator describes the devastation of war upon the psyche:

It has transformed us into unthinking animals in order to give us the weapon of instinct – it has reinforced us with dullness, so that we do not go to pieces before the horror, which would overwhelm us if we had clear, conscious thought – it has awakened in us the sense of comradeship, so that we escape the abyss of solitude – it has lent us the indifference of wild creatures, so that in spite of all, we perceive the positive in every moment, and store it up as a reserve against the onslaught of nothingness. Thus we live in a closed, hard existence of the utmost superficiality, and rarely does an incident strike out a spark. But then unexpectedly a flame of grievous and terrible yearning flares up.[2]

If you're trying to build an unstoppable war machine and glory in the manliness of the soldier, the idea that war could ruin the lives of its survivors in this way might hurt your cause. If you're a Nazi, that is.

One British psychiatrist, Lewis Yealland, suggested in 1918 that the best treatment for suffering World War I veterans was 'shaming, threats, and punishment.' For one patient rendered mute by his trauma, Yealland suggested electric shocks and berating. As the years passed after the end of the war, the interest in and compassion for these traumatised men faded. Britain was not interested in the stories of suffering men. In the United States in 1932, World War I veterans camped out on the Mall in Washington DC demanding payment of promised pensions. Instead, President Hoover ordered General Douglas MacArthur to clear out their encampments with troops, tanks, bayonets and tear gas. The veterans did not get their money.

These nations' continued interest in war, however, would revive medical interest in the neuroses of warriors. Military psychiatrists needed a way to quickly 'cure' traumatised soldiers of their mental illness so that they could be returned to combat in World War II. Psychiatrists by then had come to accept that a mental breakdown was not the result of cowardice, and could happen to any soldier. The American psychiatrists J.W. Appel and G.W. Beebe put forth the theory that the best protection a soldier had against overwhelming fear was his cohesion among fighters and between the men and their leaders. In the social group of the fighting unit, morale and cohesion could protect men's minds – as Remarque had written in *All Quiet on the Western Front*.

Medical interest in trauma faded once more with the end of World War II, until a group of American Vietnam War veterans, known as the Vietnam Veterans Against the War, met with two psychiatrists, Robert Jay Lifton and Chaim Shatan, to lobby on behalf of veterans suffering under immense psychological stress as a result of their combat experiences. Not only had these veterans witnessed worldview-shattering violence, but they had participated in it. As Dr Herman puts it: 'it was not merely the exposure to death but rather the participation in meaningless acts of malicious destruction that rendered men most vulnerable to lasting psychological damage.' In a war that could not be won, 'the standard of success became the killing itself.' Many Vietnam veterans suffer PTSD to this day.

Around the same time the veterans were lobbying in the 1970s, the women's liberation movement was inspiring new study of the psychological trauma felt not only by returning soldiers, but by women victimised in their own homes by rape and abuse. It was not at the time accepted that rape could produce the kind of trauma and traumatic stress symptoms experienced by veterans. But as a result of new understandings of trauma, the interests of the veterans' and the women's movements aligned and post-traumatic stress disorder, or PTSD, was for the first time recognised as a 'real' diagnosis in the American Psychiatric Association's DSM manual in 1980.

Think of a time you have used the word 'traumatic'. As with so many of the words of psychiatry, trauma is a word we use colloquially as well as clinically. We might call a divorce traumatic. We might call a humiliating schoolyard experience traumatic. There are any number of life's distressing blows that we might call traumatic, jokingly or not. These are the experiences that we may call everyday trauma. But that's not what trauma scientifically means – nor is it what leads to PTSD.

A genuine traumatic experience, as understood by modern trauma science, is one in which a person feels the threat of annihilation, an utter loss of control and extreme terror. Clinical trauma is caused by rape, or combat, or assault, or being abused as a child, or a terrible accident, or some other close scrape with death – or witnessing something on this scale happen to someone else.

Trauma sends the human brain into intense action, chemically and hormonally. A body under threat arouses its sympathetic nervous system, growing alert and flush with adrenaline. The region of the brain known as the amygdala releases stress hormones to increase the heart rate, and with it blood pressure and rate of breathing. The body suppresses pain and hunger and exhaustion. These physiological responses are meant to give a person faced with extreme threat a better chance at survival.

Once a threat has subsided, though, these systems are supposed to go back to normal. For most people, they will. But for some, the body will remain in this highly aroused state, as if it is still under acute stress, in the weeks, months, years and even decades after a traumatic event has concluded. This is PTSD. Every strategy the body employed in its attempt to survive in a moment of trauma carries on long afterwards. What were at the time useful adaptations become debilitating symptoms. The brain cannot settle down, and the body remains in a state of hyperarousal as if still under an acute, existential threat. According to the research of Dr Rachel Yehuda at Mount Sinai in New York, those with PTSD have paradoxically lower levels of the stress hormone cortisol. It turns out that cortisol plays a role in ending the stress response: it sends a signal that you are out of danger when a threat has passed. Those with PTSD, though, don't appear to receive the signal that they are now safe. The levels of stress hormones do not return to balance, but carry on as if still in imminent danger, still facing the threat of annihilation. The body and the mind mount a disorganised response to a threat that has long since passed.

The result is physically, psychologically and spiritually debilitating. The brain's emergency response system is recalibrated after trauma. The brain gets worse at filtering relevant from non-relevant information in any given situation. A person with PTSD may suffer nightmares and flashbacks. In a flashback, which can be triggered by any mundane sensory reminder of the trauma, a person feels as if the trauma is ongoing. Psychiatrist and trauma scientist Dr Bessel van der Kolk, author of *The Body Keeps the Score: Brain, Mind, and Body in the Healing of Trauma*, has found in studies of flashbacks that in some cases, a person may lose the ability to put thoughts and feelings into words due to a decrease in activity in a part of the brain called Broca's area, associated with speech.[3] PTSD changes the ability to think and to accurately perceive reality, cause and effect, and plan long-term. It can rob a person of the power of narrative as a means of articulating pain.

The nervous system of a person with PTSD has had its ability to cope with everyday scenarios impaired. Even mildly stressful experiences can send a traumatised person's physiological stress response haywire. This can mean sleep problems, intense startle reactions and other physical and mental health problems such as depression and anger, cardiac disease and addiction. PTSD can lead to out-of-control drinking in a futile attempt to numb unbearable pain and fear.

Whether or not a traumatised person turns to heavy drinking, out-of-control stress hormones cause physical damage to the body. Traumatised people can experience symptoms with no clear physical cause, such as migraines, chronic pain, digestive issues and chronic fatigue. Dr Van der Kolk explains that the effects of stress hormones on organs 'go on unabated until they demand notice when they are expressed as illness. Medications, drugs and alcohol can also temporarily dull or obliterate unbearable sensations and feelings. But the body continues to keep the score.' A person may try to ignore and suppress their PTSD, but their body may force them to remember – whether through long-term disease and addiction, or triggered flashbacks.

The word 'trigger' gets tossed around a lot in debates about the supposedly oversensitive young. It is a great straw man of the culture war to say that students these days demand 'trigger warnings' for graphic content in great works of literature. (Among many friends and colleagues – and one husband – who have worked in universities, the only time I have heard of this happening was when a veteran student asked to be excused from watching materials for a lesson on the 11 September 2001 terror attacks.) But what really is a trigger, medically speaking? For someone with PTSD, as Dr Van der Kolk explains: 'Triggered responses manifest in various ways. Veterans may react to the slightest cue – like hitting a bump in the road or seeing a kid playing in the street – as if they were in a war zone. They startle easily and become enraged or numb.' When a traumatised person is triggered, their stress hormones and nervous system spring into action as if they are currently under a threat that in fact ended years, even decades previously. Such flashbacks can occur decades after a traumatising incident.

And yet today, Donald Trump Jr publishes a book called *Triggered* about the pathetic sensitivity of liberals. In the minds of Trump Jr and so many other culture warriors, it is embarrassing, weak and unmanly to be triggered. They sound, in saying so, like those who thought shell-shocked World War I veterans had weak moral character one hundred years ago. It is important to remember, even when dealing with the inane writing of the former president's most inane son, that to make fun of 'triggers' is to make light of traumatised people, including traumatised war veterans. And it is this kind of belittling that may encourage a traumatised person to ignore or numb their PTSD symptoms rather than seek help.

Being 'triggered' is not something that happens to a shrill feminist who's been offended by a gingerbread *man* instead of a 'gingerbread person'. It's a medical, physical, bodily reaction to a seemingly banal part of daily life associated with an annihilating attack in the past. If a person requests a 'trigger warning' about sensitive content, it is not because they think they may be traumatised in the first place by reading a book about rape, for example. That is not how trauma, or triggers, work. The point of a trigger warning – however prevalent you really think they may or may not be – is that an already-traumatised person is susceptible to the triggers of even the most mundane things. A panic attack can be triggered by something a traumatised person 'knows is irrational,' writes Dr Van der Kolk, and yet the 'fear of the sensations keeps them escalating into a full-body emergency.' A person is not stupid to be triggered by something small. Someone who has been triggered is not weak. Their body, rather, is misfiring as a result of trauma.

Yet this is exactly how people are characterised when coping with trauma today. Recall the authors Lukianoff and Haidt and their conviction that young people, particularly on college campuses, were overly 'coddled'. In their book, they mock and belittle efforts by students at Brown University to protect victims of rape. The author Wendy McElroy had been invited to speak on campus in 2014. McElroy argues that the phrase 'rape culture' actually represses women, and students were not happy about her visit, and Lukianoff and Haidt were not happy that they were not happy about her visit. Here's how they characterised the debate:

> The logic seems to be that some Brown students believe that America is a rape culture, and for some of them, this belief is based in part on their own lived experience of sexual assault. If, during the debate, McElroy were to tell them that America is not a rape culture, she could be taken to be saying that their personal experiences are 'invalid' as grounds for the assertion that America is a rape culture. That could be painful to hear, but should college students interpret emotional pain as a sign that they are in danger?

These are words written by someone who has never worried they might be raped. It's also the writing of people who are unwilling to learn about trauma and its consequences. The authors write that the students were worried that 'any student who chose to attend the main debate could still be "triggered" by the presence of McElroy on campus and (on the assumption that students are fragile rather than anti-fragile) retraumatised.' This is why some students worked to make a 'safe space' where struggling students could get help. In their quotation-marked contempt for the word 'triggered' the authors reveal their scepticism that rape is a traumatic experience and their ignorance in the proven ways that rape victims can in fact be retraumatised. This is not something hysterical students have simply come up with, in a bid for pity. It's science. But the authors write that even PTSD sufferers are 'anti-fragile' and cite 'research on "post-traumatic growth" [which] shows that most people report becoming stronger, or better in some way, after suffering through a traumatic experience.' This is a misunderstanding of the science, which shows that for many trauma survivors, yes – incorporating trauma into one's life story can be a healing and strengthening process. But for most – MOST! – people with PTSD, they are never even diagnosed or able to process their trauma, let alone get 'stronger' from it.

In telling students they must simply become stronger from their trauma, and be 'anti-fragile', they are saying what is and is not an acceptable response to trauma, and that's simply not how trauma works. You cannot pull up your bootstraps and recover on your own. And what's more – you don't learn how to begin to feel safe again after a rape by more exposure to rape. I doubt the authors would tell a soldier with PTSD that they should feel absolutely fine – stronger, in fact – by attending a fireworks display. A rape victim does not need to hear from a person who denies the epidemic of sexual assault on college campuses and beyond to get better. The authors note that some treatments for PTSD involve gradual, controlled exposure to traumatic memories. This is true – but going to a lecture on your college campus about your trauma is not the same as therapy. You would have to be pretty cynical to believe otherwise. What is most terrible about this incident, to Lukianoff and Haidt, is that students at Brown rallied around rape survivors. That, to them, is what's wrong with the world.

It is indeed much easier to tell a traumatised person to buck up and get over it than to address the symptoms of PTSD, or the horrors that have caused it in the first place. But when someone has suffered a devastating emotional blow, telling them to get over it may only make things worse. For most people, time will indeed heal their suffering after the experience of trauma. Traumatised individuals often show enormous strength in their ability to carry on in life after shocking experiences. But being strong is not the same as fully living.

Dr Shaila Jain is a clinical psychiatrist and trauma researcher at Stanford University. In her book *The Unspeakable Mind: Stories of Trauma and Healing from the Frontlines of PTSD Science*, she lays out the way that trauma, suppressed or not, can result in the type of human behaviour that could readily be dismissed by an unkind observer as the result of poor character.[4] 'Traumatic stress cuts to the heart of life,' she writes, 'interfering with one's capacity to love, create and work – incapacity brought on not by poor lifestyle choices, moral weakness or character flaws but by a complex interplay among biology, genes and environment.' Beyond the debilitating flashbacks and nightmares characteristic of a PTSD sufferer are a muting of the things that make life wonderful. Dr Jain writes that PTSD 'renders a person's emotional life barren. It mutes happiness and yields, instead, to an irritability that keeps the suffered on the perpetual verge of withdrawals from the world and alienation from those who love them.'

Traumatic stress can affect more than a single generation. New studies show how the health consequences of traumatic stress can be passed down biologically from generation to generation. (This in addition, of course, to the way that good old-fashioned parenting can bring one generation's trauma to bear on another.)

A leader in this field of science is Dr Rachel Yehuda, whose work showed the role of cortisol in putting an end to the flight-or-fight response in the aftermath of trauma. Dr Yehuda studies the intergenerational effects of trauma, and cortisol has played a role in her ground-breaking studies. She has found that descendants of Holocaust survivors are predisposed to anxiety disorders due to altered stress hormone profiles, compared to other Jewish adults of similar profiles.[5] Holocaust survivors in general have lower levels of cortisol – while those survivors with PTSD have even less. They also have less of the enzyme meant to break down cortisol, Dr Yehuda's research has found. But the story doesn't stop there. Descendants also have lower levels of cortisol, especially in cases where their mothers suffered PTSD. The descendants also, however, have higher levels of the enzyme which breaks cortisol down. These are changes that happen to prepare the next generation for the world experienced by the parent. But in this case, descendants end up more susceptible to PTSD and more vulnerable to stress, along with physical illnesses such as hypertension.

This is the study of epigenetics. While the structure of a person's genes might not change, the way they are or are not activated can indeed be altered by life events. This is called methylation – and these epigenetic patterns can be passed on to children. Epigenetic research reminds us of the inseparability of experience and environment from biology.

An early study in the field came from a researcher at McGill University, Moshe Szyf, who looked into the effects of abuse on a child's epigenetic profile. He studies hundreds of children in Britain, both those children who had been born into extreme privilege and those who had been born into poverty. He found modifications in seventy-three genes, showing the way that psychological trauma can lead to alterations in the deepest coding of our bodies.

Dr Yehuda has also studied the effects of traumatic stress on pregnant mothers.[6] An estimated half a million New Yorkers suffered from symptoms of PTSD following the attacks of 11 September 2001. Approximately 1,700 pregnant women were directly exposed to the attacks, and a subset of these women developed PTSD. Dr Yehuda and her colleagues studied the cortisol levels of thirty-eight women who were at different stages of their pregnancies on the morning of the attacks, who were at or near the World Trade Center. The women who had developed PTSD after the attacks had lower cortisol levels than their peers who had not. A year after the attacks, when these women's babies had been born, the children of mothers with PTSD also had lower levels of cortisol than the other babies. As these children grew older, they also suffered from more intense stress responses to new situations. This study seemed to show that genes can be affected by environmental factors like trauma in utero – even when the DNA sequence itself is not changed, just the way it is expressed. Studies of mice have shown the ways these epigenetic markers can be passed down not only to children, but to grandchildren. A single traumatic event two generations previously can leave its mark on the genes of those who may not have even met their grandparents. This is to say nothing of the social dynamics of a family that has dealt with trauma – how intergenerational trauma is passed down not only biologically but through the act of parenting. Biological processes are crucial, but social practices and behaviours resulting from trauma are also passed to children.

Sometimes, the very DNA that makes a human a human contains a summary of the suffering that came before her. How can she simply 'toughen up' and 'get over' the traumas that she wasn't even alive for, let alone her own? As the poet Philip Larkin wrote in 1971:

They fuck you up, your mum and dad.
They may not mean to, but they do.
They fill you with the faults they had
And add some extra, just for you.

But they were fucked up in their turn
By fools in old-style hats and coats,
Who half the time were soppy-stern
And half at one another's throats.

Man hands on misery to man.
It deepens like a coastal shelf.
Get out as early as you can,
And don't have any kids yourself.[7]

Fifty years on, as a new field of science looks deeper into just *how* each generation fucks up the next, Larkin's poem takes on another meaning. They may not mean to pass their epigenetic profiles to you – but they do.

Sadly, PTSD is not an isolated or rare phenomenon. The rates of exposure to trauma, and of PTSD, reach widely across many groups of people in Britain, America and beyond.

PTSD is thought to affect at least seven per cent of the population in the United States, and four to five per cent of the UK. Forty per cent of American children will have a potentially traumatising experience. Dr Bessel van der Kolk lays out astonishing US statistics of trauma in childhood in his *The Body Keeps the Score*:

Research by the Centers for Disease Control and Prevention has shown that one in five Americans was sexually molested as a child; one in four was beaten by a parent to the point of a mark being left on their body; and one in three couples engages in physical violence. A quarter of us grew up with alcoholic relatives, and one out of eight witnessed their mother being beaten or hit.

These figures come from the landmark Adverse Childhood Experiences (ACE) study, which showed the vast extent of childhood trauma in America. The results of the study showed twenty-eight per cent of women and sixteen per cent of men responded that they had been made to touch or be touched in a sexual way by an adult at least five years older than them in childhood. One in eight said they had witnessed their mother be pushed, grabbed, slapped, kicked, bitten, hit with a fist or something hard, or had something thrown at her. And this is only a count of the trauma that takes place within the home, a place meant to keep a child safe from the rest of the world. Around three million children experience child abuse and neglect each year in the United States – and those are only the cases that are reported. In Britain, meanwhile, a study of English and Welsh eighteen-year-olds published in 2019 revealed almost one in three of the study's participants had been exposed to trauma at some point in their childhoods, and one in thirteen had developed PTSD as a result.[8] Those with PTSD were almost five times more likely to experience another mental health difficulty than those without. Few had sought or received mental health care.

Veterans, women and women veterans are especially vulnerable to PTSD. Twenty per cent of Americans who die from suicide each year are veterans. Twenty veterans die by suicide every day. Women veterans have a rate of suicide six times higher than civilians. Studies of American combat veterans from the wars in Iraq and Afghanistan found twenty-three per cent had symptoms of PTSD. For British soldiers, the rate of PTSD among current and former fighters in Iraq and Afghanistan has increased over the last decade, from four to six per cent.[9] And according to the Centers for Disease Control, in the US, twenty-five per cent of American women are victims of intimate partner violence, or IPV. According to some studies, sixty-four per cent of them develop PTSD as a result.[10] One trauma can lead to others, and natural disasters and wars can lead to higher rates of IPV. That said, it doesn't always take a true trauma to lead to increased IPV – something as banal as a loss by a football team has been shown to increase rates of IPV in the home.[11]

With the spectre of gun violence, the potential to experience or witness a violent trauma extends from the battlefield and the abusive home to the streets and to the classroom in America. According to Dr Jain, PTSD rates in violent American inner cities 'are comparable to the rates found in veterans of the wars in Iraq and Afghanistan.' In a study conducted by several of my own colleagues at the *Washington Post*, it was found that more than 236,000 American students had experienced gun violence at school in the years between the massacre at Columbine High School in Colorado in 1999, and the end of 2019.[12] The *Post* now keeps a database that is regularly updated with the data from new shootings, as the number of potentially traumatised children grows.

For women, the threat of sexual trauma looms over a lifetime. In the US, almost twenty per cent of women have been raped at some point in their lives. Women face higher rates than men of sexual abuse in childhood and sexual assault in adulthood. Studies in medical journals estimate that between twenty and twenty-five per cent of women are sexually assaulted over their four years of university education.[13] Rape entails a total loss of control, and a fear of annihilation, and is the most likely type of trauma to lead to PTSD. While more men than women report experiencing a traumatic event in their lives, it is women who are at a higher risk for PTSD due to the nature of women's trauma and the lack of personal and societal support for women victims of sexual assault. 'Women experience a boost in their ability to cope with a traumatic event if they can access positive social support,' Dr Jain explains, 'and the denial of such support is extra devastating.' The younger a person is when she is raped, the more likely she is to develop PTSD. And according to Dr Van der Kolk, 'more than half of all rapes occur in girls below age fifteen.'

Dr Herman explains that 'the essential element of rape is the physical, psychological and moral violation' of a person. 'The purpose of the rapist is to terrorise, dominate and humiliate his victim, to render her utterly helpless. Thus rape, by its nature, is intentionally designed to produce psychological trauma.' Dr Van der Kolk says that 'immobilisation is at the root of most traumas,' and this is certainly true of being restrained during a rape. What's more, a victim of rape is likely, unlike with other traumas, to face blame for her own trauma. Der Kolk writes of rape victims: 'They are treated with greater contempt than defeated soldiers, for there is no acknowledgement that they have lost in an unfair fight. Rather, they are blamed for betraying their own moral standards and devising their own defeat.' When a rape survivor is blamed for her own victimisation or accused of making a false report against a perpetrator, the path to healing grows ever longer, and much lonelier.

At the heart of many critiques of snowflakedom there lies a suspicion of PTSD, and of therapy itself. This can also be said for the world of psychiatry, which has fought a battle over the effects or non-effects of trauma going back to the earliest days of the field and Sigmund Freud. More than forty years since PTSD first entered the DSM as an official diagnosis in 1980, some psychiatrists, and many loud voices in the media, think that PTSD is 'overemphasised by society and over diagnosed in hospitals,' according to Dr Jain. Even in the medical establishment, the memories of trauma victims are questioned, and some may believe that victims of trauma should indeed toughen up and 'get over it'. In the court trial of disgraced movie mogul Harvey

Weinstein, his defence lawyers devoted themselves to questioning, among other things, the reliability of traumatised women's own memories. This is a very specific debate in psychiatry. But we hear echoes of this fight in campus wars, in media debates and in family homes.

I called Dr Shaili Jain to find out what a trauma scientist, clinical psychiatrist and PTSD specialist makes of the way the language of trauma has seeped into everyday life. On the one hand, as a scientist, she is wary of diluting the definition of what she calls 'big-T trauma'. Given the long history of trauma science's fight for acceptance within the medical community, the importance of a clear diagnostic definition of PTSD is crucial to the field. 'It's important for the purposes of science, and of progress of the field, that we're all talking about the same thing and that we're really precise about our definition,' she explained. This means that a smaller life event – even a debilitating one like a divorce or a bereavement – is better thought of as small-T trauma than big-T trauma. As a clinician, however, Dr Jain understands the nuance of human experience, and is always open to people's descriptions of their own distress – but warns against the conflation of the symptoms of big-T traumatic stress and regular stress, no matter how acute. There is a risk of trivialising the experience of PTSD survivors if you do this.

I asked Dr Jain if she thinks that trauma is over diagnosed or under diagnosed. 'We're probably doing both,' she told me. The trouble with studying PTSD is that historically speaking, those most susceptible to PTSD have been those without a voice – women, children and minority groups. 'Especially if the perpetrator is a more powerful person,' Dr Jain said, 'there are massive legal and sociological implications of whose story gets heard in our culture.' Nowadays, with new social media platforms giving those groups a voice on unprecedented scale, 'we are hearing from voices that were previously under-recognised,' says Dr Jain. 'It's important to hear those stories.

And I think it's important we listen first before we pass judgement on whether it's trauma with a big T or trauma with a little T. As a clinician, as a human being, I am very curious if someone tells me they feel traumatised.' The messy reality of human experience may not always fit neatly into the consistent definitions required by a researcher.

The trouble is, human beings are deeply uncomfortable hearing about other people's trauma. While it is important to separate traumatic stress from regular stress in understanding PTSD and becoming what Dr Jain calls a 'trauma-informed society', this is not the debate being waged by those who rail against snowflakes, who use language such as 'triggers' to make fun of the idea that people mentally suffer at all. It is so uncomfortable to hear about trauma that many would rather react to trauma survivors with ridicule and disbelief than compassion. Freud himself disowned his theory of hysteria because of the implications of what he had learned: that powerful people harmed women and children. 'The reality is the vast majority of people can't tolerate that discomfort,' Dr Jain explains, 'and they want to shut it down. And the best way to push it down, feeling that discomfort themselves, is by shutting up the person who's talking. So I feel like we have to see our own bias within ourselves that we don't want to hear these stories. The human brain, we're wired that way. We don't want to hear uncomfortable things, but if we want to become more trauma-informed as a society, we have to tolerate that discomfort.' One way to shut someone up, of course, is to accuse them of being a sensitive snowflake.

Dr Jain doesn't believe that young people are less resilient than previous generations, whose 'stiff upper lip approach,' she says, categorically did not work. 'It just kicked the can down the road.' While Dr Jain says there is 'no doubt' that the generations that survived two World Wars have a type of resilience in their ability to carry on with their lives after witnessing and experiencing such horrors, there's also 'a lot of avoidance, there's probably a lot of substance abuse, probably a lot of raging inside the home and family violence that was going on. So let's not glamourise it.' It is left to subsequent generations to pick up the pieces of that style of resilience – or to carry on traumatising the next generation. Part of that resilience, too, is the prevalence of shame. 'I feel like previous generations,' Dr Jain says, 'they coped with trauma with a lot of shame. They shame themselves; they shame victims. And shame is one of the really hidden emotions. It's like whack-a-mole, the minute you feel an emotion you just whack it down.' Young people today, by contrast, are generally speaking 'very comfortable expressing their feelings.' This is a good thing. While it is important for a generation to not lose what Dr Jain calls its 'grit' – the ability to get up and go after a setback – communicating feelings is always better than old-fashioned suppression of negative emotions.

Millennials and Gen Z may indeed talk about their feelings more than older generations are comfortable with – but it doesn't mean they lack grit. They just might be more honest about their sadness before coming up with a plan B. They are also more shameless – in a good way. Those who prefer a stiff-upper-lip method of dealing with life's travails would do well to look at the statistics of why Americans are dying right now, says Dr Jain: suicide and addiction. These are 'deaths of despair.' 'There's a cold hard fact,' says Dr Jain. 'We are not doing something right if American adults are choosing to end their lives, or they're taking opioid overdoses and dying that way. Part of me hopes that by encouraging a new generation of kids to be more in touch with their mental wellness, their emotional wellness, and to take care of that, we will stop stuff like that happening in future.'

There is something obviously wrong with a society that loses so many to suicide. It is also not a problem that we can necessarily therapise our way out of. Emotional wellness is important but not sufficient to thriving if you live amid inequality, poverty and violence – and in emphasising individual wellness, we can't lose sight of collective and structural problems. Yet snowflake critics would have it that overly sensitive teenagers are to blame for society's worst ills. In saying so they not only trivialise the intense suffering of people on the brink, but reproduce the shame and stigma that prevents their chance at getting help. Maintaining a stiff upper lip in times of despair may prevent those around you feeling uncomfortable when faced with your pain. But it is a steep price to pay for others' comfort with your own chance at healing.

When you learn about trauma, its scope and its devastating effects, it becomes ever more ridiculous to read books and columns about how the greatest threat to society is young people's weakness and inability to cope with daily life.

To go to therapy, or to revisit past traumas, you have to admit that it isn't always advisable to white-knuckle it through life. You have to see that the ways you have dealt with or suppressed or avoided bad feelings may have limited the scope of your human existence. You have to admit weakness. And you may even come to learn and to speak about the political conditions under which you were traumatised.

That may be exactly what people who hate snowflakes are afraid of. Maybe this is why the president's son, Donald Trump Jr, called his book *Triggered*. Or maybe he didn't consider it that deeply.

If things feel a little bleak at this point, I'm sorry. I didn't want this book to be a depressing one, but we live in depressing times. We also, though, live in a time when we understand better than ever what it takes to heal from trauma and traumatic stress – and how to build resilience against it. It's true that the project of building resilience begins in childhood – but resilience does not grow from being told, simply, to 'toughen up'.

Until the 1980s, children were assumed to be so resilient to trauma that they were largely ignored by medical researchers. This feeling extended to everyday common sense – and persists in many minds today. But if resilience is what we actually want from young people, they must not be left to suffer trauma alone, or to 'discover strength within themselves' as previous generations have so often unsuccessfully tried to do. Indeed, what may appear to be strength in those who have suffered trauma may in fact be the successful repression of pain, and a numbness to even the pleasures of life. 'In an effort to shut off terrifying sensations,' writes Dr Van der Kolk after a brain imaging study of traumatised people, they 'deadened their capacity to feel fully alive.' If strength is what we're after, there has to be another way.

The key to building resilience, according to psychiatrists, is a childhood of moderate stress. A little prince who doesn't lift a finger or do anything he doesn't want to do will, indeed, not be prepared for trauma in his future. He will also probably end up with a terrible personality, but that's a separate issue. Moderate stress, though, is not extreme stress, which can have the opposite effect and reduce resilience in the face of trauma. The stress must be ordinary and predictable, to teach a stress response system to fire up in appropriate ways, and it must be complemented by a nurturing safety net. Too much stress, though, leads to a breakdown of the equilibrium of the whole system. As everyone will end up with different experiences of stress throughout their lives, one person's trauma could be another's pittance. This is not a result of hardy character.

In children, contrary to what critics of 'coddling' might have you believe, a high sense of self instilled by parents will be an excellent yardstick later in life when someone is not treating them with the respect they deserve. If a girl is made to feel ugly or worthless in childhood, how likely is she to find, as a young woman, that a partner treating her as ugly or worthless is anything other than expected? If you believe you are incredibly special, meanwhile, you will hopefully not accept a partner who does not agree. And children who receive comfort and soothing in times of stress will learn to soothe themselves, a skill that lasts into adulthood. This kind of support is a buffer against the worst that fate can hand them. It may seem contradictory, but resilience is gained from kindness.

Dr Van der Kolk writes that children learn how to care for themselves based on what they have learned from the ways they were cared for. 'Children whose parents are reliable sources of comfort and strength,' he writes, 'have a lifetime advantage – a kind of buffer against the worst that fate can hand them.' A tough childhood does not guarantee strength against future adversity. Rather, according to Dr Van der Kolk, decades of research 'has firmly established that having a safe haven promotes self-reliance and instils a sense of sympathy and helpfulness to others in distress.'

I don't think that most commentators who decry the weakness of kids these days believe that children should experience real trauma to grow up strong. Well, some come close, especially those who advocate corporal punishment and romanticise sending young people to war. But it is easy to see how a world view which questions the safe-haven theory of building a resilient child will be the kind to excuse all kinds of bad behaviour inflicted on the young in the name of 'building character'. This extends into early adulthood, as the human brain continues to develop well into a person's twenties.

The way we think and speak about parenting matters because it seeps into everything – into schools and universities and workplaces and politics. How we think we should raise our children is a question for families, but it's also a question for governments. In both cases, children should be raised with gentleness to prepare them for a traumatic world.

Of course, parents can do plenty of harm without experiencing or inflicting 'big-T trauma' on their young. We can also speak of strategies to build resilience in children in a more general way – not just how to guard kids against developing PTSD should something awful happen to them in the future.

Parents can also do the work of breaking the intergenerational chain of unhappiness. The psychotherapist Philippa Perry devotes the first chapter of her book, *The Book You Wish Your Parents Had Read (and Your Children Will Be Glad that You Did)*, to the ways that parenting tactics are passed down from generation to generation, unwittingly or not.[14] Her fundamental argument is that we should look at the painful memories of our childhoods, and not say, 'What was good enough for me is good enough for them,' but the opposite: 'Here's how I was treated unfairly, and what I can do differently as a parent myself.' To set about this work, you have to at least perhaps admit that you didn't 'turn out just fine'. This is the first stumbling block for obvious reasons. In a society that stigmatises anything other than fineness, it's not an easy thing to say that you aren't. But 'if we don't look at how we were brought up and the legacy of that,' Perry writes, 'it can come back to bite us.' And nobody wants to be bitten by their own children.

We could even go so far as to say that being treated as a special snowflake by your parents is key to being able to function as a healthy adult later in life. 'If, when you were growing up, you were, for the most part, respected as a unique and valuable individual, shown unconditional love, given enough positive attention and had reward-ing relationships with your family members, you will have received a blueprint to create positive, functional relationships,' Perry writes. On the other hand, if you didn't have a special snowflake childhood, it can be very painful to look back. But that discomfort doesn't mean you should ignore your past.

Perry considers the ways that parents might experience triggers in everyday parenting. These may not bring on a full-blown PTSD flash-back, but rather something which sends a parent viscerally back to the feelings of their own childhood. Parents who were, as children, shouted at for making too much noise, may be overcome with deep irritation at the sound of noisy children, not just because, well, noisy children are annoying, but because they are remembering the feeling of fear and injustice they themselves felt as children being told off for noise

– an example from Perry's own family history. Parents may also repeat the same painful experiences of their youths without even meaning to. 'It is common for a parent to withdraw from their child at a very similar age to when that parent's parent became unavailable to them,' Perry observes. This is a terrifying prospect – as if parenthood weren't terrifying enough.

Many critics of snowflakes will advocate for more authoritarian parenting styles. Throughout anti-snowflake texts you find a deep interest in hierarchies generally. An overly strict parenting method, however, can lead to a parenting relationship in which authority figures must always be right, with no flexibility whatsoever. It may make them authoritarian themselves one day. 'Consistently imposing your will on your child is neither the best way to nurture morality or cooperation, nor is it a good way to have a good relationship with them,' Perry writes. On the other hand, setting no rules or boundaries for your child is a recipe for raising what my mother would call a 'holy terror'. Between these two options is what Perry calls a 'collaborative' approach. This method 'is when you and your child put your heads together to solve a problem so you're more of a counsellor than a dictator.' This is where parents and child figure out together what the problem is and how it makes everyone involved feel, and then come up with a solution together. It may sound time-consuming, but it contains neither the injustice of the authoritarian method, nor the wildness of totally lax parenting. At its root, the collaborative method says that hierarchies do exist – but the relationships of power are respectful and flexible, and while mistakes may be made, they can be addressed and fixed. Parents can't take away all the chance of pain from a child's life. This is what snowflake critics think modern parents have done. But the answer to strengthen a child's resilience to pain is with support and affirmation, not with telling a kid to buck up and get over it.

The snowflake critic assumes that kindness leads to weakness, and that telling a child they are special is a sure-fire way to ruin them. I wanted to know what Perry thought about the special snowflake panic, so I called her up. Shouldn't we worry about children thinking they're a little *too* special?

'The thing is,' Perry told me, 'everybody really, really needs to be special to at least one person. A child requires at least one parent to be a bit crazy about them because we need to feel beloved. That does not mean we are special above all others, but we need to be special to our parents. Otherwise they might as well just take any kid home from school.' It is incredibly harmful to a child who does not have one person – and it doesn't need to be a biological parent – for whom they are the specialest snowflake in the world. Who thinks the sun shines out their ass when they bring home a rubbish piece of artwork. That is the basis of our self-worth. If you do not get that in childhood, you will need to find it later in life. 'You know, there's no harm in making a kid feel good,' Perry says.

When you soothe a child who has hurt themselves, however, it is possible to overdo it. A parent who loses their senses at a child's tiniest injury is likely to teach a kid that it's *the done thing* to visit the emergency room for a scraped knee. On the other hand, though, a parent who tells their child, in so many words, to get the fuck over it, hasn't actually made hurt feelings go away. They have taught their child instead to repress and bury their feelings, where they will lurk and probably erupt in later years, or else teach a child that they cannot expect good feelings from their parents, and the relationship can end up in distance and emotional estrangement.

The way that children learn resilience, says Perry, is by going through the process of being soothed by their parents so many times that they internalise that ability: that yes, a hurt feeling is real and legitimate and respected, but also, it won't go on forever. 'The ideal parent takes the feelings seriously,' says Perry, 'but isn't overcome and overwhelmed by them. Because I think that the parent that says, "Shut up," the repressive parent, is frightened by their own emotional response. And so rather than have that triggered they'd like to shut the other person down. And all these repressed boomers are trying to shut the millennials down because they don't want to have their feelings.' Perry also doesn't think children or young people today are likely less resilient than previous generations. 'Human beings don't change that much,' she says.

When you think about the inheritance of shit today's children will soon be wading through, you have to consider that older generations' discomfort with young people is not merely due to their feelings. Young snowflakes are not merely in touch with their feelings – they are galvanised by them; just as past generations were when they were young. (And many, of course, still are.) Young people past and present look upon the shit and want to do something about it. And this is a potent source of snowflake panic.

It is clear, then, that a child who has had a loving, supportive childhood builds resilience against life's miseries – both the regular downturns and so-called big-T trauma. The same lesson follows into adulthood and encounters with traumatic stress.

People who are resilient to trauma are active in their recovery from a traumatic experience. They do not avoid or retreat or deny what happened to them or their feelings about the event. Resilient survivors maintain a sense of purpose in life and understand the temporary nature of their trauma. They are highly social, and feel they are fundamentally in control of their lives, even when unwell. Supportive relationships are fundamental not only to healing from trauma but preventing a breakdown in the first place. No matter how well a resilient trauma survivor tackles her own well-being, Dr Jain writes that 'more often than not their traits are not inherent but rather endowed, as gifts, by their early caregivers, environment and community.' An individual can only do so much to heal from traumatic stress, or to build up resilience against it. Strength comes from those around us. So does the absence of strength.

Most people do not, though, develop PTSD after a traumatic event. Many factors determine who may and may not, beyond the experience of a nurturing childhood, and much of it has nothing to do with individual character. Those at a higher risk of developing PTSD are poorer, younger, women, and those who have been victimised before or suffered previous abuse or trauma, suffered mental illness, or who dissociated during their trauma. Two people who experience the same trauma may, and probably will, react differently to it. One study referenced by Dr Herman showed that among combat veterans with PTSD, 'each man's predominant symptom pattern was related to his individual childhood history, emotional conflicts and adaptive style.' Someone who actively assists in rescue efforts, for example, has a lower chance of becoming traumatised, says Dr Van der Kolk. The ability to act and take some control in the moment of trauma may offer some protection from PTSD. In a study of veterans exposed to heavy combat in Vietnam, those who did not develop PTSD showed characteristics of active coping and strong sociability – but those Vietnam veterans who suffered adversity in their childhoods were the most likely to face long-term PTSD from their combat experiences. Extreme adversity in your early years does not necessarily make you stronger. What doesn't kill you can indeed make you 'weaker'.

What makes some people able to recover from trauma, and others succumb to PTSD or find themselves revictimised? Some of the answers are obvious. Resources. Education. A supportive family. Other factors are beyond the scope of the individual and even their support network. Does your society blame rape victims for their rape? Does it blame domestic violence victims for their predicament? The politics of a trauma shape a victim's chances for recovery. After a traumatic event has occurred, the people around the survivor can help or hurt them. According to Dr Herman, 'a supportive response from other people may mitigate the impact of the event, while a hostile or negative response may compound the damage and aggravate the traumatic syndrome.' A public figure who may think he is merely raising questions or engaging in robust debate about the causes of rape, for example, can do real harm to rape survivors attempting to recover.

As with building resilience, recovery from trauma depends on a community, not just the traumatised individual. Recovery is a group activity. You probably cannot white-knuckle your recovery alone. You must become safe, you must remember and mourn your trauma, integrating it into your life story, and then get back to regular life. And you cannot let any part of your healing depend upon your perpetrator, whether you seek repentance from or revenge upon them.

In a society that valorises masculinity, and strong, silent heroism, men in particular may feel unable to even begin the work of healing from trauma. In a society that sees withdrawal or aggression as perfectly healthy male behaviours, a traumatised man may not see the need for support at all. When asked in one study what might stop them from seeking help for their recovery from PTSD, sixty-five per cent of Iraq and Afghanistan war veterans said they feared they 'would be seen as weak.' This is what happens when a society sees feelings as weakness and stigmatises mental health. For a better chance at healing, a person needs a community to take action to support the victim – and to recognise the fact of the trauma in the first place. Yet so many traumas, whether a woman's rape or a veteran's PTSD, are stigmatised and hidden away.

Why, across history, have victims of trauma often been the subject of so much scorn? What is it that people do not like about victims? Why do many feel the temptation to forgive, believe and defend the perpetrator of a traumatic crime? Much of the time, it's simply the easiest path. 'All the perpetrator asks,' Dr Herman explains, 'is that the bystander do nothing. He appeals to the universal desire to see, hear and speak no evil. The victim, on the contrary, asks the bystander to share the burden of pain.'

Sometimes it is simply easier for bystanders and society at large to side with a perpetrator than a victim, to say that a trauma hasn't occurred or even to blame the victim, or to say that what has happened has happened and need not be worried about any longer. Victims, though, can be very powerful. As part of their recovery from trauma, they may seek justice against perpetrators or even the reform of entire political systems. A person who has survived a trauma may as a result discover new or previously unrevealed strength within themselves. As Dr Jain writes, some survivors 'may even find that they have grown emotionally or spiritually, a phenomenon referred to as post-traumatic growth. They report new life priorities, a deepened sense of meaning and an enhanced connection with others or with a higher power.' People may come to this realisation with or without the aid of therapy, but it certainly doesn't come about by someone shouting, 'DON'T BE SUCH A WEAKLING' in the wake of a traumatic event, and yet this is what snowflake critics mean when they sagely note that 'what doesn't kill you makes you stronger.' They ask that victims of trauma continue to suffer it quietly and to bottle up feelings – that this is what would show real 'strength'. But avoiding extreme feelings altogether may only make life worse. After all, strong, irrational feelings make up some of the best bits of life. What some trauma victims do instead, though, is take action.

To politicise a trauma is to place a personal experience in the context of a broader, historical fight for social justice, with an aim to prevent others from suffering the same fate as the victim. You see this in survivors of rape and sexual harassment who speak out about their experiences at the hands of powerful men: Anita Hill testifying about allegations of harassment in the Supreme Court nomination process of Justice Clarence Thomas, or Christine Blasey-Ford testifying about her alleged assault by now-Justice Brett Kavanaugh

— a testimony with trauma science at the centre of it, as Dr Ford is a trauma scientist herself. (Both Justices Thomas and Kavanaugh strenuously denied the allegations against them.) You see this politicisation of tragedy also with the efforts of students across America who have organised in the wake of mass school shootings, such as the students of Marjory Stoneman Douglas High School in Parkland, Florida. Only a month after the horrific shooting at their school which killed seventeen people, the students of Parkland organised an enormous rally in Washington demanding greater gun control. That summer, they joined up with students whose schools are plagued by more quotidian, small-scale but no less traumatising gun crime, and took their message on the road. I reported on a few of the students' stops on this national tour and was struck in speaking with them by how raw their trauma was. But in the community they formed and their action, they were taking back control of their lives with a shared purpose.

Political acts born from trauma frequently and necessarily conflict with existing structures of power. Dr Herman describes how this work can make up the final stage of recovery from trauma:

> The survivor mission may also take the form of pursuing justice. In the third stage of recovery, the survivor comes to understand the issues of principle that transcend her personal grievance against the perpetrator. She recognises that the trauma cannot be undone and that her wishes for compensation or revenge can never be truly fulfilled. She also recognises, however, that holding the perpetrator accountable for his crimes is important not only for her personal well-being but also for the health of the larger society. She rediscovers an abstract principle of social justice that connects the fate of others to her own.

A person who has been traumatised can hide their pain away. Or they can transform their grief into a sense of purpose and the ability, they hope, to help others.

Trauma, then, is political. Trauma survivors are political actors, at first disempowered but occasionally able to harness their experience for political change. Trauma is not separate from power, and to heal from it, and prevent it in the first place, you cannot look away from structures of power and the suffering in particular of marginalised groups. The flow of violence in societies – including the US and Britain – has deep impacts which can take multiple generations to heal from. You can't even begin that process if you deny the pain of victims in the first place, or the misdeeds of the perpetrator.

Even naming a crime can be politically powerful. Words have the power to shape and reshape societies. Once, there were no words for domestic violence. Even today, for several friends of mine, it was not until they learned the phrase 'domestic violence' in young adulthood that they realised something had been terribly wrong in their child-hoods. Before there was 'sexual harassment' as a phrase, there was simply an average Tuesday for a woman in the workplace. 'Date rape' and 'stalking' had to be defined and named by feminists before they could be criminalised, and for their psychological effects to be studied and acknowledged. This work was, inevitably, seen as rather *nagging* at the time – and still is. Naming crimes and traumas is in fact rather chaos-making to society as we know it, and to business as usual. Speaking about trauma is a political act.

When you learn about trauma, its scope and its devastating effects, it becomes ever more ridiculous to read books and columns about how the greatest threat to society is young people's weakness and inability to cope with daily life. When you know the numbers, you begin to look around at the people in your life and strangers you see throughout the day and understand how many trauma survivors there are. It seems a miracle that human beings are coping as well as we are. People like my grandma were left to deal with the effects of a horrible childhood, and they dealt with it. But they deserved more than mere coping, and so do we.

Those derided as snowflakes are often the ones doing the work to make the world a less traumatising place. Safe spaces and trigger warnings are all about healing people from past traumas and building resilience. An ignorant onlooker to the trend of creating safe spaces might assume the opposite: that a safe space is about preserving fragility and preventing a necessary strengthening that can only be brought about, apparently, by combative encounters with those who deny their suffering or would even seek to harm them. The idea that people who make use of safe spaces at university will forever be ignorant of hardship is a wildly privileged one. The people who make this argument do not understand the power of a safe space because, frankly, the world has been their safe space. It is ridiculous to think that for most people who do not come from an intensely privileged background, or who have not escaped the many types of trauma which disproportionately affect marginalised peoples, that they could end up soft or coddled by university. A trigger warning, meanwhile, is not just for people who may *become* traumatised by a piece of work. It is for people who have already been traumatised. The problem is the trauma, not the trigger warning. If you can comprehend the scope of traumas visited especially upon marginalised people, focusing your ire on any attempts to support and protect traumatised people becomes absurd.

What if, instead of a laughable thing, being a snowflake meant being an empathetic person? Someone who can see a person who is suffering and not assume they are suffering due to poor moral character or a spiritual weakness. Young people still have work to do expanding the horizons of our compassion. When veterans of World War I were considered shameful and weak, it took radically compassionate people to fight an age-old stereotype about honour and manliness of war and seek the root cause of veterans' suffering. It took Vietnam veterans organising in spite of their own debilitating psychological battles to try and force politicians to take their suffering seriously. It took women tearing out their hearts and placing them on the mantle of public judgement, sharing stories of harassment and rape with the hope that they would finally be taken seriously. It took Black Lives Matter protestors taking to the streets and demanding their pain be heard and for policies to be changed.

This is what snowflake critics fear: not an embarrassing over-sharing of feelings, but the political reckoning that follows.

6

Can you make a joke anymore?

Yes.

7

The Gender Panic

Content warning: this chapter is, alas, filled with references to transphobic nonsense. Turn to page 245 to not have to read through it all.

When I moved back to Britain in my mid-twenties after a sunny, blessed Californian childhood, I found myself surprised to experience some culture shock. After all, I was born in London, my parents are painfully British, and I had spent many summers visiting family across the UK while growing up. But it wasn't until living there full time as an adult, first as a student and then as a worker, that I began to notice the deep divides between countries. Specifically, I came to see how deeply traditional Britain was about gender. On the one hand, Britain is in many ways a better place to be a woman than the United States. If you want to give birth, you're less likely to die in Britain than America in the process. And you'll get time off to raise your kid – whereas there is no mandated parental leave in America, and if your American employer does give you time off, it can be counted in weeks, not months. The existence of an actual social safety net is undoubtedly beneficial to everyone, including women.

But I couldn't help but feel, in a way I did not while in America, a general air of judgement that being a woman defined who I was. Not only who I was, but the things I liked. When I studied political science courses at university in America, the class was an even mix of men and women – I didn't think about it. Our professors, too, were a mix of genders. But in a politics department in Britain, the women in any given course could be counted on one hand. It was *bizarre* – but politics was simply coded male. To receive praise for your work in this context was to be seen as a sort of scrappy, unexpectedly competent girl, as opposed to just competent.

The clammy grasp of gender norms extended to more frivolous contexts. In an American bar, you'll find men drinking wine, women drinking beer, and everyone drinking everything. In Britain, it seemed – and hear me out! – that every time I walked into a pub, almost all the women would be drinking a white wine, and almost all the men would be drinking pints. (The gin and tonic appeared to bridge this divide, sometimes.) I know this sounds silly, and I wondered if I was imagining it at times, but I kept seeing it over and over again. Preference for so many things – beverages, jobs, academic subjects – all seemed trapped in a traditional gender binary. My husband, who enjoys a crisp white wine, would send me pictures of himself out with a group of guys, the only one not drinking a pint. 'Making gender trouble,' he would text. We have come to describe this phenomenon as the 'gender pint gap'.

In Britain, it's easy to make gender trouble.* All you have to do is order the wrong drink. I was somewhat shocked, then, that my peers in grad school and then at work considered me a *wild* feminist for my basic beliefs about gender equality, and my willingness to express them. Of course, it's thrilling to be thought of as a wild feminist. But it didn't seem particularly wild to me to think that there should be as many women as men in politics, for example. I was irked by this, and stubbornly only ordered pints of bitter, because I was *ungovernable*.

* It was the feminist philosopher Judith Butler who made that phrase famous, in her book *Gender Trouble*, which argues, among other things, that gender is a performance. But I have incorporated this phrase into my day-to-day life and, rubbing my last two brain cells together, dumbed it down here to the point of ruin.

What's more, I noticed strangely traditional beliefs about gender among younger men, and not just the elderly uncles and professors and supervisors of my life. (If you're my uncle and you're reading this: don't worry, I'm talking about the other side of the family.) Indeed, a 2020 study from the Hope Not Hate Charitable Trust found that half of men aged sixteen to twenty-five believe that feminism 'has gone too far and makes it harder for men to succeed.'[1] Perhaps they had just seen me with my pint of bitter.

In a country where your apparent gender can determine even the most mundane parts of your life, then, it follows that there would be so much hostility to anyone making *actual* gender trouble. This is not to say that Americans don't punish women and LGBTQ+ people for their supposed transgressions, but what I see in Britain is a level of homophobia and transphobia that has penetrated even otherwise 'liberal' spaces. Snowflakes, as we have seen, are considered weak and pathetic, but also destructive, transgressive and threatening. And there is no faster route to instilling terror in the heart of a snowflake critic than pushing and questioning the bounds of gender, or in supporting the rights and dignity of trans and non-binary people. Shon Faye defines 'trans' in her excellent book *The Transgender Issue* as an 'umbrella term that describes people whose gender identity (their personal sense of their own gender) varies from, does not sit comfortably with, or is different from, the biological sex recorded on their birth certificate based on the appearance of their external genitalia.'[2] This term can include non-binary people – those who identify neither as men nor women. The idea that kids these days are messing around with the immutable, biological, fundamental *ancient wisdom* of sex and gender is a terrifying prospect to some who organise their lives, and their understanding of the world, around it.

This terror has led to rampant transphobia in many places – but particularly in the ranks of British media, and most notably in the wake of attempts to reform and simplify the Gender Recognition Act in the last few years. In 2004, this act was seen as the gold standard for trans rights in Europe – but nowadays, it is outdated, bureaucratic, expensive, and often humiliating to trans people, who have to receive the blessing of a board of strangers to get a new birth certificate affirming their gender. In the backlash to this reform attempt, those opposed to trans rights successfully prevented the needed reforms from taking place, and trans people in Britain saw that not only would they *not* gain new rights under a reformed GRA – but those they already had were under threat.

Those who oppose trans rights and fear the destruction of a gender binary are often conservative, of course. But some, especially in Britain, call themselves feminists, or left-wing, or both. To these people, snowflakes have taken feminism beyond what they see as the simple, reasonable, digestible idea that the world would be a better place if white women got to sit on more corporate boards. The terror of snowflakes is that they question the idea that having a vagina is central to the reality and struggle of womanhood. Snowflakes support trans people and non-binary people. Snowflakes understand that inclusivity of other genders does not oppress you but liberates you. But in Britain, a class of people who consider themselves feminists have embraced an ideology in which the opposite is true. They see trans people, and trans women in particular, as an existential threat to their womanhood, their rights and their progress. They have taken their bigotry and recast it as victimhood. These are the so-called TERFs, or 'trans-exclusionary radical feminists', which modern transphobic feminists now say is a slur akin to the n-word (it's not!). In fact, it was actually how they once identified themselves. Nowadays, they prefer 'gender critical feminist'. However you put it, though, it's a fancy way to say transphobic.

Sometimes it takes a feat of mental gymnastics to try to understand people with very different viewpoints from my own, but it's an important exercise, even when people believe awful things. To better understand the world, sometimes you have to sit down and think hard about what could make a person vote a certain way, commit a certain crime, or tell a person to die because they criticised Taylor Swift online. It's vital as a journalist to be curious about other perspectives. What makes human beings behave in all the strange and wonderful and awful ways that they do? If you want to understand the world, you have to at least try. But when it comes to those feminists in the British media who have taken it upon themselves over the course of the last decade to single out and denounce trans people, I have struggled to understand their perspective for years, even while reading their endless, moral-panic columns. Their ideology seems not only hateful, but betrays a total lack of curiosity about different kinds of people, and different ways of being in the world. How, if you seem to understand structural and interpersonal discrimination in one sense – through being a woman and feminist – are you unable to apply the same level of understanding to people even more vulnerable than you are? Perhaps it is that these feminists are largely, though not exclusively, white. The prominent ones are middle class. Many have large plat-forms. But how is it even possible to think that such a small segment of the population – and one that faces so much discrimination – is a threat to the foundations of society itself?

I was helped in my understanding when I interviewed several prominent British trans people for a video project for the *Washington Post* in the spring of 2021. I wanted to hear what it was like to live as a trans person through a moment of trans panic. Among my interviewees were bestselling YA author Juno Dawson and the journalist Freddy McConnell, who lost a 2019 court case seeking the right to be called 'father' – or even parent – on his child's birth certificate.

I asked them what they thought made Britain so uniquely transphobic. They pointed to the problem of British media. While they had often been supported by their hometowns and their families and their friends, the British media seemed determined to turn the tide of public opinion against trans people. Debate about trans peoples' rights and humanity had become so unbearably toxic that they sometimes had to disengage from the news entirely. As Freddy McConnell told me:

> You know, there's often a cycle on a weekly basis where the Sunday papers will have a big news story about some new terrible thing that trans people are doing. So you kind of like, gear up to it mentally, and you know it's going to come, and you know not to go on Twitter on certain days. In a way it dictates some of the stuff that you do, just knowing that, you know, in order to not have your day ruined, or not have this feeling of rejection heightened even more, you need to sort of avoid certain places and protect yourself in certain ways.

My interview guests also noted the way that transphobia in Britain is dressed up in overly polite or faux-scientific language. Juno Dawson explained:

> The scary thing is, you know, a lot of the most vocal transphobes in the UK are academics or journalists or writers. So they can word their transphobia very eloquently and very poetically. I always say there's two kinds of transphobia. There's just, you know, when you're on the street and some guy is like, 'Ha ha ha, that's a man,' and you can kind of roll your eyes . . . But then when you're reading all this kind of pseudoscience in the Sunday papers, there's a veneer of respectability over them.

The media discourse around trans rights in Britain, which is deeply dehumanising to trans people themselves, is relentlessly negative. The effect is that many British people who would otherwise never *think* about trans people, let alone hate and fear them, are once again fed a drip of poison from the press, telling them that *trans people are the problem* and that they're coming to get you.

Conservatives and TERFs alike will cast trans people as the new, threatening cause of all of society's ills. But being trans is nothing new – and it's not even particularly common, making up an estimated one per cent of the population. As Faye Seidler, a trans health advocate in North Dakota, pointed out in 2015, more Americans say they've seen a ghost than say they've met a transgender person.[3] Of course, we have to take into account the fact that you may not know if a person is trans, whereas it's quite obvious if someone is a ghost. The comparison comes from a 2009 Pew Research Center survey which found eighteen per cent of Americans have seen a ghost, or so they claim, while a 2015 study from GLAAD found that sixteen per cent of Americans said they knew anyone who's trans. Yet it's not ghosts that have people up in arms. (Of course, with increased trans visibility in recent years, these numbers may now be outdated. Further study is required.)

A large part of the problem is that for all the hours of television and inches of newspaper devoted to the trans 'debate' in Britain, trans people themselves are rarely heard from. When the writer Paris Lees appeared on the BBC's *Question Time* in March 2019, she pointed out the contrast between the way that British media daily casts trans people as being 'responsible for all the world's ills,' and the fact that trans people themselves are among the most vulnerable in society.[4] 'I am the only transgender person who's ever been on *Question Time*,' Lees said, 'because the conversation about us is conducted over our heads. It doesn't actually include the people who this conversation affects directly.' She went on:

> Bigotry is bigotry, whether it's dressed up as religion, whether it's dressed up as feminism ... I think there's a very loud, vocal minority who are manipulating people's concerns in the same way that people did about the fear around gay teachers and

linking it with paedophilia in the 1980s and I think it's absolutely disgusting.

Modern British transphobes simply do not make the comparison to the way that gay people have been treated in previous eras – not even those who are gay themselves, like the creators and supporters of the so-called 'LGB Alliance', which is meant to promote gay rights as separate and even at odds with trans rights. It is mostly, however, straight, cisgender (not trans or non-binary), 'feminist' women who make up the fiercest block of transphobes in Britain. It's also worth noting, though, that polls repeatedly show that women are more likely than men to support trans rights – a wrench in the argument of many TERFs that support for trans rights is rooted in misogyny.[5] The truth is, a society which defends trans rights and celebrates trans people, and difference of all kinds, is one that benefits cis women, too. If you try to block off a particular type of womanhood, you are bound to harm not only trans women, but anyone who doesn't live by whatever stereotypes and physical characteristics you have decided makes a woman. This is what British TERFs do not understand.

Transphobia is a live current in modern British media. It is an obsession. The fear and stereotyping of trans people isn't just a passive bigotry. It has become their unified theory of everything. Many transphobes seem to have taken their transphobia and let it ruin their own lives – as well as those they target. Transphobia in Britain has come to remind me of the many conspiracies gripping the United States: all-consuming, entirely baseless, and not only harmful, but embarrassing to those who engage in it.

Graham Linehan, the Irish comedian and co-creator of beloved sitcoms such as *Black Books* and *Father Ted*, is among the most ardent transphobes operating on the internet today. That is, he *was* operating on the internet – until his relentless, targeted harassment of trans people and their allies finally got him booted off Twitter. For those fearing he may have been unfairly silenced, do not worry: he was invited in early 2021 to speak before the House of Lords, where he explained how his dedication to fighting trans rights and trans people led to the break-up of his marriage.[6] I told you this would be embarrassing.

Linehan has also been spotted lurking on alternative platforms, and, for some reason, has popped up on a dating app meant for lesbian women. He was there with the aim of spotting and outing trans women who he thought should not be using the app.[7] (In fact, the app welcomes trans users, but is less keen on vicious bigots.)

Before being relegated to his personal blog, though, Linehan used to regale his hundreds of thousands of Twitter followers with a relentless barrage of transphobic nonsense. Whatever happened in the news on any given day, Linehan was there, blaming it on trans people. In the days following the defeat of the Labour Party in the 2019 UK general election, his Twitter feed was a torrent of commentary about how trans people and the politics of trans inclusion were singlehandedly ruining not just the left, but the country. This is what he always says, but Linehan was particularly *adamant* in his post-election commentary that trans people and those who support them were primarily to blame for the loss. One tweet featured a photo of an angry Malcolm Tucker, the sweary spin doctor character from Armando Iannucci's political comedy series *The Thick of It*, pointing in fury. Linehan's caption read: 'I don't care if it's fucking Christmas. Monday morning, fire anyone with pronouns in their Twitter bio.'

For British TERFs, transphobia is a complete political ideology. It is the foundation for all other political thought. For those on the left who reject trans rights, 'identity politics' no longer means civil rights advocacy, it means only the ways in which young snowflakes have decided to mess with gender. For Graham Linehan, it wasn't Brexit, it wasn't inequality, it wasn't regional austerity that led to Labour's massive defeat. It wasn't even Jeremy Corbyn. It was people who put their preferred pronouns in their Twitter bios – something trans people and their allies often do to normalise the practice of clearly stating a person's pronouns, rather than leaving people to assume them.

The tendency to catastrophise over something that *literally doesn't affect you* has spread far and wide in British politics. You can find any given article touching on gender, pronouns or trans rights, and it will be shared and re-shared across the social networks of the modern trans panic. When I published my video speaking to trans people in Britain, I received hundreds of tweets calling me an idiot, or worse. When the *Guardian* reported in early January 2020 that American linguists had voted the singular 'they' (when used to refer to non-binary people) to be the word of the decade, one Twitter user, @ Golden_Sovereign, who has a lion for a profile picture, replied: 'The gradual unravelling continues. By this madness we are set adrift.' The real wonder of the '@Golden_Sovereign' reply is the sheer *catastrophe* they (yes, I don't know their gender, so *they*) fear will befall a slight change in the English language. A language, by the way, that changes so rapidly that parents and their children sometimes have no idea what each other is talking about. A gender-neutral pronoun isn't just mildly irritating to this one Twitter user, and, unfortunately, the millions like them. No, it *unravels* us.

In 2012, I attended a community class in San Francisco called Female Sexuality, or femsex for short. It was a course that had grown out of the student-led courses called 'decals' at UC Berkeley, and also at Brown University. Its purpose was to gather together and talk about all the things we don't generally talk about – even with our friends, let alone strangers. We talked about rape, abortion, body image, and we talked about fun things too. We read papers and talked about our personal experiences. The class was mostly, but not exclusively, for women or non-binary people. Mine was entirely cis women. But as a rule in the class, we were only to use gender-neutral pronouns, in referring to ourselves, each other and our families and friends, except in cases where it was absolutely crucial to the telling of our stories. In my class, we elected to use 'phe' for he and she, and 'phe's' for his and her. Or we could use 'they' as a singular. We used 'parent' for mother or father, and 'sibling' for brother or sister, and so on.

This is, perhaps, the transphobe's worst nightmare. An *affront* to language, they might say. The destruction of hierarchy and universal order. The heralding of the end times, one *phe* at a time.

Using gender-neutral pronouns certainly didn't come naturally at first – just as learning any pronouns when you're a baby doesn't come 'naturally'. Language is learned, it is not innate. And part of learning is making mistakes. People in my femsex class would often trip up, correct themselves and laugh. It was a new experience. It caused us to think about how gender is used in our language, and how assumptions about gender touch almost everything in our lives. We realised how differently we would understand a story if we knew it was about a man or a woman. 'My friend got wasted and went home with someone they just met last night.' In your mind, imagine your friend is a man. Now, imagine they're a woman. See how much you can learn about your own world view from a gender-neutral pronoun?

Eradicating gender from our language, even for one evening a week, was a way to go about our discussions imagining people as *people* first, before their gender. It was a way to imagine, if this is just what we *did* in the English language, what it would be like if you didn't have to assume anything about someone's gender from the language you used to address them. It was tricky at first to get used to, sure. But it didn't lead to any *unravelling*. My identity as a woman was not torn from me, I was not denied the pleasures of femininity, I did not lose access to women's sports and menstrual products, I continued to paint my nails and weep softly over Jane Austen novels. My mind was not controlled by the thought police, my free speech was not curtailed, Orwell did not come calling. And ten years later, I continue to use gendered words in my normal life.

What the exercise did, though, was lead us to deeper and more criti-cal thinking about the world, as have my friendships with and expo-sure to trans and non-binary people over the last ten years, in person and online. I hope as time goes on, I will continue to think more deeply, and question more of the assumptions I carry.

One person very much *not* interested in such a project – and another one of the people who has been tragically sucked into a life-consum-ing fixation on trans people – is J.K. Rowling. The *Harry Potter* author has, for some reason, repeatedly and forcefully written, tweeted and shared statements which have offended trans people and their allies, while claiming to be defending, among other things, 'free speech'.

It all started when Maya Forstater, a researcher at a think tank called the Centre for Global Development, did not have her contract renewed because of her distasteful tweets about trans people. She took her employer to court and lost. For snowflake critics, this was a classic case of persecuting people for their right to freely express not only a point of view, but 'simple facts'.

Forstater tried to argue in court that her beliefs, and therefore her bigoted tweets about trans people, were a 'protected characteristic of philosophical belief'. She was trying to use the 2010 Equality Act to argue that her viewpoints made her a protected class and said that she could not be fired for it. She said that being forced to correctly gender trans people would be like forcing a Jewish person to eat pork. The judge, meanwhile, found that 'the claimant's view, in its absolutist nature, is incompatible with human dignity and fundamental rights of others.'[8] (This language comes from an earlier case which set the precedent for cases like Forstater's about protected beliefs.)

In response to the ruling against her, Forstater claimed: 'This judge-ment removes women's rights and the right to freedom of belief and speech. It gives judicial license for women and men who speak up for objective truth and clear debate to be subject to aggression, bullying, no-platforming and economic punishment.' But this wasn't a free-speech issue. Forstater can speak and campaign against trans rights to her heart's content, as so many prominent people do in Britain from the left and right. Indeed, she has. She can build a personal brand trading on her bigotry, as so many do. It does not mean, however, that she can insist on calling trans women men, and trans men women, without backlash. Her employer let her go for being offensive to a marginalised class of people, as they hopefully would have done if her tweets had been about Muslims, black people or gay people.

Forstater's lawyer said that had she won, it would have been a victory for people 'to express their beliefs without fear of being discriminated against.' In the end, Forstater did win an appeal which found that her beliefs *did* classify as a protected philosophical position – however, the original rule that her dismissal was legal still stands as of this writing. In the wake of other court and government decisions limiting trans peoples' rights to self-identify and to access health care, the rights of trans people appear increasingly under threat in Britain, while Forstater's celebrity has continued to rise.

The case gained wider international attention when J.K. Rowling tweeted in support of Forstater: 'Dress however you please. Call yourself whatever you like. Sleep with any consenting adult who'll have you. Live your best life in peace and security. But force women out of their jobs for stating that sex is real? #IStandWithMaya #ThisIsNotADrill.' Freddy and Juno told me about how politely worded and subtle British transphobia can be, especially when coming from the pen of a famous writer. This was such a case – implying that being trans was akin to wanting to play dress-up, which, as many trans people pointed out, diminished and delegitimised the experience of actually being trans. Rowling has insisted repeatedly that she is not transphobic, and has in fact been 'empathetic to trans women for decades' and is merely 'concerned about the consequences of the current trans activism.'[9] But as Alice Goldfuss put it on Twitter: 'The language she uses is similar to language used to minimise gay people,' for example, 'You can kiss whoever you want behind closed doors!'[10]

Many fans of J.K. Rowling and her work shared their disappointment that a woman who wrote a book about the fantastical possibilities of magic would stand up for a woman whose entire M.O. is reinforcing rigid (and scientifically wrong) conceptions of human sex. The author of a series of books about the heroism of children who stand up to bullies and a fascistic evil that loathes those who are perceived as different or weak is willing to die on the hill of a grown woman's right to tweet that trans women are not women. Maya Forstater, I'm afraid to say, is probably a Slytherin.

Throughout 2020, as pandemic and protest and political turmoil swept the world, Rowling kept popping her head above the parapet to remind people of her views. She doubled down on the choice to use her considerable influence to tell people that cis women were threatened by the advancement of trans rights. Of all things to worry about in 2020 – TWENTY TWENTY! – Rowling published a letter which was perceived by many as reiterating her transphobic beliefs. She wrote about the 'erosion of women's and girl's rights' and of the threat that trans 'activism' poses to the 'education and safeguarding' of children. She wrote that children might try to transition because of the homophobia of their families. She wrote of the fear that young girls would transition to become trans men because of the sexism they faced as girls. She said that thirty years ago, she may have been convinced to transition also. (I asked Freddy McConnell about this, in particular. He told me, 'I have to assume she's never spoken to a trans man, because trans men don't talk about our experiences in that way.')

'We're living through the most misogynistic period I've ever experienced,' Rowling concludes. She attributes this to the rise of Donald Trump and his supporters, incels (if you'll recall – online communities who resent women for not sleeping with them and are violent to women as a result), and, in the same breath, trans activists.

She frames all three groups as instances of men attacking women – when really, a majority of cis women support trans rights.

Rowling also claimed that trans women were a threat to women-only spaces, including shelters meant for survivors of domestic abuse:

> When you throw open the doors of bathrooms and changing rooms to any man who believes or feels he's a woman – and, as I've said, gender confirmation certificates may now be granted without any need for surgery or hormones – then you open the door to any and all men who wish to come inside. That is the simple truth.[11]

It isn't the simple truth, though! It's not even the complicated truth. Trans women are not fakers attempting to gain entry to shelters in order to abuse cis women. Trans women face tragically high rates of domestic abuse and assault and are therefore extremely likely to need access to safe, women-only spaces.[12] A Scottish government report from 2019 on the potential impacts of GRA reform found no evidence that trans women would, or have ever, posed a threat to cis women in women-only spaces, as it laid out in its summary:

- No evidence was identified to support the claim that trans women are more likely than cisgender women to sexually assault other women in women-only spaces. This lack of evidence is reiterated by other sources.
- This literature search did not identify any evidence supporting a link between women-only spaces being inclusive of transgender women, and cisgender men falsely claiming a trans identity to access these spaces and commit sexual violence. Other sources included in this search reiterate a lack of any evidence to support this claim.[13]

Domestic abuse shelters already screen women for abusive histories, whether they're trans or not. One domestic abuse shelter volunteer told *Pink News* that it would be 'impossible' for a cis man posing as a trans woman to enter a women's shelter.[14]

Nevertheless, of all the things which threatened women in 2020, and continue to threaten women, Rowling hung her hat upon the false, bigoted claim that if trans women had easy access to safe, women-only spaces, then 'any and all' men could charge inside to threaten and harm cis women. This idea is not grounded in truth. It is grounded in fear – in phobia – and the idea that some trans women would only self-identify as such in order to bust down the door to the women's toilets and wreak havoc within. Men who harm women don't need to go through the trouble of transition, or even self-identification, to do so. But in making this argument, Rowling adds her voice to the destructive stereotype which casts trans women as threatening, violent and not actually women. Women who have never thought about this issue, upon reading an argument like Rowling's, may well be convinced that they should be worried about trans women in women-only spaces. They might be convinced to perpetuate these false claims. They may back and vote for policies which end up harming those who often need support and safety and protection the most – trans women. This is the horror of British transphobia. That is the simple truth.

The thing is it doesn't actually hurt to support the rights and lives of trans people. And it doesn't hurt your free speech rights, or science, or the rights of women. A society which is kind to trans people is a good place for a woman to live.

Anyway, if you still want to enjoy reading Harry Potter, remember, as my former *BuzzFeed* colleague Kaye Toal said in the wake of Rowling's essay: every character in Harry Potter is actually trans. That's canon.

*   *   *

Transphobia, of course, doesn't only belong to Britain, or the TERFs of the British centre-left. British transphobes have some rather unpleasant American allies in their quest to spread fear and lies about trans people. We hear the same bad-faith arguments from TERFs as we do from the wildest fringes of the Republican party. We hear that if it is made easier and less bureaucratic for trans people to legally change the documentation of their sex, men will simply declare themselves trans to sneak into women's toilets and changing rooms to attack women. This is not a thing that happens, as we have seen. Men do attack women, but they don't pretend to be trans to do so. Of course there are trans people who are criminals. There are also left-handed people who are criminals. There are heads of state who are criminals. The problem of rape is not going to be solved by excluding trans people from the toilets matching their gender identities. Giving trans women easy access to women's facilities is a way to protect *trans people themselves* from the violence that would be directed against them if they *didn't* have that access.

The argument over bathrooms grows ever more ridiculous when you consider the fact that you almost certainly *don't know* who is trans in your bathroom. It would also be deeply weird to attempt to find out. But in attempting to enforce bathroom genders, you would inevitably harm both men *and* women who do not look sufficiently masculine or feminine according to gender stereotypes. And yet this is a key talking point of transphobes of the British left – and of American conservative politicians, who often propose and sometimes manage to enact laws banning trans people from using the bathroom they want. It's also a frequent talking point of far-right European leaders, like Hungary's Viktor Orbán, whose government ended legal recognition for trans people in 2020.

In their quest to police people's genitals at the bathroom door, British transphobes find their allies among the most terrifying and ridiculous conservative forces in the United States and around the world. They hold hands with genuine fascists and romp through a meadow of transphobia together.

For a taste of the latter's viewpoint, we can look at the American conservative author Ashley McGuire, who put out a book in 2017 titled *Sex Scandal: The Drive to Abolish Male and Female*, which lays out the conservative fear of trans people and other gender trouble quite explicitly. 'It seems like you woke up one day,' McGuire writes, 'and suddenly it was normal for kindergartens to ban Legos as sexist, for high school boys to shower in the girls' locker room, and for America to send the mothers of toddlers to defend us from our enemies.'[15] Her fear extends beyond female soldiers: 'There are people in America who consider it criminal and abusive to identify children by their biological sex. And they are coming for yours.' *They are coming for you, and they will make your child trans.*

Needless to say, the Republican Party that elected Donald Trump is also not particularly open to trans rights. The president's son, Donald Trump Jr, devotes a large section of his book, *Triggered: How the Left Thrives on Hate and Wants to Silence Us*, to reflections on his own rugged masculinity (Hunting! Butchering chickens!) and to all the greatest hits of the trans panic. This includes the claim that trans athletes will bring about the end of women's sport. This, I have to stress, is not true. Trans athletes have been allowed to compete in the Olympics since 2004, and no sport of any kind is yet to be wrecked. Nor have women's athletics been wrecked at lower levels. Nevertheless, Don Jr is deeply concerned:

So if you're a male athlete in college and you're getting your ass handed to you by all the other big, strong males in your division, you might have a way out! All you have to do is declare that you're a woman, and suddenly your competition gets smaller and less muscular. It's like magic![16]

It's magic, Trump Jr tells us, referring to something that does not happen. Though perhaps this *is* what happened with the case of Chris Mosier, a trans man who qualified for the 2020 Olympic trials in racewalking, competing against cis men, in order to get an, er, unfair advantage maybe?[17] Wait, was that not what he's talking about? Speaking of things that don't happen, Trump Jr also refers to the bathroom panic ('when the left demanded that confused old men in dresses be allowed into the same restrooms as little girls'). In both sports- and bathroom-related panics, we find bigotry that depends on a bizarre and totally unfounded belief that the *reason* some people are trans is to commit sinister crimes in toilets or triumph in various sports. They imagine that trans athletes *only* transition in order to win medals, revealing a total lack of knowledge or curiosity about the actual experiences of trans people. Trump Jr, though, is less concerned with reality, and more concerned about the supposed tyranny of gender-neutral pronouns, which he lumps together with 'every other crazy idea that the left has had – from the Green New Deal and free college to prison voting and unlimited abortions.'

These are the political allies the transphobic British feminists have chosen for themselves. The current British conservative government, too, is not stellar on trans rights. But it is the women of the 'left' whose transphobia comes as the biggest betrayal. In an era of impending climate catastrophe, and the revitalisation of the far right, and reactionary violence and discrimination against the groups including women who have made progress in recent decades – is it trans people who are the greatest threat to women? Absolutely not.

One of President Joe Biden's first acts in office was to reverse the transphobic policies enacted by the Trump presidency. An executive order would guarantee trans women the right to compete in women's athletics, and while American progressives cheered this and other trans-inclusive policies, British TERFs were up in arms. The hashtag

#BidenErasesWomen trended worldwide off the back of their outrage, claiming (incorrectly) that the inclusion of trans women in women's sports would end women's sports as we know it. The fact is, trans women have been allowed to compete in everything from high school sports to the Olympics for decades – despite countless attempts to exclude them – and the supposed plague of men 'pretending to be women in order to win sporting victories' has yet to materialise.

Perhaps because they cannot extend their understanding of structural oppression beyond their own identities, transphobic British feminists have ended up making all the same arguments as those who would seek to chip away at cis women's rights. They have made not just strange bedfellows, but destructive ones.

One of the most destructive bedfellows is the leading critic of all things snowflake, the father of YouTube demagoguery, the enforcer of gender binaries and champion of young male rage, Jordan Peterson. Grab your smelling salts, your Tums and your mace.

Before he became the godfather of simplistic viral self-help videos founded in hatred of the diversity of the human experience, Jordan Peterson was merely a psychology professor at the University of Toronto. He still is a psychology professor at the University of Toronto, but he's also so much more, and so much less. He is the author of a bestselling book, *12 Rules for Life: An Antidote to Chaos*, which according to Peterson had sold three million copies by the end of 2019. To read this book is to descend into a bewildering and slightly terrifying stream of consciousness. In his book, Peterson attempts to counter the malaise of frustrated young men through liberal reference to the Old Testament of the Bible and other such texts in search of what he and other snowflake critics often refer to as 'ancient wisdom'.

In *12 Rules for Life* Peterson does not use the term 'snowflake', but to understand the book's importance to the snowflake literature, you must place it in the context of YouTube. This is just one of the platforms in which Peterson preaches to a following of millions. His audience is dominated by disaffected young males, who in turn upload YouTube videos of Peterson's lectures and encounters with the public under titles such as, 'Jordan Peterson ruins snowflake asking a manipulated question | Cambridge Union'; '"You're a Harmful Moron" Disrespectful Snowflake insults Jordan Peterson | Watch his Epic reaction'; '"Grow The Hell Up" Jordan Peterson SCHOOLS College Snowflake'; 'Watch Snowflake Student Snaps [sic] At ANGRY Jordan Peterson, Instantly Regrets it'; and 'Jordan Peterson destroys a radical leftist snowflake with ease'. To scroll YouTube, it appears that it is Peterson's purpose in life to destroy every last snowflake in the English-speaking world. He might think so also.

Peterson rose from psychology professor to bestselling author-slash-internet star with an audience of millions thanks to, ironically, what he characterised as an attempt to restrict his free speech. In 2016, Peterson drew attention in the Canadian press for declaring that he would not use gender-neutral pronouns even if his students requested them. In the wake of his comments and ensuing protests, trans students at the University of Toronto began to receive threats from online trolls. University of Toronto administrators requested Peterson 'stop making statements that could be considered discriminatory under provincial human rights legislation,' according to Toronto's newspaper *The Globe and Mail*.[18] 'We trust that these impacts on students and others were not your intention,' the letter said. 'However, in view of these impacts, as well as the requirements [of legislation], we urge you to stop repeating these statements.' Peterson said that his job, and his career, was put at risk due to what he felt was a noble struggle against the human decency of using someone's correct pronouns. The University of Toronto, though, hosted a debate in which a panellist, the law professor Brenda Cossman, said that nothing in the bill in question 'criminalises the misuse of pronouns,' and that Peterson was therefore exaggerating his legal risk. As a result of the fracas which he insisted would silence him forever, Peterson's public profile reached unfathomable new heights. He quite literally leveraged his discrimination against trans people into a sparkling and lucrative career.

While Peterson framed his run-in with University of Toronto students and administrators as a persecution of his free speech rights, his beliefs about an immutable binary of sex make up a large part of his popular work. As he explained to Maajid Nawaz on LBC in 2018, Peterson believes those who suggest pronouns beyond 'he' and 'she' are 'playing this radical collectivist left-wing game.'[19] He believes that most of the time that people ask to be gendered according to their wishes it is 'a narcissistic power play', and insists he will 'use whatever pronoun seems to go along with the persona that they're projecting publicly' even if it is at odds with what gender they really are. 'You're trying to gain linguistic supremacy in the area of public discourse,' Peterson complains of non-binary or trans people and their allies. 'You're doing that using compassion as a guise, and you're pulling the wool over people's eyes, and you're not going to do it with me.'

Peterson's deep discomfort with the fact that gender stretches beyond a simple binary seems to stem from the way in which he constructs his entire world view around a belief in the biological, intellectual and social chasm separating men from women. It makes sense that someone who believes that all of history and all of society can be explained by this dichotomy would be uneasy with the suggestion that people can be something in between, or neither, or can be identified as the wrong gender at birth. Peterson believes in the innate suitability of men to positions of power, which flows from their deepest, biological maleness – something which may explain the attraction of disaffected young men to his work, and the comfort they take in it. It is terrifying to think of the millions of young men reading and listening to and watching Peterson's work. He has very effectively channelled the misery and disaffection of economic insecurity and aimed it at feminists and trans people. His arguments show us that those who are hostile to trans people are also hostile to cis women. They go hand in hand.

Peterson opens *12 Rules for Life* with the idea that men represent 'order' and women 'chaos' in religious mythology and other important historic texts.[20] Chaos is, among other things 'the domain of ignorance itself,' Peterson writes. (Classic women!) Peterson then delves into an argument about how dominance hierarchies are produced by groups of lobsters. Although he is a human being, Peterson warns us that 'if a dominant lobster is badly defeated, its brain basically dissolves. Then it grows a new, subordinate's brain – one more appropriate to its new, lowly position.' This is what he fears happens to subordinate human men. 'It's winner-take-all in the lobster world,' he explains, 'just as it in in human societies, where the top one per cent have as much loot as the bottom fifty per cent.' From the example of the lobster, who attracts the most mates by being at the top of this social hierarchy, Peterson advises young men to stand up tall and dominate others in order to attract women:

> The female lobsters (who also fight hard for territory during the explicitly maternal stages of their existence) identify the top guy quickly and become irresistibly attracted to him. This is brilliant strategy, in my estimation. It's also one used by females of many different species, including humans.

Peterson writes that 'dominance hierarchies' have been apparent in species for billions of years, and therefore, 'the dominance hierarchy, however social or cultural it might appear, has been around for some half a billion years. It's permanent. It's real.' This is the structure around which Peterson arranges much of his world view. 'Dominance hierarchies are older than trees,' he writes, and that's why the patriarchy is not socially constructed, and women are underrepresented in politics, I suppose. Inequality between the rich and poor, and between genders, is a natural and fair result of our biology, according to Peterson. Just ask the lobsters. Much of Peterson's book is a bizarre word salad, so it's often hard to pick out his meaning, and things are written in such a way that Peterson can claim plausible deniability about having said anything at all.

Peterson's book is meant to be an antidote to 'chaos' which is, you'll remember, characterised in religious literature as feminine, therefore chaos must be feminine. Peterson writes that creatures 'have been male or female . . . for a billion years. That's a long time.' He says that 'male and female and parent and child are categories, for us – natural categories, deeply embedded in our perceptual, emotional and motivational structures.' This is extremely simplistic, but it's also not scientifically true. Peterson stakes the history of humankind on the gender binary: 'Our most basic category – as old, in some sense, as the sexual act itself – appears to be that of sex, male and female.' And what are men, to Peterson? 'The primary hierarchical structure of human society is masculine,' he writes. 'It is because men are and throughout history have been the builders of towns and cities, the engineers, stonemasons, bricklayers and lumberjacks, the operators of heavy machinery.'

Women, on the other hand, are 'choosy maters (unlike female chimps, their closest animal counterparts). Most men do not meet female human standards,' Peterson complains, and 'it is for this reason that women on dating sites rate eighty-five per cent of men as below average in attractiveness.' This is deeply painful for men. Every time they are turned down by a 'desirable mate' of a woman, 'that's a direct encounter with chaos, and it occurs with devastating force every time they are turned down for a date.' Peterson then delves into an explanation about how Adam and Eve's personal characteristics and behaviours can explain the way that men and women are today. They are immutable. 'The first woman made the first man self-conscious and resentful. Then the first man blamed the woman. And then the first man blamed God. This is exactly how every spurned male feels, to this day.' Peterson refers to the concept of Original Sin as 'very unpopular in modern intellectual circles,' despite its full legitimacy in his mind. I apparently have a higher opinion of men than Peterson, who imagines the rejected male thus:

> First, he feels small, in front of the potential object of his love, after she denigrates his reproductive suitability. Then he curses God for making her so bitchy, himself so useless (if he has any sense) and Being itself so deeply flawed. Then he turns to thoughts of revenge. How thoroughly contemptible (and how utterly understandable).

Peterson writes as if he believes that women draw their essential worth and value from their looks and their procreative roles. ('Even the most stunning Hollywood actress eventually transforms into the Evil Queen, on eternal, paranoid watch for the new Snow White.') He believes that 'many a mother' will 'object vociferously to any command uttered by an adult male,' but will seek to ruin her son by obeying his every command, because it is the goal of every mother to produce a 'reproductively successful son.' Peterson says 'there are reasons why parents might favour sons sufficiently to eliminate female foetuses.' It goes on.

You can see in Peterson's arguments the corollary to TERF reasoning. It is a long-established standard that women are subjugated by men, and that their oppression flows from their biological function. What's more, we are all locked in a lobster battle seeking dominance, and it's bad news for weak lobsters. Women fight ferociously for male mates, men fight for dominance among each other, and it's Adam and Eve, not Adam and Steve.

The solution for all weak lobsters, according to Peterson, is to be a terrible person and/or lobster. He believes that people 'develop more self-respect' when they 'recognise in themselves the seeds of evil and monstrosity and see themselves as dangerous (at least potentially).'

This leads them to be able to resist oppression: 'They see that they have the ability to withstand, because they are terrible too.' Do you still have that mace handy? You'll need it for this next quote: 'The lust for blood, rape and destruction is very much part of power's attraction.'

Frequently Peterson sounds like he is writing from atop a horse. At other times, fancies himself a bit of a prophet ('It would be good to make the world a better place. Heaven, after all, will not arrive of its own accord. We will have to work to bring it about, and strengthen ourselves, so that we can withstand the deadly angels and flaming sword of judgement that God used to bar its entrance.') He glorifies human suffering for its own sake ('pain matters, more than matter matters') and thinks the highest type of person one can aspire to be is the one everyone else is depending on for steely strength at a funeral. It's a deeply sad thought. In Jordan Peterson's ideal binary, boys don't cry.

I share all of this with you not to make you want to die, but because Peterson is a big influence in the modern hatred of snowflakes and is leading a reactionary trend against the expansion and protection of women's rights and trans rights. His book is seen as an 'antidote' to snowflakes by many millions of people. His line of logic follows that of most snowflake critics and inspires new ones – particularly young men. He believes that children are overly coddled and must be made into strong little warriors. To counter this trend, he makes a roundabout argument for corporal punishment of children:

> To unthinkingly parrot the magic line, 'There is no excuse for physical punishment' is also to foster the delusion that teenage devils magically emerge from once-innocent little child-angels . . . And what about the idea that hitting a child merely teaches them to hit? First: No. Wrong. Too simple. For starters, 'hitting' is a very unsophisticated word to describe the disciplinary act of an effective parent.

Have you dialled 999 yet? No? OK, forget the police. Call in a plane full of armed paratroopers. Call an army of psychotherapists. Call the Hague.

Peterson takes his own inner darkness and projects it onto others. It's terrifying to think how popular this has made him. 'Perhaps the world should even be cleansed of all human presence,' he wonders. 'I believe that the person who claims never to have wished for such a thing has neither consulted his memory nor confronted his darkest fantasies.' This is the book that has resonated so deeply with millions of young men around the world – a book with a casual suggestion that humanity should be eradicated from the earth. A book that says that attempting to help others is not only misguided, but that 'the attempt to rescue someone is often felled by vanity and narcissism.' He thinks a person who tries to help another person is most likely to 'just want to draw attention to [their] inexhaustible reserves of compassion and good-will.' He does not see these qualities as worthwhile to foster or project. To Peterson, women are meant to be beautiful, and men are meant to be mighty. *12 Rules* is a deeply cynical book, and one that calls the behaviour of modern snowflakes, attempting to make the world a better place, a selfish tendency. It is a book that casts victims as undeserving of attention, let alone help. A victim is victimised as a result of their own bad moral character. And central to it all is Peterson's rage at any who would dare understand sex and gender as anything less than biologically immutable.

Again and again, Peterson returns to his fear of the ultimate chaos, the breakdown of the gender binary, which he sees as deeply destructive to society. Peterson relies completely on simple categorisations for his sense of peace. Peterson is *terrified* of change. He *longs* to bask in the comforting idea that human society can basically be explained by watching lobsters go at it in a restaurant lobster tank. 'Horror and terror lurk behind the walls provided so wisely by our ancestors,' he writes, then taking a sudden turn to wonder if it was 'really a good thing . . . to so dramatically liberalise the divorce laws in the 1960s' to make it easier for women to seek divorce from their husbands. He thinks that parents should see it is as their 'primary duty' to 'make their children socially desirable' – which is more important than 'any responsibility to ensure happiness, foster creativity, or boost self-esteem.' He believes that the demolition of 'the traditional household division of labour' has led to 'chaos, conflict and indeterminacy' in its wake. Jordan Peterson *really* doesn't want to do the washing-up.

He believes that the elevation of women closer to legal and cultural equality has damaged boys: 'As privileged beneficiaries of the patriarchy, their accomplishments are considered unearned. As possible adherents of rape culture, they're sexually suspect. Their ambitions make them plunderers of the planet.' He thinks that 'girls aren't attracted to boys who are their friends . . . they are attracted to boys who win status contests with other boys,' forgetting, as he does frequently throughout *12 Rules for Life*, about lesbians. Peterson believes that women suffer from their advancement in education and industry, because they 'have a strong proclivity to marry across or up the economic dominance hierarchy' and if they themselves are quite dominant they have a harder time finding 'mates'. Peterson writes with the energy of a man who stomps across the playground to snatch a doll from someone else's son. *You play with toy soldiers*, he hisses at the unsuspecting six-year-old.

Needless to say, Peterson also believes that universities have turned against men: Peterson believes that universities teaching about patriarchy is akin to them teaching that the world is flat. And he is terrified, *terrified*, of a world in which boys 'are socialised like girls.' He believes that boys are naturally aggressive. He believes that 'agreeable, compassionate, empathic, conflict-averse people . . . let people walk on them, and they get bitter.' He is against niceness. He believes that society is trying to destroy boys, just as mothers attempt to destroy their sons. He actually blames Hitler and Stalin's crimes on their mothers, who must have raised them poorly.

In their transphobia, TERFs have made an ally with a man who thinks that the movie *Frozen* is propaganda to convince little girls that they don't need a prince to rescue them. TERFs do not want to be policed the way that Peterson would have women controlled – but they agree in the importance and immutability and rigid binary of biological sex. They perhaps unwittingly agree on the centrality of fertility to womanhood. They share a terror, likewise, of the breakdown of the 'ancient wisdom' of men and women. Peterson and his fans fear a snowflake agenda to reduce manly men to simpering children. To allow women to neglect their motherly duties. To make Jordan Peterson admit that trans men are men, and trans women are women. To make a world where men can drink a crisp, white wine in the pub.

In September 2019, Peterson's family announced that he had been checked into rehab to recover from his dependence on the sedative, clonazepam. His daughter, Mikhaela, stressed that her father was suffering from a physical dependence – stemming from legally prescribed medication – and not a psychological addiction.[21] Whether he has suffered from a dependency or an addiction, though, does not make him morally weak. You would think so, though, if you subscribed to Peterson's clearly stated belief that people should be blamed for their own weakness, and that people can only get their lives in order by being crueller, less feeling and utterly self-dependent. I only hope that Peterson is receiving the kind of non-judgemental compassion in his moment of struggle that he consistently denies to others.

The world, it turns out, cannot be reduced to the truisms of Peterson's life's work. A person's quest for strength is fought on a battlefield more complicated than a lobster tank. And sex and gender are more complex than a lobster's romances.

*   *   *

Delving into the snowflake discourse, and reading books such as *12 Rules for Life*, I have found myself time and again writing in the margins of books: Voltaire's pants. What I really mean when I write this, though, is: Voltaire's breeches. In the first chapter of *Candide*, the young title character learns the following about the world from his instructor, Pangloss, in a lesson on what he calls 'metaphisico-theologico-cosmolo-nigology':

> Observe that noses were made to wear spectacles, and so we have spectacles. Legs were visibly instituted to be breeched, and we have breeches. Stones were formed to be quarried and to build castles; and My Lord has a very noble castle; the greatest Baron in the province should have the best house; and as pigs were made to be eaten, we eat pork all year round; consequently, those who have asserted all is well talk nonsense; they ought to have said that all is for the best.[22]

In the minds of those who argue that the gender and political and socio-economic reality of the world is reflective of some inner biological truth, the nose is made for the spectacle, not the spectacle for the nose. Voltaire's pants, in the American sense of pants, are worn by all who feel absolutely certain that the way things are is the way things ought to be. It is only natural. Everything flows from *ancient wisdoms*. My Lord has a noble castle, because he is the greatest Baron, with the best pants of all. To try and steal away his castle would be foolhardy. To criticise his wealth and power would be to defy the laws of nature. He is the best Baron, after all.

Every piece of writing in the anti-snowflake literature contains this line of logic. For Lukianoff and Haidt in *The Coddling of the American Mind*, Title IX is a foolish piece of legislation because girls simply have less interest in sports than boys. The interest gap could be due to socialisation, they admit – but if this were really true, then 'sex differences would be smaller in informal settings, such as when kids are playing in a park, compared with school settings.' To their minds, gender stereotypes could not possibly be recreated by children in a playground.

For Jordan Peterson, meanwhile, men and women have had and expressed different interests and abilities across time, and therefore, it is true that they are fundamentally different in their interests and abilities. The lobsters are horny for one another's beefy hierarchically blessed claws, and if the lobsters do it, so too must we. The very same people who profess a monk-like devotion to reason and rationality are the ones who enjoy drawing the most wildly over-simplified conclusions about the world. The ones who claim to defend 'science' repeatedly reveal their disinterest in the diversity of life and the mysteries of biology. Jordan Peterson can simply look upon a lobster and find an explanation for the human soul. This is not deep or critical thinking.

This is also where transphobes of the left and right may find themselves at odds. Those on the left who would seek to exclude trans people from their feminism believe that gender cannot be changed because gender does not *matter*. It does not predict what men and women are able or willing to do with their lives.

Both sides of the transphobic political spectrum, though, would agree in the immutable importance of a binary, biologically-determined sex. They believe in the importance of genitals and chromosomes and hormones and sex characteristics to being. Transphobes of the left believe that women's oppression stems from their physical bodies. Transphobes of the right believe that the oppression of women is justifiable due to their physical bodies, their innate abilities and preferences and weaknesses.

These are the allies that transphobes of the left have chosen for themselves. In thinking that their rights and protections must be organised purely according to their sex, they give truth to the idea that all women are, in fact, a certain way – that they are defined by their bodies and specifically their reproductive organs. If this is where women's rights stem from, it's also where women's rights can be destroyed. Voltaire's pants may be comfortable, but they are dangerous.

If you claim that having a vagina is the most important thing that makes a woman, every sexist prig will jump to agree. In joining hands with far-right ideologues in their hatred of trans and non-binary people, transphobic feminists have locked themselves in Jordan Peterson's lobster tank and thrown away the key.

Sometimes, I like to think about the things I will say and do that my future grandchildren will be offended by. What will cause them to roll their eyes and say, 'Grandma Hannah, you can't say that anymore, you stupid cow!!' as we float on our houseboat above the underwater city formerly known as London. Whatever it is, I hope I will be gracious about being corrected, smiling and saying 'Oh, I'm sorry, things just aren't how they used to be!' as I sharpen our fishing spear. (It has to be pointy, or the family won't eat.)

I think the thing that will get in trouble with my grandchildren will either be eating meat (or the fact that I USED to, back when you could) or, perhaps, my slipping into gendered words from time to time, or assuming people's gender on sight. This is a vision of the future which I'm sure would horrify many. A transphobe in 2021 would take great issue with the way that language has totally *unravelled*.

But I see it as a hopeful scene, except for the bit about the climate apocalypse, perhaps. The 'slippery slope' of overly politically correct vego-fascist gender-bending woke totalitarianism is the slope I hope we slide down. The alternative is sliding backwards into the violent conformity of the past. I want to look at my offended little grandchildren and think, 'Woo, they've got some wacky new ideas!' I don't want to look at them and wonder how we ended up more oppressive and homogenous than the world in my own young years.

I wish that British transphobic feminists, who today obsess and fear about where the acceptance and support of trans people will lead us, will someday feel the same. I wish that they would stop with their hatred and their bad-faith arguments. I wish they would realise what I understand: that my experience of womanhood has a lot more in common with other middle-class, British or American women journalists who happen to be trans, for example, than it has with women who live in different cultures or countries or in poverty or even in extreme wealth. Solidarity is not defined by a vagina, as much as I like to complain about my periods. And the real threats to cis women are also threats to trans women. They are the radicalised young men of the right, and the abusive predators of the home, and the discrimination of the workplace, and the political leaders who do not care to protect us.

We should not fear where trans rights and trans people will lead us. We should fear a future without them.

8

Snowflakes are bad for capitalism

For those who have diagnosed today's young with an incurable case of snowflakery, the problem begins in childhood. Children are coddled, and not beaten with sticks, and therefore lack character. Then, if they go on to higher education, they face the ruin of safe spaces, trigger warnings and progressive ideologies. But worst of all, for the snowflake critic, is what happens when these loathsome, vile, weeping, hysterical and authoritarian little terrors reach the workplace: they make trouble.

In some ways, this is a misguided fear. Studies show the extent to which millennials and now Generation Z put in unprecedented hours and devote themselves to work. As the divide between the rich and poor grows ever wider, there is a lot more to lose if you end up in a 'bad' job.

On the other hand, though, it's perfectly true that younger generations make trouble at work. The politics of snowflakery extends to the workplace – and that is a very good thing. Young people at work can drive their older bosses crazy. They complain about unfair work. They tell each other their salaries, and then complain about their salaries. They report harassment. They demand better treatment. They refuse to 'pay their dues' if paying their dues is a euphemism for being used and abused at work. If they are treated poorly, they quit.

This is, to some, yet another reason to blame the world's ills on young people. The political leader can look upon an economy and complain that young people do not pull their weight. The manager can look at a workplace's problems and blame not their own poor management, or ridiculous business model, but the bad attitude of kids these days. And as we have seen, who is more hateable than the young? Again and again, those with the least economic or political power make the best scapegoats for whatever ails your economy, your politics or your office.

The fact is a snowflake can be difficult to work with. A snowflake may be less willing to put their head down and ignore your transgressions. A snowflake points out harassment and discrimination when it happens. A snowflake can be bad for business, so the snowflake must be ridiculed and denigrated. A snowflake must be kept in such a precarious state at work that they dare not rock the boat. After all, everyone is replaceable.

I have never felt this more acutely than when I tried, and failed, to form a union.

There are plenty of reasons to remember 2016. Many of us will remember where we were when the Brexit referendum took a turn for the Leavers. (I was at Nigel Farage's victory party, staring at a cake shaped like a champagne bottle, complete with a cork that looked like a ball sack.) Many of us will also remember where we were when the US presidential election took a turn for the Trumpers. (I was live on-air, co-anchoring BuzzFeed's election night show, keeping it together like the fake pro that I was.) But the other thing from that year that I will remember until my dying day, when I take my last breath, clinging to a door above the climate apocalypse floodwaters like Jack in *Titanic*, was my failed attempt to get a union recognised at *BuzzFeed UK*, along with a group of friends and colleagues.

Things started out swell – we would meet in the rooms above pubs and talk about how the things that had bothered us individually were actually systemic problems. Each week, new colleagues joined us, and the union grew. People shared stories of the lack of accommodation for their mental and physical health problems, and tales of wild discrepancies in pay along lines of race and gender. We aired our grievances. We laughed a lot. The unfairness of our workplace, with its public image of a trendy and progressive haven for young people, sent us reeling. Once we had a healthy majority of our editorial team on board – those who we believed would make up our bargaining unit, or the total eligible members in a union chapel – we submitted a letter requesting voluntary recognition to our management. All hell broke loose.

There are plenty of tales I could tell you from that time. I learned a lot about my colleagues, about my company and about the way the world works. I also learned that my stomach cannot cope with stress *at all*.

But the most important thing that the experience drove home to me was the way that perceptions could suppress a union. I thought that we were being framed as coddled, awful and naïve special snowflakes, and that our goals were cast as the embarrassing, unreasonable demands of entitled young people – which is a good way to convince a good chunk of your employees to distance themselves from the common cause of a union. The company spared no expense in their effort to break up our fledgling union. They flew in the big guns – our CEO, Jonah Peretti – as well as some HR and lawyerly types. We were told that we did not need a union. After all, it's not like we were a factory, and apparently Jonah was 'not a regular CEO' because he wore hoodies to meetings. No, they would not voluntarily recognise our union. But they would increase the quality of our free snacks and lunches. After all, isn't that what we wanted? (It wasn't.)

We felt that management and their fleet of expensive union-busting lawyers could not hide their disdain for what they perceived as the tantrum of a bunch of spoiled millennial employees who ought to be grateful to work at a cool job. Myself and the other organisers were made out to be both authoritarian and incredibly naïve and frail. We were apparently wielding our unholy power over our poor, misunderstood multi-millionaire CEO, and misleading our innocent colleagues like the Big Bad Wolf. At the same time, though, we were cast as ungrateful and overly sensitive. We had taken our jobs at a cool company, and then we had asked for more. We questioned the wisdom of authority. We didn't so much challenge hierarchy, as step outside of it. This is what a union is good for: capturing power from below and creating lines of accountability that do not go through a company's HR department – whose ultimate aim is to prevent a company from being sued. That year entailed many unforgettable meetings with company management and outside lawyers, which we felt were bizarre and degrading.

In the end, our effort to gain recognition failed. After over a year of lawyering, myself and many others either left the company or were laid off (for unrelated reasons), and the bargaining unit (those who would be covered by a union contract) negotiated ever smaller to include fewer union supporters. We were beaten and exhausted. Though we started strong, we did not convince enough of our peers that they personally would benefit from a union – or that it was enough that it would benefit others. Much of that was our fault. I still think of the things we might have done better, or differently.

Later, after I had started my new job at the *Washington Post*, I heard that the US offices of *BuzzFeed* – which contain the bulk of its employees – were trying to organise their own union, and I was elated. The US organisers were bigger in number, and much more charismatic, cool and attractive than we were. They had a deep bench and maintained the incredible amount of work and energy it takes to not only recruit a union, but get it recognised, and then negotiate a contract. In the end, they won the battle for recognition – though their quest for a first contract has faced many of the same hurdles that we did. Even so, each new union in media seemed to help inspire another one that year. *BuzzFeed* was one of dozens of newsrooms in media outlets in both the US and the UK who organised unions in the late 2010s and early 2020s.

Jonah Peretti, meanwhile, has presided over several more mass layoffs, regularly deciding to cut big chunks from his staff, always in the name of getting his company 'on the fast track to profitability.' This was what he told *BuzzFeed* staffers while laying them off in 2018 and 2019, and what he told *HuffPost* staffers after he bought that company and turned around in 2021 to lay off dozens of its journalists, also. It seems that he may not have yet located the fast track to profitability, but ruthlessly firing his employees must at least look pleasing to the venture capital investors who took big bets on Jonah, the wonder boy of digital media, who wears hoodies to important meetings. I will be forever mad about the way that he and *BuzzFeed* crushed our wish for a union when it could have recognised us swiftly. He did not have to lawyer up and defeat us with such vicious decisiveness. My current job at the *Washington Post* benefits from a thriving union which has been around for nearly a century. It was a delicious pleasure to sign up for it as soon as I joined the *Post*. I laughed at how easy it was, but also how non-controversial it was. There may be a movement led by young people to form new unions in media, but we are only ever building on a very old idea.

Not even Jonah Peretti can hold back the tide of feelings that young people have about organised labour. A Pew Research Center survey from 2018 found that sixty-eight per cent of Americans aged eighteen to twenty-nine held a positive view of unions, while only about half of Americans fifty and over did so. The study also found that fewer adults under thirty years old hold a favourable view of business corporations compared to older Americans. 'Adults under thirty are the only age group,' according to Pew, 'in which a larger share has a favourable view of labour unions than of business corporations.'[1] The American union the United Auto Workers wrote in early 2019 about the increase in union interest:

> Over the past two years, we've seen unionisation efforts gain momentum among graduate students on college campuses, as well as sectors of the economy that haven't traditionally been associated with unions, including digital media, non-profits and coffee shops.[2]

The very generation with more favourable views of unions is also one characterised as being precious, needy, frail-yet-authoritarian snowflakes. The same arguments used to bust our white-collar digital media union at *BuzzFeed UK* appear in attempts from corporations to stop unions in factories and other settings. As Amazon employees in Alabama sought to become the first Amazon warehouse in America to unionise, they faced literature from management telling them that a union would simply get in the way of the relationship between management and staff. Flyers in their bathrooms from management asked them: 'Where will your dues go?'[3] They were told that their pay, benefits and retirement plans were already better than most. What more could they possibly want?

This is what managers will say to break a union, whether in a warehouse or a brightly decorated digital media office with meeting rooms named after biscuits: you should be grateful for what we're giving you.

Part of the trouble with snowflakes is that they know they deserve more. And all workers benefit when they fight for it.

The youngest members of Generation Z have only just graduated from nappies, yet the first business books about how best to manage and exploit a new generation are already upon us. They provide a rich and horrifying insight into how business leaders view the young.

A gem of this genre comes to us from Bruce Tulgan, an author who has previously written about how best to manage Generation X, of which he is a part, and millennials. The latter book is called *Not Everyone Gets a Trophy: How to Manage the Millennials*. It teaches its readers how to deliver hard truths to my own generation who, in the great American tradition, were corrupted by a childhood in which everyone was given a trophy for participation in group sports. (More on this in a minute.) But now that we've established what's wrong with millennials, it's time to ask ourselves: what's wrong with the next generation? Tulgan gives us the answer in his 2015 book, *Bridging the Soft Skills Gap: How to Teach the Missing Basics to Today's Young Talent*. The 'soft skills', which Tulgan also calls 'the old-fashioned basics', include 'professionalism, critical thinking and followership.' There are many problems which result from this, including the following list, which Tulgan says he has learned from managers attempting to wrangle Generation Z:

They are unprofessional.
They have no self-awareness.
They don't take personal responsibility or hold themselves
  accountable.
They need an attitude adjustment.
Their work habits are terrible.
Their people skills are terrible.
They don't know how to think, learn or communicate without
  checking a device.
They don't think critically. They don't know how to problem-
  solve, make decisions and plan.
They have problems deferring to authority.
They don't appreciate context and see where they fit in.
They have no sense of self-sacrifice for the greater good.
Whatever happened to citizenship, service and teamwork?[4]

Yikes! 'Today's young talent' sound rubbish indeed. The trouble, as you can probably guess, is that 'Gen Zers grew up spending most of their time ensconced in their own highly customised safety zones.' Tulgan does what so many have done before him: he constructs a fictional snowflake character on whom we can blame our grievances, and whose failings highlight our own comparative glory. This time, the snowflake is an employee who displays an entitlement, and who has a fear of danger and inconvenience. And that's not all. Tulgan shares an anecdote of a young person not being taken seriously at work despite his enormous technical skill – because he said 'like' too much. (His workplace sent him to a class instead of getting over it.) As with the many critics of snowflakes on campus, the authors writing about how best to extract profit from terrible spoiled children pinpoint a lack of respect for authority and the 'ancient wisdom' of the workplace. Gen Zers, Tulgan writes, 'expect authority figures to always be in their corner, to set them up for success and to be of service.' They are 'a rising global youth-tide of "Little Emperors" who have been told their whole lives that "all styles are equally valid".' In short, they think they're special when they're actually not.

In presenting the supposed problem that Gen Zers present to today's employers, Tulgan resorts to the same kind of critique that we often hear about snowflakey university students. He complains that Gen Zers think that 'all styles are equally valid' and says this is all part of a trend 'away from conformism and toward a broad cultural relativism.' In this, he seems to blame young people's irritating tendencies to be accepting of different kinds of people and behaviours on, I don't know, Michel Foucault. Tulgan does admit that 'cultural relativism' can be a good way to escape 'oppressively hierarchical systems and one-size-fits-all rules,' however: 'Sometimes, conforming makes a lot of sense.' The conformity he craves for the workplace, and advises in his book, has little to do with 'hard skills'. It's a generational comportment, and an uppityness. He imagines a case of a Gen Zer being interviewed to help illustrate this point. The character of the job candidate has 'impressive freshly minted credentials – especially in-demand technical skills.' She comes in for an interview and says the following speech, while staring at her phone, of course:

> I have, like, the hard skills they need? So they, like, shouldn't care so much about the soft skills. So I come in a little late or leave a little early or blow off the occasional meeting?? So what?! They should just, like, tell me what they need me to do?? Give me, like, the resources I need?? And I'll, like, get the job done?? Why do they keep, like, insisting I do everything their way?? Their way, like, makes no sense?? My way is, like, so much easier?? And I'm, like, not afraid to say so!!

I love this bit of creative writing in a business book. What a perfectly detestable imaginary person. How the style of punctuation transports us to the conference room where sits this silly girl and her in-demand technical skills. If you strip away the loathsome 'likes' and exclamation marks, however, it sort of sounds like this made-up interviewee has some great points despite her tardiness. It sounds like her managers really *shouldn't* insist she does everything their way, and really *should* give her the resources she needs. How fearless she is, for having the gumption to say her way is better! But that isn't what matters, apparently. The characteristics that might call to mind a visionary entrepreneur in an older man – lateness, lack of concern for old ways of doing things, breaking rules that don't matter – are the source of *utmost* shame in a young woman.

Who gets to think they are special in a workplace? Entire companies are founded on the cultivation of a leader's brand of rule-breaking, mischievous genius. They are college dropouts, like Mark Zuckerberg. They wear hoodies to work, like Jonah Peretti. But when young people do it – particularly if they aren't white men – they have an attitude that needs to be fixed. The way they *look* is wrong. The way they *sound* is wrong. And worst of all, according to Tulgan, they give too much weight to their 'gut feelings'. Feelings can indeed get in the way of a profitable business. (Except, I suppose, when a CEO makes a wild swerve in his strategy due to a 'gut feeling', as CEOs are wont to do.) When it comes to Gen Zers, Tulgan writes, 'their gratitude is not bottomless nor is it without conditions.' But is this such a bad thing? For Tulgan – and the kinds of bad managers every one of us has encountered at work – it absolutely is. 'Even the young superstars nowadays,' he writes, 'don't seem to come in early, stay late, work through meals and weekends and holidays, bend over backward and jump through hoops like the young superstars of yesteryear did.'

Firstly, of course these people still exist. They stay in the office late, but they also bring their work home with them and work at all hours. There is never a time of day when a millennial couldn't, or shouldn't, be working. In an economy which rewards fewer and fewer people with more, and punishes the rest with less, the pressure to work through the weekend will not make the difference between a regular life and a fabulously successful one. It may make the difference between home ownership and renting in a precarious market for your entire life. In America, it's the difference between having health care and going bankrupt if you break your arm. Not only are the stakes higher, but it's harder than ever to actually disconnect from work, thanks to the nightmares we still call phones in our pockets. During the pandemic and ensuing recession, the pressures to be working, whether at home or in person, have grown ten times more acute.

A study from the US Travel Association – a non-profit lobbying organisation for the domestic travel industry – revealed some depressing data about how hard young people work. Millennials were found to be more likely than other age groups to forfeit unused vacation days – twenty-four per cent give up their vacation time for work, despite receiving so little anyway. (American workers at the beginning of their careers are lucky to get ten days' paid time off each year.) The *Harvard Business Review* refers to this and other studies about 'work martyrdom', which have found that millennials feel more shame about taking holidays, and also shame others for doing so.[5] Millennial managers are also less likely to approve employees' time-off requests. Which makes us dickheads, yes, but not for the reasons a snowflake critic might assume.

It's dubious at best, then, to suggest that millennials are less hard-working than their older peers. But more importantly: if it were true, is it actually a bad thing if young people don't want to 'work through meals'? Is the future a place where we want to work harder, longer and for less? That may be a manager's dream – but should it be ours? Or should we hope to feel less miserable at work?

During our union drive, BuzzFeed's implicit approach was that we were simply too sensitive. We felt too much. We needed to buck up and deal with bad situations, because our managers had done the same. We should be less miserable. We should ask for less. We should feel less. (Though ironically, I have to add, one of their first responses to our letter requesting union recognition was to tell us that WE had hurt THEIR feelings.)

Feelings, it turns out, are deeply uncomfortable not just to bosses, but to snowflake haters wherever we find them.

It is perhaps the most famous line of conservative American columnist, speaker, podcaster and author Ben Shapiro: 'Facts don't care about your feelings.' He tweeted this line in February 2016, and it has received well over 140 thousand retweets. If you are a healthy and blessed enough person to not spend much or any time on Twitter, know that this is a rarely achieved level of engagement on the accursed platform. Shapiro has pinned it to the top of his profile, to ensure it does not get swept away by his dozens of daily tweets. It is central to his philosophy, and to the world view of his millions of followers: if you feel badly, we don't care.

This idea is first of all pretty meaningless. Which facts are we talking about? Which feelings? But it's also absolutely wrong. The truth is facts care very much about your feelings. And those most devoted to Shapiro feel very strongly about many things. Some seem to spend most of their time in a rage. Of course they feel a lot, and often. And those feelings lead them to decide what is, and is not, fact.

Feelings are not a little sideshow to the main event of your life. They are not something which gets in the way of the real you – they *are* you. The way we feel determines the quality of our lives. And what we believe to be facts can depend a lot on how we feel. Yale has a whole centre devoted to feelings: the Yale Center for Emotional Intelligence. Its director, Marc Brackett, wrote a book called *Permission to Feel*, which explains how we have come to be so suspicious of our feelings.

In the first place, we inherit our perspective on feelings from our parents, and then we pass our feelings about feelings to our own children. 'Our kids receive the message loud and clear, so that before long, they, too, have learned to suppress even the most urgent messages from deep inside their beings,' Brackett writes. As a consequence of this, 'we go a little numb inside.'⁶ While we think we may be successfully bottling up our feelings so as not to bother others or ourselves with our pesky emotions, they don't actually go away. They fester.

Feelings are also information in their own right. Certain feelings like fear are crucial to our survival and developed in the deepest part of our lizard brains. It's funny to think about now, but psychologists for the most part did not view emotions as all that important to their work before the 1980s. Feelings were 'extraneous noise, useless static,' explains Brackett. Even before this, many philosophers of Ancient Greece believed that emotions were 'erratic, idiosyncratic sources of information,' the very opposite of intelligence. They were what got in the way of reason, what a good thinking philosopher would aspire to. Since then, 'a great deal of Western literature, philosophy and religion ... has taught us that emotions are a kind of internal interference that gets in the way of sound judgement and rational thought.' This is the tradition that a certain strain of conservatism has picked up on. Ben Shapiro carries this mantle to us from the Ancient Greeks, or so he would have us believe. Great Men of Reason have been battling sensitive snowflakes and their meddlesome feelings since the dawn of ancient civilisation, it seems. If you do spend some time on Twitter, you will have met the acolytes of this philosophy. They're the ones who tell you that sure, eugenics might be morally reprehensible, but rationally speaking, of course it 'works'. (They are Richard Dawkins tweeting this in February 2020.)[7]

Emotions affect every part of how we interact with the world. To deny their existence or their power is silly – even if you think you are the most cool-headed rational genius brainiac ever to have walked the earth. It is also patently clear that some people are much more emotionally intelligent than others. In 1990 Peter Salovey and John Mayer defined 'emotional intelligence' as 'the ability to monitor one's own and other's feelings and emotions, to discriminate among them and to use this information to guide one's thinking and actions.' Nowadays, 'emotional intelligence' is used as an excuse for why the only woman in the office should do all the difficult emotional labour like dealing with interpersonal problems and, of course, planning the Christmas party. She's just so *emotionally intelligent*. (Note: you do not get a pay rise for being emotionally intelligent.)

Facts care so much about your feelings that your feelings shape your perception of what you might think is an objective assessment of the world. Studies have shown that teachers grade the same papers differently according to their mood at the time of marking, and that high-powered individuals 'respond with less compassion than people with less power when listening to someone describe suffering,' explains Brackett. Some of us may have encountered such people at work. They're the ones who make more money than us.

So why do we ignore feelings, good or bad?

Well, if we *did* pay better attention to our feelings, we might quit our jobs en masse. Brackett's research at Yale has found that 'high-school students, teachers and business professionals experience negative emotions up to seventy per cent of the time they are in school or at work.' This isn't a strong sign that things are going well in America. If we took these feelings seriously, what would change? A four-day week? Less pressure to pass standardised tests? More flexibility to work at home? A society that thought a lot more about feelings might be a revolutionary one.

Not only do facts care about your feelings, feelings create facts in your body. We have seen this in the effects of trauma, but even more straightforward feelings can take their physical toll as well. Anger, in particular, is linked to heart trouble in medical research. Brackett refers to research which shows that 'men reporting the highest levels of anger were over two and a half times more likely to suffer cardiac events such as heart attack than other men.' Another good reason to log off from time to time.

The feelings of young workers should be information for managers. Instead, they are seen as threatening or simply embarrassing. A key discomfort with snowflakes, especially at work, is that they demand their feelings be taken seriously. This can be awkward, yes. Feelings can be terribly uncomfortable to talk about. But beyond simple discomfort, the recognition of young workers' feelings might force a workplace to change. If a manager makes everyone feel like absolute shit, that manager might have to lose their job. If a lot of people were very, very angry about pay discrepancies, they may have to be corrected. Our failed union was, in many ways, a way to channel a lot of feelings into systemic change.

It is a powerful tool, then, to convince people that feelings are embarrassing and juvenile. Feelings of hurt and outrage, at least: in many workplaces, including newsrooms, certain feelings are romanticised and celebrated. Who doesn't love when an editor in a film about journalism rages at his young reporter about a fuck-up? This, though, is a sexier emotion than what most people feel at work, most of the time: misery.

This misery can stem from a number of places: harassment, terrible bosses and discrimination among them. Whatever the cause, though, companies faced with unhappy employees would rather recommend or subsidise various mental health apps so that staffers can sort out their broken mental health on their own time. NBC reported that when employees at Google complained about racism and sexism at work, the company told them to undergo treatment for their mental health.[8] It is easier for a company to put people on mental health leave than to address the root problems affecting their employees of colour. (A Google spokeswoman told NBC that the company supports employees who raise such concerns and investigates complaints 'rigorously'.) In other cases, as certainly happened at *BuzzFeed*, a company will tell its disgruntled employees to learn strategies of wellness and self-care. The thing is, what employees most often need is not an app that teaches guided meditation, but more money.

More money is a simple but unpopular a way to alleviate misery. The people who say that money can't buy happiness tend to be people who do not have to worry about money every day. A study published in the British Medical Journal in January 2020 found that a $1 increase in the minimum wage led to a 3.4 to 5.9 per cent decrease in the rate of suicide among eighteen- to sixty-four-year-old adults with a high school education or less.[9]

The precarity of low-wage work can devastate a life. But in our modern capitalistic hellscape, that's a cost-cutting measure that many companies are willing to take. Never did we see this more acutely than during the pandemic, when many large corporations placed their production and their profits ahead of their employees' health.

There has to be a better way.

Millennials, at least in America, have long been mocked for their supposed addiction to 'participation trophies'. I know that Britain is less organised around the cult of youth sports, so allow me to explain: when a kid in America participates in a sport, such as swimming, you get many little ribbons or trophies for your first-, second- and third-place finishers. On my neighbourhood swim team, we got ribbons all the way to eighth place: the maximum number of lanes our pool could accommodate. At the end of the season, the best swimmers got big trophies and much applause while we ate cold pasta off paper plates in the community centre. But the rest of us slowpokes, myself included, also got a trophy: a little one which simply said, you were here too, you took part, well done. I lined up my trophies and my eighth-place ribbons on top of my bookcase at home. I still love swimming to this day.

The participation trophy, though, has become central to the theory that millennials were corrupted by an overly happy childhood, and have become lazy and irritating workers as a result. The participation trophy is largely to blame for creating a generation of snowflakes, in the eyes of snowflake critics. The idea is that if all the children get a fun trophy to bring home with them from their talent show, swimming meet or art competition, all children will become convinced, forever, that it's fine to be rubbish. As a result of receiving a participation trophy, a child might not even spot the lesson that they're actually a fucking loser – and we'll all be the worse for it. In the good old days, when our noble grandparents took place in competitive sports, only the first-place runner would win the pack of cigarettes, and the rest would be sent back down the mines without supper, and that's how they won World War II. Participation trophies, on the other hand, turned us all into wild little narcissists.

I asked the psychotherapist and author Philippa Perry about the 'danger' of participation trophies. She reminded me first of all that it's actually not a bad thing to make a child feel good, but she hadn't heard of the participation trophy panic specifically and assumed it 'must be a cute little American problem.' She was right. But she shared her thoughts anyway: 'I think we must remember that children are people. And what makes us feel good, bad or particularly narcissistic and out of control will make a child feel good, bad or particularly narcissistically out of control.'

The irony might be that if you *only* give a trophy to the winner, that could lead to its own kind of trouble. 'That winner might think they're nothing without the trophy,' Perry explains, 'and then that develops narcissistic traits where the shiny outside shell counts, or what you feel on the inside counts a little bit less.' Perhaps participation trophies are the only chance we have against mass greed and exploitation. You don't have to win or crush your enemies to get something in this life. Sometimes you can just do your best, and that is fine. Perhaps participation trophies actually make us a little less competitive in things that there is no reason to be competitive about. Perhaps they let us look to our sides at the swim meet and see our comrades, not our competitors. Swimmers of the world, unite!

The wider conceptual problem with the participation trophy panic, though, is that millennial childhoods, and now Gen Z childhoods, were not and are not defined by the idea that no matter how well you did, in school or in sports or in creative pursuits, you'd be just fine. Perhaps very wealthy children could think this way, however even for them, there is, presumably, a large amount of pressure to become prime minister. Sorry to those children. For most of us, though, millennials and Gen Zers either graduated high school or college into worldwide recession or grew up in the knowledge of an economy that favoured only a few at the top. Malcolm Harris, author of *Kids These Days: Human Capital and the Making of Millennials*, argues that the millennial childhood was 'a capital project', in which endless investment and structured time was poured into those lucky enough to have attentive parents of means, in an attempt to get a return on parents' investments in the form of a wealthy or at least middle-class child. The problem is, Harris notes, millennials are the most educated generation, with the highest amount of 'human capital' – but we're also worse off, economically speaking, than our parents, grandparents and great-grandparents.

This is due to many things: crushing student debt in the United States (and in a future UK, if certain politicians get their way). We also live in a paradigm in which there is literally no time of day in which our jobs cannot reach us. Our jobs are also hollowed out: we are either paid shit wages, or flounce about within a wild and luxurious upper echelon of salary. There is little in between. Our jobs are also less stable. The fear of being fired or losing income is *incredibly* motivating. It's also crushing. Between 1948 and 2016 productivity rose among American workers by 241.1 per cent, while hourly wages only grew by 112.5 per cent. In the recovery from the 2008 recession, corporate profits saw a fifty per cent increase between 2009 and 2014, while employee compensation between 2008 and 2013 rose only 9.5% per cent. Buying a home in the cities where high-paid work can be found is out of reach unless you already come from money. We do more work for less compensation, as the boundary between work and home crumbles to dust. The pandemic only accelerated these processes.

Maybe millennials do crave participation trophies: the trophy of a safe place to live, of a stable job, of a pension and time off and dignity. These are the things that should come with participation in a modern society, whether you're a loser or a winner. And maybe the people who fear participation trophies *actually* fear a world where everyone got something to take home, even if they didn't beat the competition.

A surprisingly searing critique of participation trophies and millennials in the workplace comes from a book written by a member of Gen Z, Jonah Stillman, along with his Gen X father, David, who travels all over America consulting on generational differences in the workplace. Their book from 2017, *Gen Z @ Work: How the next generation is transforming the workplace*, actually made me feel a deep solidarity with Baby Boomers, who the Gen X/Z pair come for with as much scorn as for millennials.

The trouble with millennials, according to this father/son pairing, is that they were raised by boomers, who believed that 'every child was a snowflake – truly one of a kind.' Not only that:

> Boomer parents wanted to instil a lot of self-esteem in their Millennial children . . . The result was Millennials with delu-sional goals of being CEO and leaders who were pushed to their limits managing and even tempering Millennials' expectations about getting ahead.[10]

And yet while millennials apparently all want to immediately be CEO – they also suffer a little too much camaraderie for the authors' tastes: 'Millennials were told by Boomer parents that if everyone works together, everyone can benefit and there doesn't have to be just one winner.' This is, as you can probably guess, because of the many participation trophies we received in our childhoods. Gen Z, by contrast, is much more ruthlessly competitive, according to the authors. And folks, that's what a business needs. The Stillmans contend that the problem with millennials is that we grew up pre-recession and were jam-packed with far too much self-esteem. This means that millennials 'showed up at work and often felt that the job was lucky to have them.' Gen Z, meanwhile, grew up crushed by their parents' struggle with global recession, and as a result, they'll do anything to get ahead: 'Gen Z will show up and feel they are lucky to have a job.' I tend to think it would affect you more to graduate directly *into* a recession, as most millennials did, and Gen Z now will too, in the midst of the pandemic. But I don't know a single millennial apart from a few rich-os who doesn't feel the pressure of precarity. Also, data shows that millennials are on course to be worse off than those who came before *and* after them. But that's not the argument this father-son pair is making. Their task is to tell you how to exploit young people to work harder for less money. That's not how they put it, of course, but, well, that's why people buy such books.

While the boomers produced inefficient workers, though, the Stillmans argue that Gen Xers, being less hippy-dippy than the boomers, instilled their Gen Z children with a hard-scrabble, desperate longing for menial work. They do wonder, to be fair, whether 'all of the Xers' straight talk has gone too far,' as they have heard from many teachers 'who felt Gen Z was very serious and at times too serious.' The fundamental but unspoken tension in this inter-generational analysis, it seems, is the question of whether we want our children to be happy or whether we want them to climb a career ladder to dizzying heights.

Millennials enjoy collaboration, according to the Stillmans' studies. But the way to get Gen Z to work is to set them against each other. The book advises employers to take advantage of their unmatched digital fluency, and that Gen Z's deep digitally produced FOMO (fear of missing out) will make them 'an asset in the sales and marketing department.' Why? Because young people 'will know exactly how to make potential buyers fear that they might be missing out on something big and that they had better buy it if they want to stay on the cutting edge. Deploying FOMO will help make a potential customer feel as though what they already have will never be good enough.' Charming!

According to the authors' data, they have 'forty-two per cent of Gen Z saying they would rather finish a project on their own and get special recognition than finish the project with a group and everyone receives credit.' Millennials, meanwhile, 'will likely feel offended' when Gen Z arrives in their workplaces 'and doesn't immediately join in for a round of kumbaya.' The authors call Gen Z's apparent hard-won scrappiness, in the face of crushing economic precocity in their childhoods, 'resilience'. But what kind of resilience is this? If you are to buy the Stillmans' argument, you would be thrilled to learn that Gen Z, despite a few wacky digital-dependent ways, are primed for exploitation. The Stillmans write: 'what others would see as just a bad third quarter, Gen Z might see as a death sentence.' This is a desperately sad vision of work.

But are Gen Z really so resilient and cut-throat? Or are they just terrified of the working world they are about to inherit – one which, after the pandemic, is more unequal than ever before?

When Millennials and Generation Z enter the workforce, they are usually met, as I have seen in ridiculous business books and personal experience alike, with scorn and judgement. (I presume the same will be true when today's babies are tomorrow's interns.) This can be for the way they talk, for their tendency to see themselves as special and/or get easily upset in the manner of a snowflake, or if they dress too ~kooky~ for an old-fashioned workplace. But they also are derided for their ideas about what might be possible from the world of work. A snowflake in the workplace wonders aloud: 'What if we didn't have to work so hard?' And most of them ask this while working basically non-stop, with little hope in sight for home ownership, freedom from debt or a stable life. This isn't even necessarily a vision of the future. The thing young people may long for may even look like the past, when a forty-hour work week was developed with the understanding that every employee had a nice little wife at home, padding around the kitchen, taking care of the cooking, cleaning and child-rearing. We long for a time when one salary could buy a dignified life for an entire family.

In August of 2019, Microsoft's Japan office conducted an experiment with their employees: what if they only worked for four days a week? It was called the Work-Life Choice Challenge Summer 2019, in which 2,300 Microsoft employees got the same pay they had before – but five Fridays off in a row.[11] By the end of the month, the company found that its employees were not only forty per cent more productive, getting more work done in a shorter amount of time, but they were happier, too. They also took fewer unexpected days off, and the company saved money on utilities. Ninety-three per cent of employees reported that they liked the four-day week. (The other seven per cent were probably sucking up.) Similar experiments have produced similar results – whether lessening the hours or days worked each week.

Consider this: what if better technology and innovation meant people had to work less, not more? The trait that apparently makes the snowflake such a bane to managers is a tendency to ask for more. For more care from their employer, more accommodation for their differences and abilities. More time for themselves and more flexibility. Less rigid hierarchies at work. What if *this* was a sign of progress, rather than employees squeezed further into misery and depression? Sadly, though, our fearless economic leaders instead see increased productivity bought by a larger workforce and technological gains as a way to push everyone even further, to generate ever more profit for themselves. It can only be so long before a new generation of workers objects to this arrangement.

The reasons people hate snowflakes – a sensitivity, a fragility, an obsession with 'woke'-ness – are all bad-faith arguments not particularly grounded in reality, as we have seen. But they're also traits that make a snowflake a terrible capitalist. A true snowflake isn't greedy enough, isn't profit-obsessed and isn't willing to sacrifice their morality or their health to get ahead. Snowflake critics fear that this really could obliterate the working world as we know it.

Many of the anti-snowflake books and columns and breathy podcast episodes say the world is on the brink of ruin, chaos and horror, while it was in fact very nice and good in the commentator's own childhood. Conversely, the world was also an impossibly difficult place in the commentators' own childhoods, while kids today have it easy. Do not dwell too long on this, it is simply so. Either way you look at it, what causes a snowflake critic the greatest concern is never that Bad Things Occur, but rather, The Reaction To Bad Things Is Too Extreme.

What people choose to get mad about reveals everything about their politics and their privilege. Of course, there are many problems in this hell world, and we can all choose what hills we want to die on. But the anti-snowflake discourse is riddled with rage not at bad things, but at reactions to bad things. They see the problem as people 'piling on' those who have been racist online. The actual problem is that people are racist, and with social media, we get to witness white people making the kinds of statements they might normally reserve for all-white company. They see the problem as young people being too difficult at work, when the actual problem is that much work is awful and endless and wages are stagnant even as the cost of buying a first home slips ever more out of reach.

The things people choose to get mad over also reveal the dividing and stupefying force of social class. After university, I worked at the Arab Cultural and Community Center in San Francisco for two years, tutoring kids who had recently arrived from Yemen or Syria and were living in social housing in the Tenderloin neighbourhood of San Francisco. While their families kept immaculate homes in the building, children who lived in this housing witnessed daily violence and poverty on their streets. They had a wisdom about drugs that outpaces my own to this day. At eight years old, they could tell what was being dealt out the window of our tutoring classroom. As educators and social workers, my colleagues and I had to be on alert for more insidious traumas our kids might be facing, and so we were trained in how to spot signs of physical and sexual abuse of children. Each lesson was a depressing look into the crimes faced by children with abusive home lives. Abuse can and does derail a life forever.

Each day, the training ended at around the same time that Terry Gross's show *Fresh Air* began to play on NPR. (For those not familiar, Terry Gross hosts an hour-long public radio program in the US featuring interviews with important cultural figures. It's a bit like Radio 4's *Desert Island Discs*, without the island or the discs.) This meant that when my colleague Shiva and I, utterly depressed, would get into my car to return to our office from the abuse trainings, we would hear the intro to Gross's program. After one particularly grim lecture about sexual abuse of children, we turned on the radio to hear Gross introduce a man who had made it his life work to improve Google Maps or something. Shiva and I burst into despairing laughter. I threw my arms in the air and yelled, 'THIS IS NOT WHAT THE PROBLEM IS!' It became a theme.

Obviously, arts programming is good, and Terry Gross is wonderful, and people can care both about technology development and abused children. But after that incident, Shiva and I began to encounter more and more moments of saying to each other 'that's not what the problem is'. In 2012, the Tenderloin neighbourhood where we worked was experiencing the first cautious encroachments of gentrification. One day, after hours of struggling with the kids in our care, who laboured through large piles of homework in a language they were only just beginning to understand, living in overcrowded apartments with the ghosts of the wars of their home countries, Shiva and I walked down Market Street to find a new pop-up. A 'pop-up' is usually a temporary business in an otherwise disused, often post-industrial space. This one was in an empty former restaurant. We could see many a bearded and beanied hipster inside sitting at long rows with typewriters. Curious, we asked the man at the door what the gathering was for. 'This is a device-free space,' he smugly explained. 'People aren't allowed to have their phones. Instead they have to interact with each other.' Behind him, we could see people quietly tapping away at typewriters, ignoring each other. We thanked him politely and walked away. Once out of earshot, we turned to each other with a wild look in our eyes and whispered: 'That's not what the problem is.'

Again, there are so many problems a person is entitled to worry about day to day. But if a person worries about, say, *the kids these days are on their phones too much*, and not also, for example, *millions of children in our supposedly rich country live in desperate poverty*, you are not a person concerned about the betterment of society. You are a person who enjoys grumbling about the people who are concerned with the betterment of society.

This is, I think, an endemic problem with media, especially in Britain. The people who write books, who write columns, who go on the radio to hold forth about the issues of the day, are impossibly removed from the worst of Britain's problems. They are largely white and middle class. They are removed, and do not even know themselves to be removed.

It's fine and natural to worry about young people. They're there to be worried about. They throw themselves off roofs into swimming pools and take drugs and finger each other in parking lots. It's all very stressful, I get it. But we should be excited about the protests of students and union organisers whose intention is greater equality and justice in society and in their workplaces – even if you think they have gone about it wrong. History is not linear, and the progress for workers that has been won across time must be actively defended each and every day. Young people happen to have the most energy to do this.

And even if your young colleagues irritate you when they advocate for themselves and their colleagues – *that's not what the problem is.*

As I write this, strands of messenger RNA are percolating throughout my body, teaching my immune system how to recognise a new threat, and to protect me from COVID-19. Less than a year after a novel coronavirus wreaked havoc on the world, a stunning, futuristic feat of science has brought us a way to stop this pandemic. The success of mRNA vaccines has opened up a new world of possibility in vaccinations for other kinds of disease.

In mid-2019, I visited the vaccination labs at the National Institutes of Health as a producer on an assignment for the *Washington Post*. My colleague, the science journalist Anna Rothschild, interviewed the nation's leading infectious disease expert, Dr Anthony Fauci, about his excitement for the future of mRNA vaccines. They sounded, then, like a distant fantasy. Not long afterwards, they were a reality, and a world-saving one. (He also said his greatest fear was a global pandemic. He was right!)

The pandemic changed everything in the world, and it changed everything about work. It heightened shocking divides between rich and poor, those who could work from home, and those who had to show up and risk their lives. On one side of the spectrum, it showed that much professional work could be done without commutes, and expensive clothes, and time away from family and children. On the other, it showed that when it comes down to it, many businesses are willing to accept the sickness and death of their employees in order to protect profits and productivity.

When we finally leave the pandemic behind us (I hope!), we have a choice to decide if the lesson of the pandemic is that workers can work less and enjoy life more, or if it's that workers can be exploited to a level never before achieved. Is the lesson that people can work less while protecting not only productivity, but their happiness – or is it that they can be used, and even killed, in a crisis?

To make sure it's not the latter lesson we take away from this terrible time, it will take the insistence of young people that they deserve dignity at work. That even in a precarious economy, they deserve to be treated with respect, free from harassment and discrimination, and most of all, to be paid what they're worth.

The project of denigrating young people, and calling them snow-flakes, is a way to denigrate the values that they demand and fight for: of equality, of respect, and of the right to log off and enjoy a life outside of work – just as previous generations could. Making fun of these demands, or casting snowflakes as entitled and ungrateful, only serves the rich and the powerful.

Nobody wants their boss or their colleagues to think they're a snowflake. But it's snowflakes who will make work less miserable for all of us.

Conclusion

With Donald Trump's disappearance from politics and public life – for now, anyway – it may be tempting to believe that we will also get a reprieve from the kind of nonsense culture-war discourse that he fuelled with such skill and energy. Nobody knows better than the former president how to use simple, derogatory language to skewer his political enemies and arouse the passions of his tens of millions of supporters. Trump entered office on a tide of resentment at an unequal society, carefully laundered into votes for his toxic brand of politics. He is the greatest living proof of the fact that being accused of racism, sexism and all-around 'political incorrectness' will not get you banished from public life – nor 'cancelled' – but elevated to enormous cultural power. With Trump gone – *for now* – will the culture wars also wither?

My most rational, logical, deepest lobster brain knows that they will not. The machine that fed and was fed by Trumpism is stronger than ever. Media channels of every variety have come to use culture-war arguments as a sustaining life force, generating outrage based on stories that, like so many Great Snowflake Panics we have seen, are either totally fictitious or whipped into a bad-faith argument. The only difference, in a post-Trump era, is that without the firehose of news to occupy us, ridiculous claims about snowflakes and students and cancelling and free speech and *the mob* will have even more room to thrive. An outrage news cycle that in the Trump era would have been quickly knocked off the front pages – for instance, the one about the estate of children's author Dr Seuss deciding to stop publication of several of his lesser-known books which contain racist imagery – can thrive for *weeks* instead of hours. The Trump years were a constant barrage of terrible news, one thing after another, and often many things in one day. With him gone, it's up to media to not get dragged into moral panics because there is simply not much else going on. I don't have faith that media, particularly in Britain, is up to that task.

To that end, we must travel through this stupid world holding tightly and confidently to our sense of selves, not letting powerful, petty interests define what young people are. We must confidently believe in what we know about ourselves. And here's what we know:

We know that the term 'snowflake' is wielded to distract, to belittle, and to diminish the arguments, identities and political power of young people, poor people, LGBTQ+ people and people of colour. We know that the fear and hatred of snowflakes can not only suck people in, it can obsess people. We know that the term snowflake has its origins in the far right and has arrived in the mainstream. We know how the language of mental health has been used to make fun of young people. We know that calling someone a snowflake is a way to silence people who push and break the boundaries of the status quo. We know that it's a way to discount the actions and speech of people of colour who demand active change to a racist society, and to trans and non-binary people whose very existence threatens an old-fashioned understanding of gender. We know it's a way to ridicule workers who want a fair deal. We know that when a white person is called a snowflake by another white person, it is an attempt to embarrass and chastise them in the hopes they will abandon their allyship. We know that many people with very large platforms in media and politics are more concerned with the feelings of statues than the feelings of people.

We know that if you are called a snowflake, you have very likely said or done something to push against the constraints of centuries of expectations about your place in society. Congratulations! You have probably been very irritating to someone who needs very badly to be irritated.

We also know that to be a snowflake is to be a lifelong student, and to have the tenacity to keep on learning about yourself and the world, even when it makes you uncomfortable. The snowflake critic cringes every time they see a news story about seemingly over-the-top student protests. The snowflake may cringe at first, too, but knows that anything that makes you cringe might, if you dig a little deeper, teach you something about the world that you didn't know before.

Don't get me wrong, at the end of all this, I still believe that snow-flake is an extremely silly term. It means so many different silly things to so many different silly people, that sometimes it means very little at all. But being silly doesn't mean this word is harmless. In its simplicity and flexibility, 'snowflake' can be a powerful term indeed.

Treasured reader, if you've made it to the bitter end of this journey into the heart of snowflakery, I offer you a challenge. From now on, when you are called a snowflake, or someone around you is called a snowflake, or if someone even *implies* that they are disgusted, angry or uncomfortable with snowflake activities, I want you to ask yourself why. Better yet, ask *them* why they have used that term. What you may learn may say more about them than about you.

The term snowflake is a weapon to neutralise a challenge to the status quo, from outside or from within. And in every example I have heard of someone being called a snowflake, there seemed to be no good way to respond. In some instances, particularly online, it can be possible or amusing to simply ignore it. But it's less easy when the person calling you a snowflake is a colleague or a relative. And worst of all, a person who calls you a snowflake is probably not just a good old-fashioned arsehole. I mean, they probably *are* a good old-fashioned arsehole, but in calling you a 'snowflake' rather than a 'prick' or an 'idiot', they may be something even worse. They may be revealing their membership of or at least interest in the politics of the alt-right. Maybe they heard it in *Fight Club*. Maybe they saw it in a column in the *Sunday Times*. Or maybe they read it on a white nationalist forum. Maybe they want to hurt you, or maybe they just want to get a rise out of you, or both. You can't know, and that's threatening, and being threatened is the point.

The next time you are called a snowflake – or consider calling someone else one – I want you to think about who you have threatened with your speech or behaviour – or what you feel threatened by. Ask yourself what could have forced someone to reach for a silly insult with a dark political origin. Ask yourself what and who you are protecting when you wield the term yourself. The next time you are called a snowflake, you might like the answers to these questions. The next time you call someone a snowflake, you might not.

Perhaps the only way to react to being called a snowflake, if it does upset you, is to say so. And then, when they point out that – *Ha! See how sensitive you are?* – then you can say, maybe, yes, but I'd rather be too sensitive than a racist, a twat, a bigot, a homophobe, a petty and vindictive and cruel person flailing fruitlessly against the tide of their own irrelevance. Being a snowflake isn't the worst thing to be. Chances are, if you are called a snowflake, it's evidence that you are a principled and compassionate person.

Snowflakes push against the constraining forces of society. They blow apart expectations of race, class and gender. They fight against the inequities of capitalism. They see feelings not as distractions from, but tools in the quest for greater knowledge of ourselves and of others.

Can the fiercest snowflake critics ever be convinced to step away from their all-encompassing world views, which pin all manner of ills on the snowflake? I'm not sure they can. But I'm also not hopeless, because I think that if *most* people understand that they shouldn't worry about snowflakes, or roll their eyes at them, or believe everything they hear about them, then that will be enough. We can develop a societal immunity to nonsense. We can find the antidote to the poison that bad actors in politics and media are slipping into our daily diets.

I'm hopeful that someday it will be embarrassing for snowflake critics to look back on the things they claimed about today's young people. Perhaps they will even pretend to have always supported the snowflake's project of reducing the sum of human misery. I'm hopeful that snowflakes themselves will have the last laugh and will not stop being exactly who they are.

We need snowflakes too much to continue to diminish and ridicule and persecute them in this way. We need to support the snowflakes in our lives, and understand them, and learn from them. We need them to thrive and enter politics and media and become good teachers and examples for whatever wild and inscrutable generation comes next. And more than that, we need to become snowflakes ourselves.

Otherwise, we're all fucked.

References

INTRODUCTION

1 Aristotle. 'Book II – Chapter 12: Aristotle's Rhetoric.' Accessed June 20, 2021. https://kairos.technorhetoric.net/stasis/2017/honeycutt/aristotle/rhet2-12.html.

CHAPTER ONE

1 Stolworthy, Jacob. 'Collins Dictionary's 10 Words of the Year, from "Snowflake Generation" to "JOMO".' *The Independent*, November 3, 2016. https://www.independent.co.uk/arts-entertainment/books/news/collins-dictionary-s-10-word-year-brexit-and-snowflake-generation-jomo-a7395121.html.
2 'Snowflake Generation Definition and Meaning | Collins English Dictionary.' Accessed March 7, 2021. https://www.collinsdictionary.com/dictionary/english/snowflake-generation.
3 'The American Heritage Dictionary Entry: Snowflake.' Houghton Mifflin Harcourt Publishing. Accessed March 10, 2021. https://ahdictionary.com/word/search.html?q=snowflake.
4 'Snowflake, n.' In *OED Online*. Oxford University Press. Accessed March 7, 2021. https://www.oed.com/view/Entry/183512.
5 Harrison, George. 'What Does Snowflake Mean?' *The Sun*, December 4, 2020. https://www.thesun.co.uk/news/5115128/snowflake-term-generation-meaning-origin-use/.

6 Reavis, L. U. *Saint Louis, the Future Great City of the World* . . . Barns, 1876.

7 'No, "Snowflake" as a Slang Term Did Not Begin with "Fight Club".' Accessed March 7, 2021. https://www.merriam-webster.com/words-at-play/the-less-lovely-side-of-snowflake.

8 Grace to You. 'Concerning Spiritual Gifts, Part 3.' Accessed March 14, 2021. https://www.gty.org/library/sermons-library/1850/.

9 Palahniuk, Chuck. *Fight Club*. New York: W.W. Norton & Co, 2005 (1996).

10 'Fight Club Author Chuck Palahniuk Takes Credit for "Snowflakes".' *Evening Standard*, January 24, 2017. https://www.standard.co.uk/news/londoners-diary/londoner-s-diary-chuck-palahniuk-i-coined-snowflake-and-i-stand-by-it-a3448226.html.

11 Schwartz, Dana. 'Why Trump Supporters Love Calling People "Snowflakes".' *GQ*, February 1, 2017. https://www.gq.com/story/why-trump-supporters-love-calling-people-snowflakes.

12 Tait, Amelia. 'The Myth of Generation Snowflake: How Did "Sensitive" Become a Dirty Word?' *The New Statesman*. Accessed March 7, 2021. https://www.newstatesman.com/politics/uk/2017/01/myth-generation-snowflake-how-did-sensitive-become-dirty-word.

13 Silman, Anna. 'For the Alt-Right, Dapper Suits Are a Propaganda Tool.' *The Cut*. Accessed March 7, 2021. https://www.thecut.com/2016/11/how-the-alt-right-uses-style-as-a-propaganda-tool.html.

14 Levin, Josh. 'The Year America's Most Famous White Supremacist Went Mainstream.' Slow Burn: David Duke. Accessed March 14, 2021. https://slate.com/podcasts/slow-burn/s4/david-duke/e1/david-duke-1989-district-81.

15 Evans, Robert. 'Shitposting, Inspirational Terrorism, and the Christchurch Mosque Massacre.' *Bellingcat*. March 15, 2019. https://www.bellingcat.com/news/rest-of-world/2019/03/15/shitposting-inspirational-terrorism-and-the-christchurch-mosque-massacre/.

16 Harkinson, Josh. 'Meet the White Nationalist Trying to Ride the Trump Train to Lasting Power.' *Mother Jones* (blog). Accessed March 7, 2021. https://www.motherjones.com/politics/2016/10/richard-spencer-trump-alt-right-white-nationalist/.

17 Relman, Eliza. 'Steve Bannon Says Ivanka Trump Is "Dumb as a Brick".' *Business Insider*. Accessed March 7, 2021. https://www.businessinsider.com/steve-bannon-says-ivanka-trump-is-dumb-as-a-brick-2018-1.

18 Coppins, McKay. 'Channeling Breitbart from Behind the Resolute Desk.' *The Atlantic*, August 28, 2017. https://www.theatlantic.com/politics/archive/2017/08/breitbart-behind-the-resolute-desk/538239/.

19 Sky News. *Debate: Sexism in Science*, 2015. https://www.youtube.com/watch?v=kBiS4qTsjCg&t=445s.

20 Channel 4 News. *Richard Spencer Interview: How Alt-Right Are Testing the Limits of Free Speech at US Colleges*, 2017. https://www.youtube.com/watch?v=Yc55Xr_avR8.

21 Harkinson, Josh. 'Meet the White Nationalist Trying to Ride the Trump Train to Lasting Power.' *Mother Jones* (blog). Accessed March 7, 2021. https://www.motherjones.com/politics/2016/10/richard-spencer-trump-alt-right-white-nationalist/.

22 Yiannopoulos, Milo. 'Milo Yiannopoulos: Why I'm Winning.' Breitbart, November 24, 2015. https://www.breitbart.com/the-media/2015/11/23/why-im-winning/.

23 Helmore, Edward. 'Milo Yiannopoulos Resigns from Breitbart News over Paedophilia Remarks.' *The Guardian*. February 22, 2017. http://www.theguardian.com/us-news/2017/feb/21/milo-yiannopoulos-resigns-breitbart-pedophilia-comments.

24 Peters, Jeremy W., Alexandra Alter, and Michael M. Grynbaum. 'Milo Yiannopoulos's Paedophilia Comments Cost Him CPAC Role and Book Deal.' *The New York Times*, February 20, 2017. U.S. https://www.nytimes.com/2017/02/20/us/politics/cpac-milo-yiannopoulos.html.

25 Jeb Lund. '"I Support Fat-Shaming" Says Barney-Wearing-a-Teen's-Poplin Top, Wonka-Accident Amazing-Gobstopper-Ass Motherfucker Https://T.Co/EEZ5dtIhPU.' Tweet. *@Mobute* (blog), November 30, 2015. https://twitter.com/Mobute/status/671390539070242816.

26 Beauchamp, Zack. 'Milo Yiannopoulos's Collapse Shows That No-Platforming Can Work.' *Vox*, December 5, 2018. https://www.vox.com/policy-and-politics/2018/12/5/18125507/milo-yiannopoulos-debt-no-platform.

27 Alan White. 'Stunned to Learn Milo Is Now Selling Bottles of Milk Thistle Extract at $20 a Pop on Infowars Https://T.Co/4ZQPkcN7fk.' Tweet. *@aljwhite* (blog), February 21, 2018. https://twitter.com/aljwhite/status/966331474495574016.lion.

28 Bokhari, Allum. 'The Regressive Left Are Losing on American Campuses.' *Breitbart*, March 21, 2016. https://www.breitbart.com/tech/2016/03/21/regressive-left-on-defensive-on-campus/.

29 Fox, Claire. *'I Find That Offensive!'* Biteback Publishing, 2016.

30 Ellis, Emma Grey. 'The Alt-Right Found Its Favourite Cartoonist—and Almost Ruined His Life.' *Wired*. Accessed July 27, 2021. https://www.wired.com/story/ben-garrison-alt-right-cartoonist/.

31 Garrison, Ben. 'Ben Garrison Cartoons – Posts | Facebook.' February 13, 2019. https://www.facebook.com/RealBenGarrisonCartoons/posts/aocs-bar-drink-up-suckers-new-bengarrison-cartoon-for-socialismneverworks-ocasio/2152686838124948/.

32 'Attack of the Cry Bullies – Grrr Graphics.' Accessed March 7, 2021. https://grrrgraphics.com/attack-of-the-cry-bullies-new-ben-garrison-cartoon/.

33 Brent Bozell. 'Unlike the Snowflake Left Four Years Ago, Today Conservatives Were Able to Survive without Having to Hug Teddy Bears, Scream into Pillows, Fill in Coloring Books, Find Crying Rooms and Have Therapy Sessions.' Tweet. @BrentBozell (blog), January 20, 2021. https://twitter.com/BrentBozell/status/1352016478850191362.

34 Lavin, Talia. 'The Far Right's Ironic Snowflake Problem.' The Village Voice, April 26, 2018. https://www.villagevoice.com/2018/04/26/the-harpy-the-far-rights-ironic-snowflake-problem/.

35 Zilinsky, Jan, Jonathan Nagler, and Joshua Tucker. 'Analysis | Which Republicans Are Most Likely to Think the Election Was Stolen? Those Who Dislike Democrats and Don't Mind White Nationalists.' Washington Post. Accessed March 14, 2021. https://www.washington-post.com/politics/2021/01/19/which-republicans-think-election-was-stolen-those-who-hate-democrats-dont-mind-white-nationalists/.

36 Jewell, Hannah. 'Anthony Scaramucci Thinks Trump's "kookoo lala" Tweets Are Holding Him Back.' Washington Post, Accessed July 25, 2021. https://www.washingtonpost.com/video/politics/anthony-scara-mucci-thinks-trumps-kookoo-lala-tweets-are-holding-him-back/2019/07/22/61804c49-9ce0-4b97-b48f-c4edac78b68f_video.html.

37 Schwartz, Dana. 'Why Trump Supporters Love Calling People "Snowflakes".' GQ, February 1, 2017. https://www.gq.com/story/why-trump-supporters-love-calling-people-snowflakes.

38 Nicholson, Rebecca. '"Poor Little Snowflake" – the Defining Insult of 2016.' The Guardian, November 28, 2016. Politics. https://www.theguardian.com/science/2016/nov/28/snowflake-insult-disdain-young-people.

CHAPTER TWO

1 Silverman, Rosa. 'Of Course Oxford Should Serve Its Students Octopus – Not a Snowflake Diet of Anti-Aspirational Mush.' The Telegraph, January 18, 2019. https://www.telegraph.co.uk/news/2019/01/18/course-oxford-should-serve-students-octopus-not-snowflake/.

2 Coren, Giles. 'Uni Is a Safe Space for Alphabetti Spaghetti.' *The Times*, Accessed March 14, 2021. https://www.thetimes.co.uk/article/uni-is-a-safe-space-for-alphabetti-spaghetti-m5vrrgvt0.

3 Sitwell, William. 'Take Octopus off the Menu? What Utter Cretinous Stupidity.' *The Telegraph*, January 18, 2019. https://www.telegraph.co.uk/food-and-drink/news/take-octopus-menu-utter-cretinous-stupidity/.

4 Stefano, Mark Di. 'This Vegan Journalist Pitched to Waitrose Food Magazine, And The Editor Replied Proposing A Series About Killing Vegans.' *BuzzFeed*. Accessed March 9, 2021. https://www.buzzfeed.com/markdistefano/waitrose-food-killing-vegans-freelance-journalist.

"Waitrose Food: Editor William Sitwell Resigns Over 'Killing Vegans' Row." *BBC News*, October 31, 2018. UK. https://www.bbc.com/news/uk-46042314.

5 Ibbetson, Ross. 'Students at Oxford University Are Latest to Demand Clapping Is Banned.' *Mail Online*, October 23, 2019. https://www.dailymail.co.uk/news/article-7605991/Snowflake-students-Oxford-University-latest-demand-clapping-banned.html.

6 Piers Morgan. "H @OxfordSU_WEO, Re Your Ban on Clapping to Stop Students with Anxiety Being Triggered, & Use of Silent 'jazz Hands' Instead.. a) Performing 'Jazz Hands' Is Racist. b) Your New Rule Excludes Blind People, so Will Make Them Feel Marginalised. c) Grow a Pair You Imbeciles." Tweet. @piersmorgan (blog), October 24, 2019. https://twitter.com/*piersmorgan*/status/1187348107836579840.

7 Cook, Chris, and Ella Hill. 'A College with Secrets.' *Tortoise*, February 18, 2020. https://www.tortoisemedia.com/2020/02/18/campus-justice-trinity-hall/.

8 Trinity Hall. 'Statement from Trinity Hall.' Accessed July 28, 2021. https://www.trinhall.cam.ac.uk/news/statement-from-trinity-hall-updates/.

9 Croxford, Rianna. 'What It Is Like for a Black Student to Go to Cambridge.' *Financial Times*, May 31, 2018. https://www.ft.com/content/cad952d2-215d-11e8-8d6c-a1920d9e946f.

10 University of Cambridge. 'Increase in Black Student Numbers.' October 11, 2019. https://www.cam.ac.uk/news/increase-in-black-student-numbers.

Hazell, Will. 'Proportion of Black and Minority Ethnic Students Going to Oxford Rises to Record High in 2020.' inews.co.uk, February 4, 2021. https://inews.co.uk/news/education/oxford-university-black-minority-ethnic-students-record-high-858051.

11 Beauchamp, Zack. 'One of the Most Famous Incidents of Campus Outrage Was Totally Misrepresented.' *Vox*, November 5, 2019. https://www.vox.com/identities/2019/11/5/20944138/oberlin-banh-mi-college-campus-diversity.

12 Patel, Vimal. 'Colleges Are Losing Control of Their Story. The Banh-Mi Affair at Oberlin Shows How.' *CHE*, October 31, 2019. https://www.chronicle.com/article/colleges-are-losing-control-of-their-story-the-banh-mi-affair-at-oberlin-shows-how/.

13 Licea, Melkorka, and Laura Italiano. 'Students at Lena Dunham's College Offended by Lack of Fried Chicken.' *New York Post* (blog), December 18, 2015. https://nypost.com/2015/12/18/pc-students-at-lena-dunhams-college-offended-by-lack-of-fried-chicken/.

14 Friedersdorf, Conor. 'The New Intolerance of Student Activism.' *The Atlantic*, November 9, 2015. https://www.theatlantic.com/politics/archive/2015/11/the-new-intolerance-of-student-activism-at-yale/414810/.

15 Tran, Linh K. 'The "Real" Americans.' *Daylalinh* (blog), February 2, 2017. https://daylalinh.wordpress.com/2017/02/02/the-real-americans/.

16 Licea, Melkorka, and Laura Italiano. 'Students at Lena Dunham's College Offended by Lack of Fried Chicken.' New York Post (blog), December 18, 2015. https: / / nypost.com / 2015 / 12 / 18 / pc - students - at - lena - dunhams - college - offended - by - lack - of - fried - chicken / .

17 Nichols, Tom. *The Death of Expertise: The Campaign against Established Knowledge and Why It Matters*. 1st edition. Oxford University Press, 2017.

18 Friedersdorf, Conor. 'How Campus Activists Are Weaponizing "Safe Space".' *The Atlantic*, November 10, 2015. https://www.theatlantic.com/politics/archive/2015/11/how-campus-activists-are-weaponizing-the-safe-space/415080/.

19 Obaro, Tomi. 'Before Syracuse, There Was Mizzou.' *BuzzFeed News*, November 26, 2019. https://www.buzzfeednews.com/article/tomiobaro/mizzou-football-boycott-protests-2015-racism.

20 Jones, Maya A. 'Lil' Joints: The Final Season.' *The Undefeated* (blog), May 31, 2016. https://theundefeated.com/videos/spike-lees-lil-joints-2-fists-up/.

21 Kingkade, Tyler. 'The Incident You Have to See To Understand Why Students Wanted Mizzou's President To Go.' HuffPost, 19:26 500. https: / / www.huffpost.com / entry / tim - wolfe - homecoming - parade _ n _ 56402cc8e4b0307f2cadea10.

Ledford, Joe. 'University of Missouri System President Says He

Handled Student Protests Poorly.' *The Kansas City Star*. Accessed August 8, 2021. https://www.kansascity.com/news/politics-government/article43438974.html.

22 Svrluga, Susan. 'U. Missouri President, Chancellor Resign over Handling of Racial Incidents." *Washington Post*. Accessed August 8, 2021. https://www.washingtonpost.com/news/grade-point/wp/2015/11/09/missouris-student-government-calls-for-university-presidents-removal/.

23 Kertscher, Tom. 'Pro-Sheriff David Clarke Group Says Clarke Called Black Lives Matter Hate Group, Terrorist Movement.' *PolitiFact*, April 17, 2017. https://www.politifact.com/factchecks/2017/apr/17/sheriff-david-clarke-us-senate/pro-sheriff-david-clarke-group-says-clarke-called-/.

24 Nelson, Libby. 'Yale's Big Fight over Sensitivity and Free Speech, Explained.' *Vox*, November 7, 2015. https://www.vox.com/2015/11/7/9689330/yale-halloween-email.

25 Svrluga, Susan. 'Students Accuse Yale SAE Fraternity Brother of Saying "White Girls Only" at Party Door.' *Washington Post*. Accessed March 7, 2021. https://www.washingtonpost.com/news/grade-point/wp/2015/11/02/students-accuse-yale-sae-fraternity-brothers-of-having-a-white-girls-only-policy-at-their-party/.

26 Christakis, Erika. 'My Halloween Email Led to a Campus Firestorm – and a Troubling Lesson about Self-Censorship.' *Washington Post*, October 28, 2016. Opinions. https://www.washingtonpost.com/opinions/my-halloween-email-led-to-a-campus-firestorm--and-a-troubling-lesson-about-self-censorship/2016/10/28/70e55732-9b97-11e6-a0ed-ab0774c1eaa5_story.html.

27 Contributing Writers. 'Voices from the Movement.' *DOWN Magazine* (blog), November 10, 2015. https://downatyale.com/voices-from-the-movement/.

28 Lukianoff, Greg, and Jonathan Haidt. *The Coddling of the American Mind: How Good Intentions and Bad Ideas Are Setting Up a Generation for Failure*. Penguin Books, 2018.

29 Dupuy, Beatrice. 'Most Americans Didn't Approve of Martin Luther King Jr before His Death.' *Newsweek*, January 15, 2018. https://www.newsweek.com/martin-luther-king-jr-was-not-always-popular-back-day-780387.

30 Izadi, Elahe. 'Black Lives Matter and America's Long History of Resisting Civil Rights Protesters.' *Washington Post*, April 19, 2016. https://www.washingtonpost.com/news/the-fix/wp/2016/04/19/black-lives-matters-and-americas-long-history-of-resisting-civil-rights-protesters/.

31 Walker, Victoria M. 'Here's Why Kendall Jenner's Pepsi Ad Is So Controversial.' *Washington Post*, 2017. https://www.youtube.com/watch?v=bTivpgMkGKA.

32 Ohlheiser, Abby. 'The UC Davis Pepper-Spraying Cop Gets a $38,000 Settlement.' *The Atlantic*, October 23, 2013. https://www.theatlantic.com/national/archive/2013/10/uc-davis-pepper-spraying-cop-gets-38k-settlement/309629/.

CHAPTER THREE

1 Grant, Jonathan, Kirstie Hewlett, Tamar Nir, and Bobby Duffy. 'Freedom of Expression in UK Universities | The Policy Institute | King's College London.' Accessed March 11, 2021. https://www.kcl.ac.uk/policy-institute/research-analysis/freedom-of-expression-universities.

2 'Zimmer and Isaacs – Report of the Committee on Freedom of Expression.Pdf.' Accessed June 20, 2021. https://provost.uchicago.edu/sites/default/files/documents/reports/FOECommitteeReport.pdf.

3 Riley, Charlotte Lydia, ed. *The Free Speech Wars: How Did We Get Here and Why Does It Matter?* Manchester University Press, 2021 (2020). p.19.

4 Siraj Datoo. 'The Irony of This Is That by My First Year at University, the British Government Had Enacted a Policy That Meant Any Muslim Who Said Anything That Criticised Government Policy Could Be Subject to Scrutiny and Have Their Names Passed on to Authorities.' Tweet. *@dats* (blog), March 8, 2020. https://twitter.com/dats/status/1236560751440977920.

5 The Free Speech Union. 'Home.' Accessed March 11, 2021. https://freespeechunion.org/.

6 Bland, Archie. 'Students Quit Free Speech Campaign over Role of Toby Young-Founded Group.' *The Guardian*, January 9, 2021. Media. https://www.theguardian.com/media/2021/jan/09/students-quit-free-speech-campaign-over-role-of-toby-young-founded-group.

7 LII / Legal Information Institute. 'Fighting Words.' Accessed March 7, 2021. https://www.law.cornell.edu/wex/fighting_words.

8 Strossen, Nadine. *HATE: Why We Should Resist It With Free Speech, Not Censorship*. 1st edition. New York, NY: Oxford University Press, 2018.

9 Hudson Jr, David L. 'Patriot Act | Freedom Forum Institute.' September 2012. https://www.freedomforuminstitute.org/first-amendment-center/topics/freedom-of-speech-2/libraries-first-amendment-overview/patriot-act/.

10 'Words of Freedom: Video Made from Mario Savio's 1964 "Machine Speech". *Berkeley News*, November 30, 1AD. https://news.berkeley.edu/ 2014/09/30/words-of-freedom-video-made-from-mario-savios-1964-machine-speech/.

11 Cohen, Robert, and Reginald E. Zelnik, eds. *The Free Speech Movement: Reflections on Berkeley in the 1960s.* 1st edition. Berkeley: University of California Press, 2002. p.515.

12 University of California. 'How Students Helped End Apartheid.' May 4, 2018. https://www.universityofcalifornia.edu/news/how-students-helped-end-apartheid.

13 '11.20.2009 – Chancellor's Message to Community: Wheeler Hall Protest Ended Peacefully.' Accessed July 28, 2021. https://www.berkeley.edu/news/media/releases/2009/11/20_wheeler-rjb.shtml.

14 Public Affairs, UC Berkeley. 'Campus Panel Issues Report on November 2009 Protest Response.' *Berkeley News*, June 16, 2010. https://news.berkeley.edu/2010/06/16/prb/.

15 Wong, Julia Carrie. 'UC Berkeley Cancels 'Alt-Right' Speaker Milo Yiannopoulos as Thousands Protest.' *The Guardian*, February 2, 2017. World news. https://www.theguardian.com/world/2017/feb/01/milo-yiannopoulos-uc-berkeley-event-cancelled.

16 Wan, William. 'Milo's Appearance at Berkeley Led to Riots. He Vows to Return This Fall for a Week-Long Free-Speech Event.' *Washington Post*. Accessed March 7, 2021. https://www.washingtonpost.com/news/grade-point/wp/2017/04/26/milos-appearance-at-berkeley-led-to-riots-he-vows-to-return-this-fall-for-a-week-long-free-speech-event/.

17 Staff, Lillian Holmes|. 'Looking into UC Berkeley's History of Activism.' The Daily Californian, April 9, 2017. https://www.dailycal.org/2017/04/09/looking-into-uc-berkeleys-history-activism/.

18 Hiltzik, Michael. 'Column: Are College Campuses Growing More Intolerant of Free Speech? The Numbers Say No.' *Los Angeles Times*, March 13, 2017. https://www.latimes.com/business/hiltzik/la-fi-hiltzik-campus-speech-20170313-story.html.

19 Baer, Ulrich. *What Snowflakes Get Right: Free Speech, Truth, and Equality on Campus.* New York, NY, United States of America: Oxford University Press, 2019.

20 Southern Poverty Law Center. 'Charles Murray.' Accessed March 7, 2021. https://www.splcenter.org/fighting-hate/extremist-files/individual/charles-murray.

21 Charles Murray. 'Just One Little Quote from Me to Substantiate the "White Supremacist" Charge, Please. Just One.' Tweet. @*charlesmurray*

(blog), April 20, 2019. https://twitter.com/charlesmurray/status/1119552582358269953.

22 Egginton, William. *The Splintering of the American Mind: Identity Politics, Inequality, and Community on Today's College Campuses*. 1st edition. Bloomsbury Publishing, 2018.

23 Siegel, Eric. 'The Real Problem with Charles Murray and "The Bell Curve".' Scientific American Blog Network. Accessed March 11, 2021. https://blogs.scientificamerican.com/voices/the-real-problem-with-charles-murray-and-the-bell-curve/.

24 Strauss, Valerie. "Analysis | Why This 1852 Frederick Douglass Speech – 'What to the Slave Is the Fourth of July?' — Should Be Taught to Students Today." *Washington Post*. Accessed October 2, 2021. https://www.washingtonpost.com/education/2020/07/04/why-this-1852-frederick-douglass-speech-what-slave-is-fourth-july-should-be-taught-students-today/.

25 Serwer, Adam. 'A Nation of Snowflakes.' *The Atlantic*, September 26, 2017. https://www.theatlantic.com/politics/archive/2017/09/it-takes-a-nation-of-snowflakes/541050/.

26 Hussain, Murtaza. 'The Real Cancel Culture: Pro-Israel Blacklists.' *The Intercept*, October 4, 2020. https://theintercept.com/2020/10/04/israel-palestine-blacklists-canary-mission/.

27 Trilling, Daniel. 'Why Is the UK Government Suddenly Targeting "Critical Race Theory"? *The Guardian*, October 23, 2020. http://www.theguardian.com/commentisfree/2020/oct/23/uk-critical-race-theory-trump-conservatives-structural-inequality.

28 Ingraham, Christopher. 'Republican Lawmakers Introduce Bills to Curb Protesting in at Least 18 States.' *Washington Post*. Accessed March 7, 2021. https://www.washingtonpost.com/news/wonk/wp/2017/02/24/republican-lawmakers-introduce-bills-to-curb-protesting-in-at-least-17-states/.

29 ICNL. 'US Protest Law Tracker.' Accessed March 7, 2021. http://www.icnl.org/usprotestlawtracker/.

30 Axelrod, Tal. 'Tennessee Governor Signs Bill Increasing Punishments for Certain Protests.' Text. *The Hill*, August 21, 2020. https://thehill.com/homenews/state-watch/513201-tennessee-governor-signs-bill-increasing-punishments-for-certain.

31 UK Parliament. "Police, Crime, Sentencing and Courts Bill." Accessed October 2, 2021. https://bills.parliament.uk/bills/2839.

32 Goldwater Institute. 'Campus Free Speech: A Legislative Proposal.' Accessed March 7, 2021. https://goldwaterinstitute.org/article/campus-free-speech-a-legislative-proposal/.

33 Hiltzik, Michael. 'Column: How a Right-Wing Group's Proposed "Free Speech" Law Aims to Undermine Free Speech on Campus.' *Los Angeles Times*, May 30, 2018. https://www.latimes.com/business/hiltzik/la-fi-hiltzik-free-speech-20180530-story.html.

34 'Campus Free-Speech Legislation: History, Progress, and Problems | AAUP.' Accessed August 8, 2021. https://www.aaup.org/report/campus-free-speech-legislation-history-progress-and-problems.

35 Glaude, Eddie. 'The Real Special Snowflakes on Campus.' *Time*. Accessed March 7, 2021. https://time.com/4958261/eddie-glaude-special-snowflakes/.

36 Todd. 'University of Wisconsin Approves Free Speech Policy That Punishes Student Protesters' *Chicago Tribune*,' October 26, 2017. https://www.chicagotribune.com/nation-world/ct-university-of-wisconsin-protest-punishment-20171006-story.html.

37 UK Parliament. "Higher Education (Freedom of Speech) Bill." Accessed October 2, 2021. https://bills.parliament.uk/bills/2862.

38 Harris, Malcolm. *Kids These Days: Human Capital and the Making of Millennials*. Little, Brown and Company, 2017.

39 Glaude, Eddie. 'The Real Special Snowflakes on Campus.' *Time*. Accessed March 7, 2021. https://time.com/4958261/eddie-glaude-special-snowflakes/.

CHAPTER FOUR

1 'Statues to Get Protection from "Baying Mobs".' BBC News, January 17, 2021. https://www.bbc.com/news/uk-55693020.

2 Felicia Sonmez. 'Speaking on the Floor of the House of the Representatives, Rep. Jim Jordan (R-Ohio) Bemoans "the Cancel Culture That Only Allows One Side to Talk." As He Opens the House Debate for Republicans, He Declares That You "Can't Even Have a Debate in This Country." Tweet. *@feliciasonmez* (blog), January 13, 2021. https://twitter.com/feliciasonmez/status/1349411331640872965.

3 Sathnam Sanghera. 'This Is Incredible and Depressing. The National Trust Did an Important, Intelligent and Deeply Relevant Thing by Exploring the Colonial History of Its Properties. Even This Is Turned into a Culture War by the Charity Commission. We Are So Fucked Up About Our History. #EmpireLand Https://T.Co/2Zzrsc0Xfg.' Tweet. *@Sathnam* (blog), October 24, 2020. https://twitter.com/Sathnam/status/1319911879817519104.

4 Butler, Patrick. 'National Trust Report on Slavery Links Did Not Break

Charity Law, Regulator Says," *The Guardian*. March 11, 2021. http://www.theguardian.com/uk-news/2021/mar/11/national-trust-report-uk-slavery-links-did-not-break-charity-law-regulator-says.

5 Sunder Katwala. 'Telegraph Letter from 28 Conservatives, Challenging the Idea of Portraying "Multiple Perspectives on History" https://T.Co/BtdY3WO7ze.' Tweet. @*sundersays* (blog), November 9, 2020. https://twitter.com/sundersays/status/1325750156487237633.

6 keewa. 'The UK Is a Country with a Deep and Lingering Sickness in Its Soul Https://T.Co/CTAOTaMqzN.' Tweet. @*keewa* (blog), August 23, 2020. https://twitter.com/keewa/status/1297629662978478080.

7 Oliver, Neil. "I Solemnly Swear, It's Time to Get Serious about Having a Laugh." *The Times*, July 19, 2020. Accessed November 18, 2021. https://www.thetimes.co.uk/article/i-solemnly-swear-its-time-to-get-serious-about-having-a-laugh-pw2rqvz8l

8 West, Ed. 'Ed West: So Far, 2020 Has Proved My Most Pessimistic Expectations to Be Horribly True. How Very Satisfying.' Conservative Home. Accessed March 7, 2021. https://www.conservativehome.com/platform/2020/08/ed-west-so-far-2020-has-proved-my-most-pessimistic-expectations-to-be-horribly-true-how-very-satisfying.html.

9 Gray, John. 'JOHN GRAY: Not Exaggeration to Compare "Woke Movement" to Red Guards.' *Mail Online*, July 19, 2020. https://www.dailymail.co.uk/debate/article-8537583/JOHN-GRAY-not-exaggeration-compare-methods-new-woke-movement-Maos-Red-Guards.html.

10 Turner, Janice. 'The Woke Left Is the New Ministry of Truth.' *The Times*, July 11, 2020. Comment. Accessed August 18, 2021. https://www.thetimes.co.uk/article/the-woke-left-is-the-new-ministry-of-truth-vmrgt823b.

   As seen in: Declan Cashin. "A Tyrannical Minority Decide What We're Allowed to Say", Argues the Person with a Weekly Column in the Times Https://T.Co/W8UvW8njRa.' Tweet. @*Tweet_Dec* (blog), July 11, 2020. https://twitter.com/Tweet_Dec/status/1281886796549414913.

11 Turner, Janice. 'Children Sacrificed to Appease Trans Lobby.' *The Times*, November 11, 2017. Comment. Accessed July 29, 2021. https://www.thetimes.co.uk/article/children-sacrificed-to-appease-trans-lobby-bq0m2mm95.

12 Hope, Christopher. 'Roads to Be Named after Victoria Cross Heroes in Latest Tory Plan for "War on Woke".' *The Telegraph*, January 23, 2021. https://www.telegraph.co.uk/politics/2021/01/23/roads-named-victoria-cross-heroes-latest-tory-plan-war-woke/.

13 Waterson, Jim. 'BBC Journalists Told Not to "Virtue Signal" in Social Media Crackdown.' *The Guardian*, October 29, 2020. Media. https://www.theguardian.com/media/2020/oct/29/bbc-journalists-virtue-signalling-social-media-crackdown.

14 Harper's Magazine. 'A Letter on Justice and Open Debate.' July 7, 2020. https://harpers.org/a-letter-on-justice-and-open-debate/.

15 Robert Reich. 'I Declined to Sign the Harper's Letter Because Trumpism, Racism, Xenophobia, and Sexism Have Had Such Free Rein and Baleful Influence in Recent Years That We Should Honour and Respect the Expressions of Anger and Heartache Finally Being Heard.' Tweet. @*RBReich* (blog), July 8, 2020. https://twitter.com/RBReich/status/1280885837081661441.

16 Kim, Richard. 'Richard Kim on Twitter: 'Okay, I Did Not Sign THE LETTER When I Was Asked 9 Days Ago Because I Could See in 90 Seconds That It Was Fatuous, Self-Important Drivel That Would Only Troll the People It Allegedly Was Trying to Reach -- and I Said as Much." July 7, 2020. https://webcache.googleusercontent.com/search?q=cache:gU0R6L3Vq4MJ:https://twitter.com/richardkimnyc/status/1280592642645114880+&cd=1&hl=en&ct=clnk&gl=us.

17 Glenn Greenwald. '1/ Regarding the Apparent Fact That the Letter's Organiser Wanted to Have Me Sign but the Luminaries Actually in Control Cancelled Me (I Was Never Asked), It's Been Obvious from the Start That the Letter Was Signed by Frauds, Eager to Protect Their Own Status, Not the Principles.' Tweet. @*ggreenwald* (blog), July 18, 2020. https://twitter.com/ggreenwald/status/1284467879774244865.

18 CNA. "Full Text: Sister Dede Byrne's Speech at the 2020 Republican National Convention." Catholic News Agency. Accessed October 2, 2021. https://www.catholicnewsagency.com/news/45617/full-text-sister-dede-byrnes-speech-at-the-2020-republican-national-convention.

19 Mark Joseph Stern. 'Here Is Justice Alito Complaining That the Supreme Court's Same-Sex Marriage Decision Has Crushed the Free Speech of Anti-LGBTQ Advocates. Https://T.Co/0eH9QsxMTU.' Tweet. @*mjs_DC* (blog), November 13, 2020. https://twitter.com/mjs_DC/status/1327070227339874306.

20 Sharf, Zack. 'Louis C.K. Reacts to Parkland Shooting Joke Controversy, Jokes About Masturbation in New Set." *IndieWire* (blog), January 17, 2019. https://www.indiewire.com/2019/01/louis-ck-jokes-about-jerking-off-parkland-schooting-comment-1202036287/.

21 Ryzik, Melena, Cara Buckley, and Jodi Kantor. 'Louis C.K. Is Accused by 5 Women of Sexual Misconduct." *The New York Times*, November

9, 2017. Arts. https://www.nytimes.com/2017/11/09/arts/television/louis
-ck-sexual-misconduct.html.

Miller, Liz Shannon. 'Louis CK and Others Didn't Just Allegedly Harass Women – They Silenced Them.' *IndieWire* (blog), November 10, 2017. https://www.indiewire.com/2017/11/matthew-weiner-louis-ck-harassment-victims-1201895994/.

22 Ronson, Jon. *So You've Been Publicly* Shamed, 2016.

23 Mettler, Katie. 'Nobody Is Buying Mark Halperin's Book. The Disgraced Journalist's Publisher Lambasts "Cancel Culture".' *Washington Post.* Accessed March 12, 2021. https://www.washingtonpost.com/arts-entertainment/2019/11/07/nobody-is-buying-mark-halperins-book-disgraced-journalists-publisher-lambastes-cancel-culture/.

24 Wong, Julia Carrie. 'Journalist Mark Halperin Apologizes over Sexual Harassment Allegations," *The Guardian.* October 28, 2017. http://www.theguardian.com/tv-and-radio/2017/oct/27/mark-halperin-sexual-harassment-allegations-apology.

25 Hagi, Sarah. 'Cancel Culture Is Not Real – At Least Not in the Way People Think.' *Time*, November 21, 2019. https://time.com/5735403/cancel-culture-is-not-real/.

26 D. Clark, Meredith. 'DRAG THEM: A Brief Etymology of So-Called 'Cancel Culture'. *Communication and the Public 5*, no. 3–4 (September 1, 2020): 88–92. https://doi.org/10.1177/2057047320961562.

27 'Andrew Cuomo Apologises, Says He Didn't Know He Was Making Women Uncomfortable and Rejects Calls to Resign' *CNNPolitics*, Accessed July 29, 2021. https://www.cnn.com/2021/03/03/politics/andrew-cuomo-harassment-press-conference/index.html.

28 Sue, Derald Wing, Christina M. Capodilupo, Gina C. Torino, Jennifer M. Bucceri, Aisha M. B. Holder, Kevin L. Nadal, and Marta Esquilin. 'Racial Micro Aggressions in Everyday Life: Implications for Clinical Practice.' *American Psychologist 62*, no. 4 (2007): 271–86. https://doi.org/10.1037/0003-066X.62.4.271.

29 Geronimus, Arline T., Margaret T. Hicken, Jay A. Pearson, Sarah J. Seashols, Kelly L. Brown, and Tracey Dawson Cruz. 'Do US Black Women Experience Stress-Related Accelerated Biological Aging?: A Novel Theory and First Population-Based Test of Black-White Differences in Telomere Length.' *Human Nature (Hawthorne, N.Y.)* 21, no. 1 (March 10, 2010): 19–38. https://doi.org/10.1007/s12110-010-9078-0.

30 Chae, David H., Amani M. Nuru-Jeter, Nancy E. Adler, Gene H. Brody, Jue Lin, Elizabeth H. Blackburn, and Elissa S. Epel. "Discrimination, Racial Bias, and Telomere Length in African-American Men." *American*

Journal of Preventive Medicine 46, no. 2 (February 1, 2014): 103 -11. https://doi.org/10.1016/j.amepre.2013.10.020.

31 *Piers Morgan | The Ben Shapiro Show Sunday Special Ep. 64.* Accessed March 7, 2021. https://soundcloud.com/benshapiroshow/sundayspecialep64.

32 Shapiro, Ariel. 'The Highest-Earning Stand-Up Comedians Of 2019.' *Forbes.* Accessed March 7, 2021. https://www.forbes.com/sites/arielshapiro/2019/08/16/the-highest-earning-stand-up-comedians-of-2019/.

33 James Felton. '@Jacob_Rees_Mogg There's a Huge Difference between "No One Laughed at My Shit Joke" and "Snowflakes Have No Sense of Humour" You Fucking Potato.' Tweet. *@JimMFelton* (blog), July 16, 2019. https://twitter.com/JimMFelton/status/1151053903754137600.

34 Ricky Gervais. 'Please Stop Saying "You Can't Joke about Anything Anymore". You Can. You Can Joke about Whatever the Fuck You like. And Some People Won't like It and They Will Tell You They Don't like It. And Then It's up to You Whether You Give a Fuck or Not. And so on. It's a Good System.' Tweet. *@rickygervais* (blog), September 14, 2019. https://twitter.com/rickygervais/status/1172874651019763712.

35 Garbus, Martin. *Tough Talk: How I Fought for Writers, Comics, Bigots, and the American Way.* Crown, 2010 (1998).

36 Merrett, Robyn. 'New SNL Star Shane Gillis Offers to Apologise to "Anyone Who's Actually Offended" Over Racial Slur.' *PEOPLE.com.* Accessed March 14, 2021. https://people.com/tv/shane-gillis-offers-apology-after-using-racial-slur-resurfaced-video/.

37 Staff, MTV News. 'Sebastian Maniscalco Recasts Lil Nas X's Horse As An Emotional Support Animal In VMAs Monologue.' *MTV News.* Accessed March 14, 2021. http://www.mtv.com/news/3136540/sebastian-maniscalco-vmas-monologue/.

38 Nwanevu, Osita. 'The "Cancel Culture" Con.' *The New Republic*, September 23, 2019. https://newrepublic.com/article/155141/cancel-culture-con-dave-chappelle-shane-gillis.

39 Wilson, John K. *The Myth of Political Correctness: The Conservative Attack on Higher Education.* Duke University Press Books, 1995, p. 8. As seen in:

    Becca Lewis. 'Here's a Quote from a Commencement Speech given by George H.W. Bush in 1991, Mere Months after the Brutal Beating of Rodney King. The More Things Change . . . Https://T.Co/2UaV4TGs0z.' Tweet. *@beccalew* (blog), July 11, 2020. https://twitter.com/beccalew/status/1281960715658555395.

40 Krishnamurthy, Meena. 'What Martin Luther King Jr Really Thought About Riots.' Jacobin, September 6, 2020. https://jacobinmag.com/2020/09/martin-luther-king-riots-looting-biden.

41 Martin Luther King III. 'As My Father Explained During His Lifetime, a Riot Is the Language of the Unheard.' Tweet. *@OfficialMLK3* (blog), May 28, 2020. https://twitter.com/OfficialMLK3/status/1266040838628560898.

42 King Jr., Martin Luther. "'I Have A Dream' Speech, In Its Entirety." *NPR*, January 18, 2010. Race. https://www.npr.org/2010/01/18/122701268/ihave-a-dream-speech-in-its-entiret.

43 King Jr, Martin Luther. 'Letter from a Birmingham Jail.' First published 1963. Accessed March 14, 2021. https://www.africa.upenn.edu/ArticlesGen/letterBirmingham.html.

44 Scribd. 'Questions About Civil Rights Protests 1960s | Gallup (Company) | Opinion Poll.' Accessed March 7, 2021. https://www.scribd.com/doc/308461037/Questions-About-Civil-Rights-Protests-1960s.

45 Bidol, Pat A. *Developing New Perspectives on Race: An Innovative Multi-Media Social Studies Curriculum in Racism Awareness for the Secondary Level*. New Perspectives on Race, 1972.

As seen in: Sivanandan, Ambalavanar. *Communities of Resistance: Writings on Black Struggles for Socialism*. Verso, 1990.

46 DiAngelo, Robin. *White Fragility: Why It's So Hard for White People to Talk About Racism*. Beacon Press, 2018. p.47.

47 Gonyea, Don. 'Majority Of White Americans Say They Believe Whites Face Discrimination.' *NPR.org*. Accessed March 14, 2021. https://www.npr.org/2017/10/24/559604836/majority-of-white-americans-think-theyre-discriminated-against.

48 Mohdin, Aamna. 'Up to 40% of Britons Think BAME People Do Not Face More Discrimination.' *The Guardian*, December 20, 2018. World news. https://www.theguardian.com/world/2018/dec/20/up-to-40-of-britons-think-bame-people-do-not-face-more-discrimination.

CHAPTER FIVE

1 Herman, Judith. *Trauma and Recovery: The Aftermath of Violence--from Domestic Abuse to Political Terror*. New York: Basic Books, 1997 (1992).

2 Remarque, Erich Maria. *All Quiet on the Western Front*. Translated by Brian Murdoch, 2010.

3 Kolk, Bessel van der. *The Body Keeps the Score: Brain, Mind, and Body in the Healing of Trauma*. 1st edition. Penguin Books, 2014.

4 Jain, Shaili. *The Unspeakable Mind: Stories of Trauma and Healing from the Frontlines of PTSD Science*. Reprint edition. Harper, 2019.

5 Yehuda, Rachel et al. 'Holocaust Exposure Induced Intergenerational Effects on FKBP5 Methylation.' *Biological Psychiatry* Volume 80, no. Issue 5 (n.d.): 372–80.

6 Costandi, Mo. 'Pregnant 9/11 Survivors Transmitted Trauma to Their Children.' *The Guardian*, September 9, 2011. Science. https://www.theguardian.com/science/neurophilosophy/2011/sep/09/pregnant-911-survivors-transmitted-trauma.

7 Larkin, Philip. "This Be The Verse." From *High Windows* Faber and Faber Ltd. 1974.

8 Lewis, Stephanie. 'Burden of Trauma and PTSD in Young British People Revealed – New Research.' *The Conversation*. Accessed March 7, 2021. http://theconversation.com/burden-of-trauma-and-ptsd-in-young-british-people-revealed-new-research-112168.

9 Kelland, Kate. 'Rates of Post-Trauma Stress Rise in British Military Veterans.' *Reuters*, October 7, 2018. https://www.reuters.com/article/us-health-ptsd-military-idUSKCN1MH12E.

10 Centers for Disease Control and Prevention. "Preventing Intimate Partner Violence | Violence Prevention | Injury Center," November 5, 2021. https://www.cdc.gov/violenceprevention/intimatepartnerviolence/fastfact.html.

11 Card, David, and Gordon B. Dahl. 'Family Violence and Football: The Effect of Unexpected Emotional Cues on Violent Behaviour.' *The Quarterly Journal of Economics* 126, no. 1 (2011): 103 -43.

12 Cox, John Woodrow, Steven Rich, Allyson Chiu, John Muyskens, and Monica Ulmanu. 'Analysis | More than 240,000 Students Have Experienced Gun Violence at School since Columbine.' *Washington Post*. Accessed March 7, 2021. https: / / www.washingtonpost.com / graphics / 2018 / local / school - shootings - database / .

13 Senn, Charlene Y., Misha Eliasziw, Paula C. Barata, Wilfreda E. Thurston, Ian R. Newby-Clark, H. Lorraine Radtke, and Karen L. Hobden. "Efficacy of a Sexual Assault Resistance Program for University Women." *New England Journal of Medicine* 372, no. 24 (June 11, 2015): 2326–35. https://doi.org/10.1056/NEJMsa1411131.

14 Perry, Philippa. *The Book You Wish Your Parents Had Read (and Your Children Will Be Glad That You Did)*. 1st edition. UK: Penguin Life, 2019.

CHAPTER SEVEN

1 Barr, Sabrina. 'Half of Generation Z Men "Think Feminism Has Gone Too Far".' *The Independent*, August 4, 2020. https://www.independent.co.uk/life-style/women/feminism-generation-z-men-women-hope-not-hate-charity-report-a9652981.html.

2 Faye, Shon. *The The Transgender Issue: An Argument for Justice*, 2021.

3 Michelson, Noah. 'More Americans Claim To Have Seen A Ghost Than Have Met A Trans Person.' *HuffPost*, December 21, 2015. https://www.huffpost.com/entry/more-americans-claim-to-have-seen-a-ghost-than-have-met-a-trans-person_n_5677fee5e4b014efe0d5ed62.

Williams, Joe. 'More Americans Claim to Have Seen a Ghost than a Trans Person.' *PinkNews – Gay News, Reviews and Comment from the World's Most Read Lesbian, Gay, Bisexual, and Trans News Service* (blog), December 18, 2015. https://www.pinknews.co.uk/2015/12/18/more-americans-claim-to-have-seen-a-ghost-than-a-trans-person/.

4 BBC. 'BBC One – Question Time, 2018, 22/03/2018.' Accessed August 18, 2021. https://www.bbc.co.uk/programmes/b09x008x.

5 Stone, Jon. 'Majority of Women Support Self-Identification for Transgender People, Poll Finds.' *The Independent*, July 13, 2020. https://www.independent.co.uk/news/uk/politics/uk-women-support-self-identification-transgender-people-boris-johnson-gra-a9616136.html.

6 ryan john butcher. 'Graham Linehan Just Admitted to the House of Lords That His Fight against Trans People's Rights Placed His Marriage under "Such a Strain That My Wife and I Finally Agreed to Separate" Sad Https://T.Co/Td8xNHpkUc.' Tweet. *@ryanjohnbutcher* (blog), March 9, 2021. https://twitter.com/ryanjohnbutcher/status/1369311631029776390.

7 Kelleher, Patrick. 'Graham Linehan Joined a Queer Women's Dating App to Share Trans People's Profiles. It Backfired, Badly.' *Yahoo News*, February 21, 2021. https://uk.news.yahoo.com/graham-linehan-joined-queer-women-132516955.html.

8 Bowcott, Owen. 'Judge Rules against Researcher Who Lost Job over Transgender Tweets.' *The Guardian*, December 18, 2019. Society. https://www.theguardian.com/society/2019/dec/18/judge-rules-against-charity-worker-who-lost-job-over-transgender-tweets.

9 J.K. Rowling. 'The Idea That Women like Me, Who've Been Empathetic to Trans People for Decades, Feeling Kinship Because They're Vulnerable in the Same Way as Women – i.e., to Male Violence – "Hate" Trans

People Because They Think Sex Is Real and Has Lived Consequences – Is a Nonsense.' Tweet. *@jk_rowling* (blog), June 6, 2020. https://twitter.com/jk_rowling/status/1269406094595588096.

10 bletchley punk. 'She Is Taking a Very Real and Concrete Issue (the Acceptance of Trans People as Humans with Full Rights and Respect in Society), Minimizing It to Some Surface Level Features (Appearance and Names), and Then Abdicating Any Responsibility.' Tweet. *@alicegoldfuss* (blog), December 19, 2019. https://twitter.com/alicegoldfuss/status/1207734458213748736.

11 Rowling, J.K. 'J.K. Rowling Writes about Her Reasons for Speaking out on Sex and Gender Issues.' *jkrowling.com* (blog), June 10, 2020. https://www.jkrowling.com/opinions/j-k-rowling-writes-about-her-reasons-for-speaking-out-on-sex-and-gender-issues/.

12 Office of Justice Programs. 'Sexual Assault: The Numbers | Responding to Transgender Victims of Sexual Assault.' Office For Victims of Crime, June 2014. https://ovc.ojp.gov/sites/g/files/xyckuh226/files/pubs/forge/sexual_numbers.html.

13 Scottish Government. 'Potential Impacts of GRA Reform for Cisgender Women: Trans Women's Inclusion in Women-Only Spaces and Services.' GRA EQIA Literature Search, November 2019. https://www.gov.scot/binaries/content/documents/govscot/publications/foi-eir-release/2020/01/foi-202000011201/documents/foi-202000011201-document-5---earlier-version-of-literature-review/foi-202000011201-document-5---earlier-version-of-literature-review/govscot%3Adocument/FOI-202000011201%2BDocument%2B5%2B-%2BEarlier%2BVersion%2Bof%2BLiterature%2BReview.pdf.

14 Parsons, Vic. 'Domestic Abuse Workers Once and for All Shut down the Insidious Myth That Trans Women Are a Threat to Women's Refuges.' *PinkNews* (blog), September 8, 2020. https://www.pinknews.co.uk/2020/09/08/trans-women-refuges-domestic-abuse-myth-debunked-womens-aid-diana-james/.

15 McGuire, Ashley. *Sex Scandal: The Drive to Abolish Male and Female.* Illustrated edition. Regnery Publishing, 2017.

16 Trump Jr, Donald. *Triggered: How the Left Thrives on Hate and Wants to Silence Us.* Illustrated edition. Center Street, 2019.

17 Minsberg, Talya. 'Trans Athlete Chris Mosier on Qualifying for the Olympic Trials.' *New York Times*, January 28, 2020. Sports. https://www.nytimes.com/2020/01/28/sports/chris-mosier-trans-athlete-olympic-trials.html.

18 Lum, Fred. 'Jordan Peterson Creating Climate of "Fear and

Intimidation": U of T's Faculty Association.' Accessed March 13, 2021. https://www.theglobeandmail.com/news/national/jordan-peterson-creating-climate-of-fear-and-intimidation-u-of-ts-professors-say/article36924134/.

19 LBC. *Jordan Peterson Meets Maajid Nawaz | Interview in Full | LBC*, 2018. https://www.youtube.com/watch?v=IMBfT38xbhU.

20 Peterson, Jordan B. *12 Rules for Life: An Antidote to Chaos*. Random House Canada, 2018.

21 Beyerstein, Lindsay. 'What Happened to Jordan Peterson?' *The New Republic*, March 10, 2020. https://newrepublic.com/article/156829/happened-jordan-peterson.

22 Voltaire. *Candide*, 1759.

CHAPTER EIGHT

1 'More See Decline of Unions as Bad for Working People than Good in US.' *Pew Research Center* (blog). Accessed March 7, 2021. https://www.pewresearch.org/fact-tank/2018/06/05/more-americans-view-long-term-decline-in-union-membership-negatively-than-positively/.

2 UAW. 'Millennials and Unions.' January 24, 2019. https://uaw.org/millennials-and-unions/.

3 Greene, Jay. 'Amazon's Anti-Union Blitz Stalks Alabama Warehouse Workers Everywhere, Even the Bathroom.' *Washington Post*, February 2, 2021. https://www.washingtonpost.com/technology/2021/02/02/amazon-union-warehouse-workers/.

4 Tulgan, Bruce. *Bridging the Soft Skills Gap: How to Teach the Missing Basics to Today's Young Talent*. 1st edition. Jossey-Bass, 2015.

5 Carmichael, Sarah Green. 'Millennials Are Actually Workaholics, According to Research.' *Harvard Business Review*, August 17, 2016. https://hbr.org/2016/08/millennials-are-actually-workaholics-according-to-research.

6 Brackett, Marc. *Permission to Feel: Unlocking the Power of Emotions to Help Our Kids, Ourselves, and Our Society Thrive*. Celadon Books, 2019.

7 Richard Dawkins. "It's one thing to deplore eugenics on ideological, political, moral grounds. It's quite another to conclude that it wouldn't work in practice. Of course it would. It works for cows, horses, pigs, dogs & roses. Why on earth wouldn't it work for humans? Facts ignore ideology." Twitter, February 16, 2020. https://twitter.com/RichardDawkins/status/1228943686953664512

8 Adams, Char, and April Glaser. 'Complaints to Google about Racism

and Sexism Met with Therapy Referrals.' *NBC News*, March 7, 2021. https://www.nbcnews.com/tech/tech-news/google-advised-mental-health-care-when-workers-complained-about-racism-n1259728.

9 Kaufman, John A, Leslie K. Salas-Hernández, Kelli A. Komro, and Melvin D. Livingston. 'Effects of Increased Minimum Wages by Unemployment Rate on Suicide in the USA.' *Journal of Epidemiology and Community Health* 74, no. 3 (March 1, 2020): 219. https://doi.org/10.1136/jech-2019-212981.

10 Stillman, David, and Jonah Stillman. *Gen Z Work: How the Next Generation Is Transforming the Workplace.* Harper Business, 2017.

11 Paul, Kari. 'Microsoft Japan Tested a Four-Day Work Week and Productivity Jumped by 40%.' *The Guardian*, November 4, 2019. Technology. https://www.theguardian.com/technology/2019/nov/04/microsoft-japan-four-day-work-week-productivity.

Acknowledgements

This book was an enormous faff to research, write, edit, and put out into the world, only made more stressful by the biological and political horrors of 2020 and beyond. The following are just some of the people who made this process tolerable, and sometimes even a delight.

Thank you to my agent Charlie Viney, who plucked me from obscurity and thrust me into riches and international superstardom (or at least that's how it felt). You are a great advocate and an even better lunch companion.

Thank you to all those at my publisher, led by the extremely cool Hannah Black. Thank you, Hannah, for making me an author. Thank you to Sophie Lazar for your wise and careful editing. You took a turd of a manuscript and polished it up beautifully. Thank you Erika Koljonen for answering all of my silliest questions, and helping me through every complicated and/or terrifying step of the publishing process.

Thank you to Maria Garbutt-Lucero for your publicity skills, and Katy Blott for your marketing prowess – these two fields fill me with terror, and I'm lucky to have your help. Thank you Joanne Myler for your fabulous cover design, which I love, and Matthew Everett for your production, which I also love. Thank you Saba Ahmed for your proofreading, ensuring that my mom can't ruin Christmas dinner by pointing out mistakes.

Thank you to those who read entire chapters with an expert eye. My brilliant mother-in-law Dr. Margaret Wetherell, and internet culture reporting queen Sarah Manavis, prevented me from sounding like an idiot in several key chapters. Thank you Freddy McConnell for your crucial help and advice, Kelly Oakes for your endless solidarity, and Mary Beth Albright both for reading a chapter and for regularly liquoring me up and stuffing me full of cheese.

Thank you to Bim Adewunmi for your wonderful friendship, as well as your swift advice in my various moments of book panic. Thank you Kaye Toal for permission to include your excellent Harry Potter joke. Thanks to Dave Jorgenson for an additional piece of Harry Potter trivia, which I did not end up using, but was interesting nonetheless. (It was about werewolves.) Thank you Jack Powell for helping me remember some key details from a decade ago (yikes!) and, retroactively, for your love and support while I wrote my *first* book.

Thank you for the emotional encouragement of Laura Gutiérrez, who sends me supportive fridge magnets, and Aisha Gani, my saving grace of a friend during the worst of the pandemic. Gena-mour Barrett, I had a small editing breakthrough on your famous green sofa. Thanks for letting me stay in your perfect house. Now finish your book! Secure the yacht! Emily Burtch, I probably wrote some of this in your delightful company. I can't even remember. But either way, you and papa Bobby Burtch are exemplary supporters and salespeople and I appreciate you forever.

Thank you Flo Perry for letting me stay on your surprisingly comfortable air mattress on a visit to my publisher.

Thank you Chris Casey, who fixed my bike the weekend I was writing acknowledgements, and also Erica Lee, Tim Wright, Mirjam Voerkelius and little Elias, who together formed a little social safety net throughout COVID, as we shivered sitting in the snow around a bonfire eating frozen takeaway and assessing the end of the world. This was key to maintaining sanity, it turns out.

Thank you to my colleagues at the *Washington Post* with whom I floundered through this horrific time in history, including my bosses Lauren Saks, Michelle Jaconi and Micah Gelman, who offered unequivocal support throughout my authordom. A big shoutout to my Guild colleagues, who are energetic, compassionate and extremely chic. Also, um, hello to T.J. Ortenzi, thank you for your support—and here's your name in exchange for that piece of promised gossip. I beg you!

Thanks to those who I interviewed and quoted in these pages, including all you anonymous beauties, and the non-anonymous Dr. Shaili Jain, Tom Ward, Natalie Eskrick, Philippa Perry, Amna Saleem, Roisín McCallion, Juno Dawson, and Freddy McConnell.

Thank you to the many authors, journalists and random tweeters who I cited. Please peruse my bibliography and read the books therein. Or at least the good ones.

A note: those who I interviewed for this book, or who otherwise helped with it, may agree with parts of this book but not others – do not take their help or involvement as an endorsement, unless they tell you otherwise!

Similarly, if anything is foolish in this text, it's my fault and not theirs. This much should be clear.

Uncle Gordon, thanks for confirming the font is nice. I know you love to see your name in a book, so here it is again: Gordon Chesterman.

Jonathan Potter and Alexa Hepburn, thanks for the frequent oysters and even more frequent accommodation. I believe I reached a low point of writing in your downstairs bedroom, but you were there to lift me out of it with fine wines and fine company.

Simeon and Amy Jewell and your babies, thank you for your eternal support and your lifts from the airport.

ACKNOWLEDGEMENTS

Thank you to my parents, to whom I dedicate this book. My dad, Chris Jewell, was one of the very first readers. Thank you for telling me it was in fact good, and allowing me to air out some family drama in the introduction. And thank you to my mother, Jane Jewell – I am so glad the funny mummy is my mummy, and that you were happy to find the typos *before* publication this time. Everything I've been able to do in my life has been thanks to your exceptional parenting.

And finally, thank you to my husband Sam Wetherell, the very first reader and source of reassurance. Writing and editing and existing in a time of plague and fear and isolation was extremely unnerving, even before they had to board up the CVS. But being trapped in a small, one-bedroom apartment with you in a pandemic has only confirmed my excellent choice in life partner, friend, and personal chef. I'm so glad we got married in a Las Vegas drive-through. I love you even though you get crumbs on the sofa. You get the next book's dedication, but only if you stop it with the crumbs.